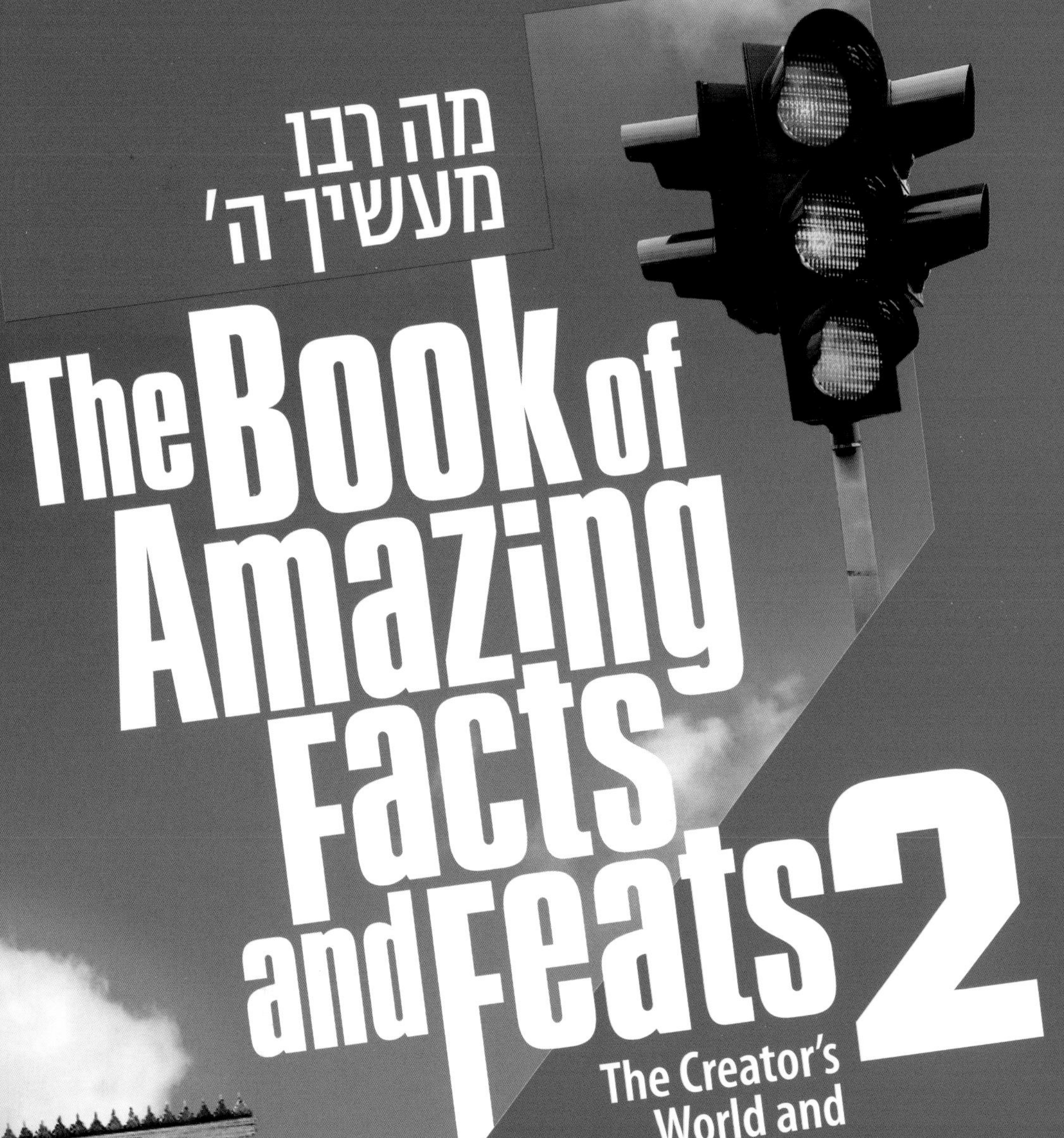

מה רבו
מעשיך ה׳

The Book of Amazing Facts and Feats 2

The Creator's World and All That Fills It

Nattan Hurvitz and
Aharon Yosef Hoffman

FELDHEIM
JERUSALEM · NEW YORK

This book contains words from the Written and Oral Torahs, as well as statements from our Sages; therefore, it requires *genizah* and should be treated respectfully.

Every effort has been made to verify the accuracy of the world records and amazing facts in this book. Nevertheless, it is said: "Who can understand unintentional errors?" The publisher is not responsible for any mistake that may be found in this book; any emendations will be accepted with thanks.

To contact us: seeim10@gmail.com

Originally published in Hebrew as *Sefer HaSe'em v'HaNifla'ot*, volume 2 (2009)

Translated into English by Nehemiah Klein
Research: Gabi Chayun and Yitzchak Hurvitz
Text Graphics and Design: Assaf Brill, Ayin Roeh Hafakot
Page Layout of English Edition: Eden Chachamtzedek
Additional Annotations: David and Natan Hoffman

The authors wish to thank attorney Dr. Mark Friedman
for his legal advice and encouragement

First published 2011

ISBN 978-1-59826-769-3

FELDHEIM PUBLISHERS
POB 43163/ Jerusalem, Israel

208 Airport Executive Park
Nanuet, NY 10954

www.feldheim.com

10 9 8 7 6 5 4 3 2 1

Printed in Israel

Introduction

Beholding amazing phenomena awakens the heart to the realization that the entire world in which we live is one of miracles and wonders. The seemingly dull and gray routine of our daily lives becomes lit up, reminding us that the eyes of Hashem are always focused on us.

World records can be viewed as a map of the world's "borders" — mankind's extreme acts and events. We read of people who are able to accomplish more and more, to go higher and farther and thus better themselves, yet we realize how ridiculous and foolish are others who are willing to waste their precious time on trivialities and the pursuit of honor, which often has a bitter ending.

For us believing Jews, the events in the history of mankind, the behavior of nations and the workings of their wars, the thoughts that occupy the hearts of kings and leaders, and the discoveries by sages of the other nations, all teach us to appreciate the privilege of being able to wake up every morning to the sweet words of Torah — while others spend sleepless nights on trivialities, toiling but receiving nothing in return. We run to behold the sweetness of Hashem, while they run toward emptiness.

This book is filled with many good and interesting things, and we pray that we not be the cause of any mishap or misunderstanding. May we merit to strengthen our readers' *emunah*, and may each and every one of us realize that all acts which take place under the sun are simply miracles and wonders guided by Divine Providence. Hashem alone made, makes, and will make everything; the entire world is dependent only on "the One Who spoke and the world came into being."

Nattan Hurvitz and Aharon Yosef Hoffman

ABBREVIATIONS USED IN THIS BOOK

¢ = cent
$ = American dollar
€ = euro
₣ = French franc
% = percent
£ = pound sterling
# = number
c = circa (approximately)
cm = centimeter
col. = colonel
dB = decibel
DM = Deutschmark
est. = estimated
ft = foot
ft^2 = square feet
ft^3 = cubic feet
ft/m = feet per meter
ft/sec = feet per second
gal = gallon
hp = horsepower
in. = inch
kg = kilogram
km = kilometer
km/h = kilometers per hour
km^2 = square kilometers
kT = kiloton
kW = kilowatt
kWh = kilowatt hours
lb = pound
lt. col. = lieutenant colonel
m = meter
m^2 = square meters
m^3 = cubic meters
mi = mile
mi^2 = square miles
mm = millimeter
mpg = miles per gallon
mph = miles per hour
mT = megaton
mW = megawatt
NIS = New Israeli Shekel
rpm = revolutions per minute

HOLY MEN, HOLY BOOKS, AND HOLY PLACES

The Hearts of Kings and Nobles 8
From Generation to Generation 10
Center of the World 12
People of the Book 14
Warriors 18
Facts and Feats in Tanach 20

MANKIND

Population 26
Names 30
Healer of All Flesh 34
Mail and Communication 38
Inventions 44

NATIONS AND GOVERNMENTS

Nations of the World 48
Governments 54
A Common Language and a Shared Purpose 58
Lawbreakers 62

THE WORLD

Energy 68
The Power of Nature 72
Tragedies 76
"If Hashem Will Not Protect" 78

STRANGE, YET INTERESTING

Unusual Talents 86
Large and Small 90
A Time to Play 94

WHO NOURISHES ALL

"Not by Bread Alone ..." 100
"Drink Sweet Beverages" 104
Fruit of the Land 108
"His Palate Is Sweet" 112
From the Fat of the Land 116

Contents

ARMIES AND WARS

Men of War 120
Fighter Aircraft 124
Battleships 130
Submarines.................... 132
Tanks 134
Cannons and Guns 136
Bombs and Missiles 138
Unconventional Weapons 140
Nuclear Warfare............... 142

WHO BY CHARIOT

Cars 146
Trains......................... 154
History of Flight 156
Jets........................... 160
Air Transport.................. 164
Ships 166
Motorcycles 170
Bicycles...................... 172

The Hearts of Kings and Nobles 8

From Generation to Generation 10

Center of the World 12

People of the Book 14

Warriors 18

Facts and Feats in Tanach 20

Holy Men, Holy Books, and Holy Places

Whatever the *tanna'im* and *amora'im* said is reliable and truthful.

Therefore, if you come across anything that looks wrong or inappropriate, don't be disturbed, because all of the words of our Sages are absolute truth. Each letter is pure gold and silver. What in their eyes appeared so simple and obvious, in our feeble minds appears fantastic, mystical, and hidden.

Because of our long exile and the passage of time, Chazal decided to write down the hidden aspects of our Torah, so they wouldn't become lost to future generations. They wrote using types of riddles so that their words had hiddden meanings which could only be figured out by those holding the keys needed to understand them. These Sages passed on the keys to their faithful students who they trusted would protect them from falling into the wrong hands.

At times, the Sages' words were hidden through phrases usually meant for a different context, or with parables, or by attributing incidents and actions to the wrong characters....Sometimes they seem to contradict themselves, because their full meaning has not been grasped. Only someone who fully understands the context within which these words were written will be able to uncover the absolute truth behind each saying.

At times our Sages presented their words in a simplistic manner — almost like a folk tale — but this was just camouflage for profound and elevated ideas. Only someone who can make his thoughts soar to lofty heights will be able to understand the monumental ideas behind the seemingly simple words.

Other times, Chazal presented their ideas in a clear and simple manner in order to make the reader think he understood, so that he will not look for the hidden secrets and meanings hidden in these same words....

Above all, one must understand that all the words of Chazal are based on the fact that the physical world is activated through spiritual powers and every matter in this lowly world is influenced from above — while at the same time physical acts leave an impression in the spiritual realm. Whoever does not accept this point will never understand the words of Chazal and their views, even one iota.

In addition, all Torah writings should not only be understood with their plain meaning — they also allude to prophecies regarding the future, acts from the past, and much more.

Each person will therefore interpret *midrashim* as well as he can, based on the principles he has learned from his teachers.

The men who wrote down the Shas and the *midrashim* went to great lengths to collect all of Chazal's writings. They evaluated each one in the presence of others. Only those that were thought to be appropriate were recorded in the collections of *midrashim*. Thus, all the *midrashim* recorded by the *tanna'im* and the *amora'im* are absolutely true, each idea sifted by the dedicated compilers.

Based on *Ma'amar al HaHaggados* by the Ramchal (HaRav Moshe Chaim Luzzatto)

LIFESPAN OF A KING

We generally do not find in Tanach or in the writings of Chazal the number of years a king, prophet, or kohen gadol lived. The book of *Melachim* records for us the age of a king at the beginning of his reign and the number of years he ruled. With this information we can calculate the number of years he lived, though not exactly, because the years of his reign were not counted from the anniversary of his becoming king but rather from Rosh Chodesh Nisan — the New Year for kings of Yehudah and the kingdom of Yisrael.

More than half the Jewish kings did not die a natural death. Some of them were killed in battle, others died from illness, while still others were assassinated.

Not a single king, including those who died of natural causes, merited reaching the age of 70 except King David. While Azaryah ben Amatzyah lived for 68 years and Menashe ben Chizkiyahu lived for 67 years, the majority of kings died between the ages of 40 and 55. The average life expectancy of Jewish kings who met a natural death was 44 years.

Most important of all is the fact that kings who "did what was proper in the eyes of Hashem" lived an average of 51 years, while those who "did what was evil in the eyes of Hashem" lived an average of 38 years.

The spring of Gichon, where Jewish kings were anointed

SHAUL, THE FIRST JEWISH KING

The first king of the Jewish nation was Shaul ben Kish from the tribe of Binyamin. Shaul was anointed by the prophet Shmuel at the age of 59 and ruled for 2 years. Some say that he ruled for 18, or perhaps 20, years. Still others say that after David was anointed he had the status of a king without a crown.

Shaul knew that he was the *gilgul* (reincarnation) of Lemech (comprised of the same Hebrew letters as *melech* — king), who had killed Kayin 77 generations earlier. Shaul killed himself in order to atone for this sin, as it is written, "If revenge for Kayin was taken after 7 generations, then Lemech after 77!" (*Bereishis* 4:24).

SHAUL, THE LAST JEWISH KING

HaRav Shaul Wohl, born in Padua, Italy, in the year 1545, was the son of HaRav Shmuel Yehudah Katzenellenbogen, known as the Maharshik. He studied in Padua before moving on to *yeshivos* in Poland, finally settling in Brisk. During that time, the Polish Prince, Nikolai Christoff Radziwell, traveled the land dressed as a simple peasant. When he got to Padua, he realized that he had run out of money. Shaul's father, the Maharshik, gave him food, drink, basic necessities, and enough money for the return trip to Poland.

Upon Prince Radziwell's return to Poland, he formed a close relationship with Shaul Wohl, who soon became the prince's closest advisor. Polish law required that the king be chosen by the noble class. However, when the king, Stephen Batori, died, the Polish nobles could not decide between Duke Maximillian, son of the German Caesar, and Prince Sigmund III, son of Johannes, king of Sweden, for the next Polish king. Late that night, Prince Radziwell suggested a temporary compromise: HaRav Shaul Wohl would temporarily become king, in order that the Polish people not remain even one night without a ruler.

Shaul Wohl ruled Poland for one day. The very night he became king, he declared all the anti-Jewish decrees null and void. The following morning he suggested that Prince Sigmund III be crowned as the next king of Poland, and his suggestion was accepted. HaRav Shaul Wohl merited to live a long life. He died in the year 1617 at the age of 72.

Tomb of the prophet Shmuel in Ramah, outside of Yerushalayim

LONGEST ROYAL DYNASTY

The longest-lasting family of monarchs was the Davidic dynasty. Their first ruler was David. He was followed by 21 descendants: Shlomo (whose reign lasted 17 years), Rechavam (17 years), Aviyah (3 years), Asa (41 years), Yehoshafat (25 years), Yehoram (8 years), Achazyahu (1 year), Yehoash (40 years), Amatzyah (14 years), Uziyahu (52 years), Yosam (16 years), Achaz (16 years), Chizkiyahu (29 years), Menashe (55 years), Amon (2 years), Yoshiyahu (31 years), Yehoachaz ben Yoshiyahu (3 months), his brother Yehoyakim ben Yoshiyahu (11 years), Yehoyachin ben Yehoyakim (3 months), Tzidkiyahu ben Yoshiyahu, who was the brother of Yehoachaz and Yehoyakim as well as the uncle of Yehoyachin (11 years), and Gedalyah ben Achikam (52 days). The Davidic dynasty reigned over Yehudah for a total of 450 years.

LONGEST DYNASTY OF KINGS OF YISRAEL

The longest-lasting monarchy among the kings of the (northern) kingdom of Yisrael was the dynasty of Yehu ben

The Hearts of Kings and Nobles

LONGEST-LIVING KING

At the time of creation it was decided that King David would live only 3 hours. But David lived longer than any other Jewish king! The 70 years of his life were given to him as a gift by Adam HaRishon. An extra 70 years were donated jointly by Avraham (5 years), Yaakov (28 years) and Yosef (37 years). Given that David hardly slept at night (he is known to have slept the amount a horse sleeps), it can be said that he lived 2 times 70 years — 70 years of days and 70 years of nights.

David was anointed king in the year 2803 (958 B.C.E.) at the age of 29 by the prophet Shmuel. He ruled over Yehudah in Hebron for 7½ years, and for another 33 years he reigned in Yerushalayim as king of all of Israel. The 6 months in which he was afflicted with *tzara'as* as punishment for the incident with Batsheva are not included in the count. Therefore, he is considered to have reigned for 40 years.

Ir David, the City of David, c. 1920

Yehoshafat ben Nimshi, who was anointed by the prophet Elisha in the year 3083 (678 B.C.E.). Yehu had been the military chief-of-staff of King Yehoram ben Achav. He was sent by Eliyahu HaNavi and Elisha to destroy the house of Achav and eradicate all the *avodah zarah* which Achav had set up with the counsel of his wife Izevel.

Yehu ruled over the kingdom of Yisrael for 28 years and was followed by four generations of descendants: his son Yehoachaz (17 years), Yoash ben Yehoachaz (16 years), Yeravam ben Yoash (41 years), and Zechariah ben Yeravam, who a mere 6 months following his becoming king was assassinated by Shalom ben Yavesh.

LONGEST REIGN

Menashe ben Chizkiyahu, king of Yehudah, ruled longer than any other Jewish king. During the first 22 years he was evil and actively went against Hashem's word — going so far as to place an idol in the *Heichal* of the Beis HaMikdash! However, after the king of Bavel came and locked him in a copper vat under which he lit a fire, Menashe cried out to Hashem to save him. The angels closed the windows of the heavens so his prayer wouldn't reach Hashem. However, Hashem dug a tunnel under His Holy Throne and Menashe's prayer went up through the tunnel and was accepted. After he did *teshuvah*, Menashe ruled for another 33 years, bringing his reign to a grand total of 55 years.

SHORTEST REIGN

After assassinating his master Elah ben Basha, king of Yisrael, Zimri entered the palace and took over the kingdom. However, the army was totally against his kingship and instead appointed Omri, the military chief-of-staff who waged war against Zimri. Zimri responded by burning down the royal palace while he himself was inside, bringing about his own death. Zimri's rule lasted a total of 7 days.

The shortest reign of a king of Yehudah was that of Gedalyah ben Achikam, the last king before the destruction of the first Beis HaMikdash. His rule lasted only 52 days.

THE ONLY FEMALE RULER

All the kings of Yehudah descended from the house of David with the exception of Asalyah bas Achav king of Yisrael. In addition, she was the only woman to rule during the time of the Tanach. Asalyah was married to Yehoram ben Yehoshafat, king of Yehudah. After Yehoram died from a serious illness, his son Achazyahu was anointed king at the age of 22.

While Achazyahu made a visit to his uncle Yehoram ben Achav, king of Yisrael, Yehu ben Yehoshafat arrived with orders from Eliyahu HaNavi to assassinate King Yehoram and eliminate the wicked rule of Achav and his sons. Achazyahu was injured during the assassination and later died from his wounds. When word reached his mother Asalyah, sister of Yehoram king of Yisrael, she used witchcraft and a deadly drug to destroy the entire house of David — all except Yehoash, youngest son of Achazyahu. And then she forcibly took the throne for herself.

FIRST SHOFET

The first of the *shoftim* (judges) was Osniel ben Kenaz from the tribe of Yehudah. Osniel became a *shofet* in the year 2516 (1245 B.C.E.), at the end of the Period of the Elders (*Zekeinim*). At that point, the Jewish nation was led by Calev ben Yefuneh, Pinchas ben Elazar, the sons of Eldad and Meidad, and the 70 elders. Osniel ben Kenaz was a *talmid chacham* (Torah scholar) as well as a great warrior. After he captured the town of Kiryat Sefer, he was given Achsah, the wise and righteous daughter of Calev, for a wife. Osniel rescued the Jewish people from subjugation under Cushan Rishatayim and served as their *shofet* for 40 years.

LONGEST-REIGNING SHOFET

Ehud ben Gera from the tribe of Binyamin ruled longer than any other *shofet*. He led the Jewish nation for 80 years (62 according to the Vilna Gaon). Ehud ben Gera was a disciple of Osniel ben Kenaz. He saved the Jewish nation from subjugation under Eglon, king of Moav. Ehud ben Gera is the only Jewish leader known to have been left-handed.

THE ONLY FEMALE JUDGE

The prophetess Devorah was the only female judge (*shofetess*). Devorah was from the tribe of Naftali and she freed the Jewish people from being enslaved to Yavin, king of Canaan, and his chief-of-staff Sisera. She ruled the Jewish nation for 40 years and was 1 of only 2 women whose song composed through *ruach hakodesh* is recorded in Tanach. (The other is Chanah.)

Tomb of Devorah, in Kadesh Naftali

DID YOU KNOW?

In the last few years, scientists in laboratories researching old age have identified the aging gene of fruit flies and have managed to alter it. As a result of this genetic change, the life expectancy of the flies has doubled and they remain physically young until their death. Because of these experiments, researchers now believe that old age is controlled by a genetic mechanism that allocates our life span artificially and actually shortens our "true" life expectancy.

The researchers concluded that man's life expectancy should really be 1,000 years and that the body has the ability to preserve its youthfulness until the day of death. In fact, beginning with Adam HaRishon and for the next 10 generations, many people lived for more than 900 years in perfectly good health, displaying no signs of old age. Noach, for example, had his first child at the age of 500 and only began building the ark at the age of 600.

Researchers are trying to solve the mystery of precisely at what point in history life spans shortened and what was the cause. The answer is found in the Torah. The Torah says that because of the sins in Noach's generation — mainly pride — Hashem decreed regarding man: "His days shall be 120 years" (*Bereishis* 6:3). Limiting the maximum life expectancy to 120 years was meant to humble man. (Based on the commentary of the Ba'alei HaTosafos on the Torah.)

This shortening of man's life span was a gradual process. Noach, who was the 10th generation from Adam HaRishon, lived for 959 years. His son Shem lived for 600 years, and Shem's son Arpachshad lived for 438 years. Avraham Avinu, who was the 10th generation from Noach, lived for 175 years. The maximum life expectancy of man decreased to 120 years — today's maximum lifespan — with Moshe Rabbeinu, who was the 26th generation from Adam HaRishon.

In the time of the *Avos*, people did not show any signs of old age — their hair didn't even turn white. Chazal relate that after Yitzchak's birth, Avraham saw that people couldn't distinguish between the two of them in spite of their 100-year age difference. Avraham therefore prayed for old age in order that man would learn to honor and respect his elders.

There were also no illnesses at that time — death would come suddenly and without warning. Yaakov asked Hashem to take away sudden death in order to give people the opportunity to repent before they died. Hashem granted the requests of both Avraham and Yaakov.

OLDEST PERSON TO HAVE A BRIS MILAH

The oldest person to have a *bris milah* was Avraham Avinu, who underwent circumcision a the age of 99. This act came with tremendous self-sacrifice.

In our days, the oldest person to have a *bris milah* was an 83-year-old man who had immigrated from the Soviet Union to Eretz Yisrael in the 1950s and was placed by the Jewish Agency on a kibbutz in the north. He innocently asked about arranging a *bris milah* for himself (*bris milah* was forbidden in the USSR), but the kibbutz members said that there was no longer any need for this in Eretz Yisrael. With *siyata diShmaya*, in his old age he wa taken care of by a man who happened to be a believing Jew. During one of their conversations, the elderly gentleman related that he was very interested in finally having a *bris milah*. The caretaker contacted the organization called *Bris Yosef veYitzchak*, and at the age o 83, the Russian immigrant finally merited entering into the covenant of Avraham Avinu.

Holy Men, Holy Books, and Holy Places
From Generation to Generation

LONGEST-LIVING HUMAN BEING

Mesushelach, who was the 8th generation from Adam HaRishon, lived longer than any other human being — 969 years. He served Adam HaRishon for 243 years and learned 900 *sedarim* of Mishnah. Every sentence he uttered contained 233 parables in praise of Hashem. Mesushelach's merit protected his generation his entire life. When he died, a great noise was heard, which was the sound of his being eulogized in Heaven. Hashem delayed the start of the Flood for seven days in order to allow this *tzaddik* to be properly eulogized and mourned. (*Yalkut Shimoni*, *Bereishis* 42)

LONGEST-LIVING WOMAN

The woman who lived longer than any other woman in history was Serach, daughter of Malkiel and Hadurah. After her husband Malkiel died, Hadurah, the granddaughter of Eiver, married Asher the son of Yaakov Avinu. Although Serach is referred to as Asher's daughter, she was really his adopted daughter. Born in the year 2214 (1547 B.C.E.), Serach is famous for giving Yaakov the wonderful news that his beloved son Yosef was still alive and was ruler over the entire land of Egypt. When Yaakov heard the news from Serach, he blessed her that the angel of death would never be able to overpower her. Seven hundred and seven years later, her great wisdom saved the residents of Avel Beis Ma'achah when she handed over Sheva ben Bichri — a rebel against King David — to Yoav. In the merit of Yaakov's blessing, Serach entered Gan Eden during her lifetime. (*Kallah Rabbasi* 3:23)

OLDEST PARENTS

Noach begat his eldest son at the age of 500. Yocheved gave birth to Moshe Rabbeinu at the age of 130, and Chanah, mother of the prophet Shmuel, was 130 when Eli the Kohen told her she would have a baby.

A REALLY GREAT-GRANDFATHER

Adam HaRishon lived to see Lemech ben Mesushelach, who was the 9th generation of his offspring. When Adam HaRishon died at the age of 930, Lemech was 56 years old. Lemech begat Noach 126 years later, at the age of 182.

ENTERING GAN EDEN IN THEIR LIFETIMES

Nine people entered Gan Eden during their lifetimes. The first of them was Chanoch, whom Hashem removed from this world before he could sin. After him came Eliezer, who entered as a reward for being a loyal servant to Avraham.

Serach bas Asher was the next person to enter Gan Eden while still alive as reward for reviving Yaakov Avinu's spirits by telling him that Yosef was still alive. Bisya daughter of Pharaoh was rewarded for drawing Moshe Rabbeinu out of the water. Eved-Melech of Kush — who was Baruch ben Neriyah — pulled the prophet Yirmeyahu out from the pit and revived him. Chiram king of Tzor provided King Shlomo with workers and raw materials for construction of the Beis HaMikdash. These 6 were followed by the son of Rabbi Yehudah HaNasi, Eliyahu haNavi, and the Mashiach. (*Derech Eretz Zuta* 1)

THE ONLY ONE TO RETURN FROM GAN EDEN

Yitzchak Avinu is the only person to have entered Gan Eden in his lifetime and later return to this world. After the *Akeidah*, Yitzchak went to recover in Gan Eden. He stayed there for the next three years, returning to the world at the precise moment Eliezer brought Rivkah to Eretz Yisrael. The Chida explains that when Rivkah met Yitzchak she noted that he was *hadur*. While the word usually implies a sense of dignity, it can also come from the word *hadran*, which implies a return. Rivkah had spotted Yitzchak returning from Gan Eden in the manner of all who descend from Heaven — head down and feet up. (*Chizkuni*, *Bereishis* 26)

GREATEST NATURAL POPULATION GROWTH

In the year 2238 (1523 B.C.E.) Yaakov and his family, totaling 70 people, went down to Egypt. Two hundred and ten years later, the Jewish nation, which numbered 600,000 men, left Egypt. Four-fifths of the Jewish nation had died during the plague of darkness (*makkas choshech*). A quick calculation reveals that before the plague of darkness there must have been at least 3 million Jewish men in Egypt. Adding the women and children, the total is approximately 15 million people — more than 214,285 times the 70 who initially went down to Egypt!

In the opinion of Rabbi Nehorai, only 1 out of every 5,000 Hebrews left Egypt. This means there were 3 billion Jewish men in Egypt before the plague of darkness! The *Midrash HaGadol* states that only 1 out of 600,000 men merited leaving Egypt.

CITY WITHOUT CORPSES

After the death of Yehoshua, Yosef's descendants decided to capture the city of Luz. The entrance to the city was hidden and its location kept a secret. So Yosef's descendants placed guards around the area and succeeded in capturing a man who had left the city. They promised to save the man and his family if he would reveal the entrance to the city. The man showed them the entrance, which was hidden inside a hollow tree trunk. He then took his family to the land of Chittim where they built a city named Luz, after the city they had come from.

In the merit of the kindness this man showed the descendants of Yosef, the angel of death never passed through the new Luz. When the people reached old age and decided it was time to leave this world, they would go beyond the city walls and die over there. The city of Luz was also left completely intact. It did not suffer the exile of Sancheriv nor the destruction of Nebuchadnezzar.

GREATEST NUMBER OF VISITORS IN ONE CITY

Twelve million *olei regel* (pilgrims) lodged in Yerushalayim for approximately 10 days. Each one required enough room to both sleep and conduct the Seder. Most of us would expect homeowners to cash in on the demand and rent out space at high prices. However, the law in Yerushalayim forbade renting houses or beds. In addition, nobody felt crowded, and no one ever said, "There is not enough room for me to stay in Yerushalayim" (*Pirkei Avos* 5:7).

Imagine — 12 million *olei regel* in one city! Compare this to today's population of 7 million in the entire Eretz Yisrael and the 700,000 people living in Yerushalayim and surrounding areas. (*Pesachim* 64b)

BREAD FIT FOR A KING AND WINE FLOWING LIKE WATER

The Gemara in tractate *Eiruvin* teaches us that the average person's daily food consumption corresponds to the daily amount of manna that fell in the Desert. This means that the average adult consumes approximately 4.4 lb (2 kg) of food per day. Therefore, during their 10-day stay in Yerushalayim, the 12 million *olei regel* consumed a total of 528 million lb (240 million kg) of food. In addition, they required an estimated 3.2 million gal (12 million liters) of wine for their four cups at the Seder, Kiddush and Havdalah, and 1.6 million additional gal (6 million liters) for the wine offerings which accompanied their sacrifices. Compare the 4.8 million gal (18 million liters) of wine needed for those 10 days to today's statistics: the entire population of Eretz Yisrael consumes 12 million gal (45 million liters) of wine and grape juice per year. (*Eruvin* 81a)

"WOOL MOUNTAINS"

The *korban Pesach* had to be eaten when a person was already full from eating meat. Therefore, Jews had to offer a *chagigas arba asar* on Erev Pesach and eat it before the *korban Pesach*. At least four *chagigah* sacrifices accompanied each *korban Pesach* — which was 4.8 million additional animals.

According to the Rambam, every person was required to offer *shalmei simchah*, and adult males were also obligated to bring *olos reiyah* and *shalmei chagigah*. Although each of these sacrifices could be brought by a group of people, many *olei regel* offered more than 1 animal for this purpose. It can safely be estimated that the total number of animals brought for *shalmei simchah*, *olos reiyah*, and *shalmei chagigah* totaled approximately 6 million.

Olei regel took advantage of being in Yerushalayim to bring other offerings they needed to sacrifice during the course of the year, such as a *korban chatas*, *asham*, *ma'aser sheini*, and other *nedarim* and *nedavos*. Adding together all these animals, it can be estimated that at least 24 million — probably even more — animals were brought to Yerushalayim for sacrificing.

In order to supply this huge amount of animals, the Sanhedrin instructed animal merchants to gather all the cows, goats and sheep from towns surrounding Yerushalayim. The masses of wooly sheep covering the mountains made it seem as if the mountains were painted white. Of course, the 24 million animals in Yerushalayim and the vicinity — not to mention the animals which brought the *olei regel* to Yerushalayim — needed straw to eat and water to drink!

Today, the meat consumption in Eretz Yisrael is estimated at 33 lb (15 kg) per person per year, totaling approximately 97,000 tons of meat produced from the slaughter of 200,000 animals. Most of the meat sold is cattle.

ABOVE TIME AND SPACE

The entire area referred to as *Har HaBayis* encompassed 500 x 500 *amos* — 820 x 820 ft (250 x 250 m), totaling 551,650 ft^2 (51,250 m^2). The empty area free of any building was the *Ezras Yisrael* and *Ezras Kohanim*, whose area was 221.5 x 180.5 ft (67.5 x 55 m), totaling 40,058 ft^2 (3,721.5 m^2). In the 3.5 hours allotted for offering the *korban Pesach*, 1.2 million men along with their 1.2 million goats or lambs would pass through this area.

The *korban Pesach* was slaughtered in three rounds while Hallel was sung. In each of the first two rounds the Levi'im managed to complete the entire Hallel twice while all the *korbanos* were slaughtered and offered. The third group was smaller in size, and everything was finished before the Levi'im even reached *"Ahavti ki yishma"* the first time around. This means that an estimated 530,000 men along with 530,000 animals filled the *Azarah* in the first two groups, while the final group contained "only" 132,500 men and animals.

Twelve Levi'im stood outside the gate and another twelve Levi'im stayed inside. They were there to maintain order, limiting each square meter to only 140 men accompanied by 140 animals.

THE QUICK AND NIMBLE KOHANIM

The moment the *Azarah* filled up, the doors were locked and the work began. Next to the base of the *mizbeach* — whose length was 66 *amos* (96 ft or 29.3 m), stood 66 rows of Kohanim. The Kohanim stood on special platforms to prevent their clothing from becoming covered with blood. They each held a basin used for collecting the blood of the *korban* from the slaughtered animal. Each basin would get passed from one Kohen to the next until it reached the *mizbeach*. Five hundred and thirty thousand animals were divided among the 66 columns, which meant that in each column 8,030 animals were slaughtered in the 90 minutes allotted for each of the first 2 rounds of offerings. This translates to a maximum of .66 seconds per animal.

The work was carried out with lightning speed. The representative of each group offering a *korban* would go to the end of the row to have his animal slaughtered. A Kohen would immediately collect the blood in the designated basin and the person who had brought the sacrifice would quickly leave the area to make room for the next sacrifice. The basins practically flew along the entire row of Kohanim; the basins in each row were either entirely gold or entirely silver. The Kohen who received the blood would pass the full basin to the Kohen next to him closer to the *mizbeach*. After passing a full basin to one side, the Kohen would receive an empty one whose contents had been emptied upon the *mizbeach* from the other side. The basins flew by with such speed that it was impossible to figure out how they were being passed from one hand to the other. For 90 minutes non-stop, one could only see one long line of silver or gold extending from the area where the *korban* was slaughtered all the way to the other end where the blood was poured. Eventually the *Azarah* was filled with 1.2 million liters of blood, which reached a height of almost 14 in. (35 cm).

Immediately after an animal was slaughtered it was hung on designated hooks and then skinned — this too had to be carried out incredibly quickly. Whoever couldn't find a hook would lay the animal between his shoulder and another person's shoulder. The *emurim* (sacrificial portions) were removed and immediately placed in a *keli shareis* (service vessel), so that the Kohanim would be able to offer them before sunset and clean the floor of the *Azarah* as well.

The animal had to be roasted — and it needed to be roasted in a sanctified area. Because the rooftops were not sanctified, every *korban Pesach* was roasted on the ground floor. One of the miracles of Yerushalayim was that no one ever said that he couldn't find an oven in which to roast his *korban Pesach* (*Avos d'Rabbi Nasan*).

YERUSHALAYIM — HEIGHT OF PURITY

Several decrees were passed so the streets of Yerushalayim would always remain *tahor* (ritually pure). There were no projections

Center of the World

jutting out from buildings (no porches and not even any drainage pipes), to prevent people from accidentally becoming *tamei* (ritually impure) through *tum'as ohel* (being under the same overhead covering as a corpse). Public garbage dumps were forbidden (lest there be found insects that could transmit *tum'ah*—spiritual impurity—to someone who came into contact with them), and special cleaning crews kept Yerushalayim so clean that there was not even the slightest speck of dirt anywhere.

Because a large number of the *olei regel* had come from far away, whoever suspected that he may be *temei meis* (impure from a corpse) would proceed to the "*taharah* street" on the third and seventh days following his arrival, where he would be sprinkled with purification waters. He would then be *tahor* in time for his Pesach offering. With so many visitors wanting to insure they were *tahor*, this street looked like a river.

It was forbidden to enter the Beis HaMikdash without first immersing in a *mikveh*. This meant that the 1.2 million representatives of the groups assigned to each *korban Pesach* immersed on the 14th of Nisan. In addition, all of the estimated 6 million men immersed on the morning of Yom Tov so they could daven *Shacharis* in the Beis HaMikdash and offer their *olos reiyah*.

The Rosh explains that the time required to immerse and dry oneself is equivalent to the time it takes to walk 50 *amos* — 27 seconds. This means that the immersion of 6 million men would take about 45,000 hours. Assuming that this was all carried out in a space of 5 hours, this meant that 9,000 *mikvaos* were required for the city of Yerushalayim.

In fact, excavations in the Old City have revealed that practically every house in the ancient city of Yerushalayim contained its own *mikveh*. In comparison, in the entire Eretz Yisrael there are approximately 3,000 *mikvaos* in operation today.

STOREHOUSES OF THE BEIS HAMIKDASH

On Erev Yom Tov, 4.8 million *korbenos chagigas arba asar* were offered (see p. 12). An additional 6 million *shalmei chagigah*, *olos reiyah*, and *shalmei simchah* were offered on the morning of Yom Tov. These *korbanos* were accompanied by *nesachim* (wine-offerings) and *menachos* (flour-offerings). The Torah writes that the minimum *nesachim* and *menachos* was that for a lamb-offering — an *isaron* of fine-flour (approximately 2.2 quarts or 2.4 liters of flour), .25 *hin* of oil (about a quart, or slightly more than 1 liter) and another .25 *hin* of wine.

Based on the calculation of 10.8 million *korbanos*, the storerooms in the Beis HaMikdash contained 133,480 ft^3 (37,800 m^3) of oil and wine, and 83,923 ft^3 (23,760 m^3) of flour for the *korbanos* of the first day alone. Storing such a large volume requires storerooms with an approximate length and width of 226 ft (69 m) and a height of 33 ft (10 m) — or 1,300 average size rooms.

In the Beis HaMikdash there were 2 counters. At 1 counter sat cashiers who would collect money and give receipts, while those at the 2nd counter would distribute *nesachim* and *menachos* in exchange for a receipt. On the first day of Yom Tov, 6 million people patiently waited their turn at these counters. Even if we assume that everything worked like clockwork and everyone received their receipt within 1 second, the distribution would have taken 1,666 hours — nearly 70 days. Tens of people were therefore assigned to each counter and would work in pairs to insure quick distribution.

MIRACLES OF THE MIZBEACH

Six million *shalmei chagigah* were offered on the morning of Yom Tov. They were accompanied by 13 million quarts (14.4 million liters) of flour for *menachos* and an additional 6.3 million quarts (6 million liters) of oil for *nesachim*, which were completely consumed upon the *mizbeach* on the same day. The volume of the *menachos* and *nesachim* was enough to fill 500 rooms. If we were to place the entire amount on the top of the *mizbeach* at one time (an area 39 x 39 ft or 12 x 12 m), the top of the *mizbeach* filled with oil and flour would reach a height of 41 stories.

The 2 million *olos reiyah* were also consumed entirely upon the *mizbeach*. If we were to assume that the weight of an average sheep was 44 lb (20 kg), this means that an additional 88 million lb (40 million kg) of meat had to be entirely burnt. On the first day of Pesach, 6.3 million quarts (6 million liters) of wine used for the *nesachim* were poured into a designated cup on the *mizbeach* and from there poured into the *shisin* (a hollow area under the *mizbeach*).

SMOKELESS FIRE

By the laws of nature, burning this amount of meat, flour, and oil would need a fire large enough to burn down an entire city — certainly large enough to fill the entire city of Yerushalayim with smoke. However, the fire which burned up the *korbanos* during the days of King Shlomo in the first Beis HaMikdash came down from Heaven and looked like a lion lying upon the *mizbeach*. One could touch the fire, and it was as bright as the sun. This miraculous fire would consume liquids such as oil and the moisture from the meat as if they were nothing more than dry pieces of wood, without emitting any smoke.

Despite the fact that there was a heavenly fire, there was a mitzvah to light the pyre every day. Only the energy emanating from nuclear reactors and laser apparatus could even remotely resemble such a fire.

FIRST BOOKS

The first mention of any book is found in *Parashas Bereishis*: "This is the book of the descendants of Adam" (*Bereishis* 5:1). R' Yehudah son of R' Shimon said that before Hashem breathed life into Adam HaRishon, he was shown all future generations, the sages and leaders, until the end of time. This is alluded to in the verse: "Your eyes saw my unshaped form and in Your book all were recorded" (*Tehillim* 139:16).

The commentary *Matnos Kehunah* explains that Adam HaRishon had with him a book which he received from Heaven. The *amora* Shmuel claimed to have had the privilege of browsing through Adam HaRishon's book and noticed his name with a comment that he would become a *chacham* but would not be referred to as Rabbi Shmuel.

The second book ever to appear was *Sefer Raziel HaMalach*. According to the Zohar, Hashem handed the book to Adam HaRishon via His angel Raziel, the one appointed over the hidden areas of the Torah. While still in Gan Eden, Adam HaRishon bequeathed this book to his son and to all of his descendants, until it finally reached Avraham Avinu.

Rabbi Nachman of Breslov claims that the *sefer* known today as *Raziel* is not the one the angel gave to Adam HaRishon. He adds that the claim that this book is a *segulah* to save one from fire is not true, and in fact there have been known cases of fires in which the book itself was consumed.

GOOD THINGS COME IN SMALL PACKAGES

Together with his staff of researchers, Professor Uri Sivan, head of the Institute for Nanotechnology at the Technion in Haifa, managed to write all 304,901 words of the Tanach in an area of .5 m^2. They accomplished this feat with the help of a concentrated ionic beam. In order to read this miniature Tanach, the print had to be magnified 10,000 times.

FIRST KNOWN BOOK ON KABBALAH

The Chida records in his book, *Shem HaGedolim*, that the first known book on the subject of Kabbalah was *Sefer HaBahir*, written by the *tanna* R' Nechnuyah ben HaKaneh.

LONGEST COMPOSITION BY A TANNA

The Zohar contains only a small part of the Torah wisdom of the *tanna* R' Shimon bar Yochai. It is the longest known *tannaic* composition. The Zohar was completed by R' Shimon's *talmidim* (disciples), and was then placed in *genizah* where it remained for approximately 1,000 years until the period of the Ramban. The Zohar contains *Midrash HaNe'elam*, hidden secrets of the Torah; *Sifri d'Tzniusa*; *Idra Rabba* and *Idra Zuta*; and *Raia Meheimna*. It also cites *mishnayos*, as well as *beraisos* and *toseftas*, which until then had been in the hidden portions of the Torah.

LONGER THAN THE ENTIRE EARTH

R' Eliezer and R' Yehoshua said: "If all the seas were ink and the marshes were quills and the heavens and earth parchment, and all the people were scribes, they would not be able to write down all the Torah that we learned. But for all that, we did not take away (from our teachers' knowledge) even the amount a paintbrush takes away from the sea."

R' Akiva said: "I am not on the level of my teachers, who took from their teachers' knowledge. What I took from my teachers is the equivalent of a person smelling an *esrog*, where the smeller enjoys the fragrance without taking away one bit from the *esrog*; similar to one who lights one candle from another."

(*Shir HaShirim Rabbah* 1)

DID YOU KNOW?

The five books of the Torah were dictated by Hashem to Moshe Rabbeinu. Some say that the final eight verses which describe Moshe's death were written with tears by Moshe Rabbeinu, while others hold that Yehoshua bin Nun wrote them.

The book of *Yehoshua* was written by Yehoshua himself, with the last part being written by Elazar HaKohen and his son Pinchas.

The book of *Shoftim* was written by the prophet Shmuel, who also wrote the book of *Shmuel* up until the description of his death. The rest of the book was written by the prophet Nasan and the *chozeh* (seer) Gad.

The book of *Melachim* was written by the prophet Yirmeyahu, who also wrote the book of *Yirmeyahu*.

Unlike the other books of the prophets, the book of *Yeshayahu* was not written by Yeshayahu himself, but rather by King Chizkiyahu and an assistant. Rashi explains that the other prophets were able to write their books as the time of their death drew near, something Yeshayahu was not given the chance to do because he was killed by Menashe King of Yehudah.

Tosafos hold that King Chizkiyahu himself did not actually write the book of *Yeshayahu*, but rather it was written by colleagues who outlived him. Yet Chizkiyahu is credited with writing it, as reward for having strengthened Torah learning during his reign as king.

The book of *Yechezkel* was written by the *Anshei Knesses HaGedolah*. Yechezkel himself was unable to write it because he prophesied in Bavel and it was not permitted to record this prophecy outside of Eretz Yisrael. The *Anshei Knesses HaGedolah* also wrote the *Trei Asar* (the Twelve Prophets).

Megillas Ruth was written by the prophet Shmuel.

The book of *Tehillim* was written by King David. In addition to David's psalms, the book contains the words of ten other sages. Some of these sages lived many years before him: Adam HaRishon, Malki Tzedek, Avraham Avinu, Moshe Rabbeinu and the three sons of Korach. The other three sages lived during his lifetime: Heyman, Yedusun, and Asaf, who were among the Levi'im who sang in the Beis HaMikdash.

The book of *Iyov* was written by Moshe Rabbeinu.

Mishlei, *Koheles*, and *Shir HaShirim* — all the words of wisdom of King Shlomo — were actually recorded by King Chizkiyahu and his assistant.

Megillas Eichah was written by the prophet Yirmeyahu.

The book of *Daniel* and *Megillas Esther* were written by the *Anshei Knesses HaGedolah* — one of whose members was Mordechai.

The books of *Ezra* and *Divrei HaYamim* were written by Ezra the Scribe.

People of the Book

FIRST WRITTEN WORK OF THE ORAL TORAH

Once the Sages allowed recording the Oral Torah, the first book containing Oral Torah to be published was *Pirkei d'Rabbi Eliezer*, written by the *tanna* R' Eliezer ben Hyrcanus — the *rebbi* of R' Akiva.

GREATEST NUMBER OF LESSON REVIEWS

The *tanna* R' Preida had a student to whom he would have to repeat each lesson 400 times before he understood it. One day R' Preida was called to perform a mitzvah in the middle of a lesson. Before leaving he taught the student the usual 400 times, but he still did not understand the lesson. R' Preida asked him why today was different. The student answered, "From the very moment they told you that there is a mitzvah for you to do, I couldn't concentrate, because every moment I said that now you will get up and leave."

R' Preida sat down again and taught him another 400 times. Then a heavenly voice said, "Do you want 400 years to be added to your life, or do you prefer that you and your generation merit the World to Come?" R' Preida said, "That I and my generation merit the World to Come." Hashem said, "Give him both." (*Eiruvin* 54b)

CITY WITH THE LARGEST NUMBER OF SCHOOLS

The city of Beitar had 400 synagogues, each equipped with 400 teachers who each taught 400 schoolchildren — 64 million schoolchildren in all. When enemies entered the city, the children would drive them away by pricking them with the sharp sticks used to point to words during class. (*Gittin* 58a)

WHERE THERE'S LIFE, THERE'S HOPE

A child who acts unruly toward a great man can rise to greatness, as the verse states (*Iyov* 11:12), "Let one who is a wild donkey be reborn as a man." (*Otzar Yad HaChochmah*)

DID YOU KNOW?

The amount of wisdom an adult has is in proportion to how much he cried as a child: the more a child cries, the more wisdom he will have as an adult. Crying helps clarify thoughts. (*Nofes Tzufim*)

Cheder, early 1900s

MISHNAH STATISTICS

The Shas (Talmud) is divided into six sections, known as *sedarim*: *Zera'im*, *Mo'ed*, *Nashim*, *Nezikin*, *Kodashim*, and *Taharos* — with a total of 63 *masechtos* (tractates). The *sedarim* with the largest number of *masechtos* are *Mo'ed* and *Taharos*, with 12 *masechtos* each. *Taharos* has the most chapters — 126, followed by *Kodashim* with 89 and *Mo'ed* with 88.

Nashim contains the least number of *masechtos* — 7, and the least number of chapters — 71.

MOST CHAPTERS IN MISHNAH AND GEMARA

Maseches Keilim — the first tractate in *seder Taharos* — contains the largest number of chapters — 30. Because there is no *Gemara Keilim*, the largest number of chapters in Gemara (24) is found in *maseches Shabbos*, which is the first tractate of *seder Mo'ed*.

LARGEST MASECHES

In *dapim* (double-pages): *Bava Basra* — 176.

In words: *Berachos*, packed into only 64 pages — 68,843. (However, there there are discrepancies between editions.)

SHORTEST AMUD (SINGLE PAGE) OF GEMARA

Bava Kama 77a contains only two lines of Gemara and only three lines of Rashi. The remainder of the page is filled by two entries of Tosafos, each bearing the same introductory words (*divrei hamaschil*).

LONGEST RASHI IN SHAS

The longest Rashi in Shas — in *Yevamos* 9b, *"Veha'amar Rav Yehudah amar Rav"* — contains 817 words.

FIRST SHAS TO BE PRINTED

Twenty-three *masechtos* of the Talmud Bavli (the Babylonian Talmud), containing the commentaries of Rashi and Tosafos, were first printed in the year 1484 by the Soncino press in Italy. The printing was done in secret and was spread over a period of 6 years.

LAYOUT OF THE DAF

The layout of a *daf* (double-page) of Gemara as we know it today has remained constant through 50 worldwide printing editions. The first appearance was in the Venice edition, published in 1523. It was in this edition that the commentary of Rabbeinu Asher first appeared along with the Gemara.

THE BA'ALEI TOSAFOS

The period of the Ba'alei Tosafos began around the year 1240 and lasted about 200 years. Most of the approximately 300 Ba'alei Tosafos lived in Ashkenaz and France, with a few of them in England and Italy. Their commentary covered 30 *masechtos* of Talmud Bavli, and some of them wrote commentaries on the Torah as well. Much of their work focused on trying to arrive at a clear understanding of Rashi. In their great humility they referred to themselves simply as Tosafos ("additions"), implying that they were simply adding to Rashi's commentary and explaining his intent.

The Ba'alei Tosafos were Rashi's grandsons, great-grandsons, disciples and disciples' disciples. Many of them had the privilege of discussing the issues and their commentary with Rashi himself.

Rabbeinu Yaakov ben Meir, known as Rabbeinu Tam, was a grandson of Rashi. He is considered the greatest of the Ba'alei Tosafos. The Rivash writes about him in a letter: "All of the sages of Israel are as insignificant as a garlic peel or a sesame seed when compared to even the least of his disciples."

HaRav Yitzchak Eizik Yehuda Yechiel from Saprin writes that even the least of the Ba'alei Tosafos was so great that he was able to revive the dead.

THE MAHARAM OF ROTHENBURG

Rabbi Meir ben Baruch, the Maharam of Rothenburg (1215–1293), was a well-known, German Ba'al Tosafos. His most famous student was the Rosh. In 1286, while trying to move to Eretz Yisrael in order to escape Germany's persecution of the Jews, the Maharam was betrayed by a Jewish convert to Christianity and imprisoned in the Ensisheim Fortress in Alsace (an area on the eastern French-western

Graves of the Maharam of Rothenburg and Alexander ben Salomon Wimpfen

German border). The king demanded a ransom of 23,000 silver marks for the Maharam's freedom. The money was raised, but the Maharam refused to be redeemed because he knew it would encourage more kidnapings of rabbis (see Mishnah *Gittin* 4:6).

The Maharam died in prison 7 years later, but the government wouldn't release his body. Fourteen years after this, a man named Alexander ben Salomon Wimpfen paid a large sum of money for the Maharam's body, and a year later was buried next to him in the Jewish cemetery in Worms, Germany.

WORLD'S LARGEST TEHILLIM

The world's largest and most expensive sefer *Tehillim* was created by Judaica artist Shuki Freiman of Jerusalem. This unique, 5-volume set was commissioned by Jay and Jeanie Schottenstein, who were also involved in its planning and design.

Jay Schottenstein

The *Tehillim* are written on parchment (*klaf*), each page showing the Hebrew text with a facing English translation. Each page is decorated differently, with several colors as well as gold leaf.

Each volume is 20 in. (52 cm) high, 14 in. (37 cm) wide, and 3 in. (8 cm) thick. The letters are over 0.5 in. (1.7 cm) high. And each book weighs 17.6 lb (8 kg).

It took a special artisan 1.5 months to hand-sew the parchment together and insert it into each $4,000 cover. The entire *Tehillim* project took 4 years, and cost an estimated $600,000.

Front cover of *Tehillim*

World's largest *Tehillim* in comparison to volume 1 of this book

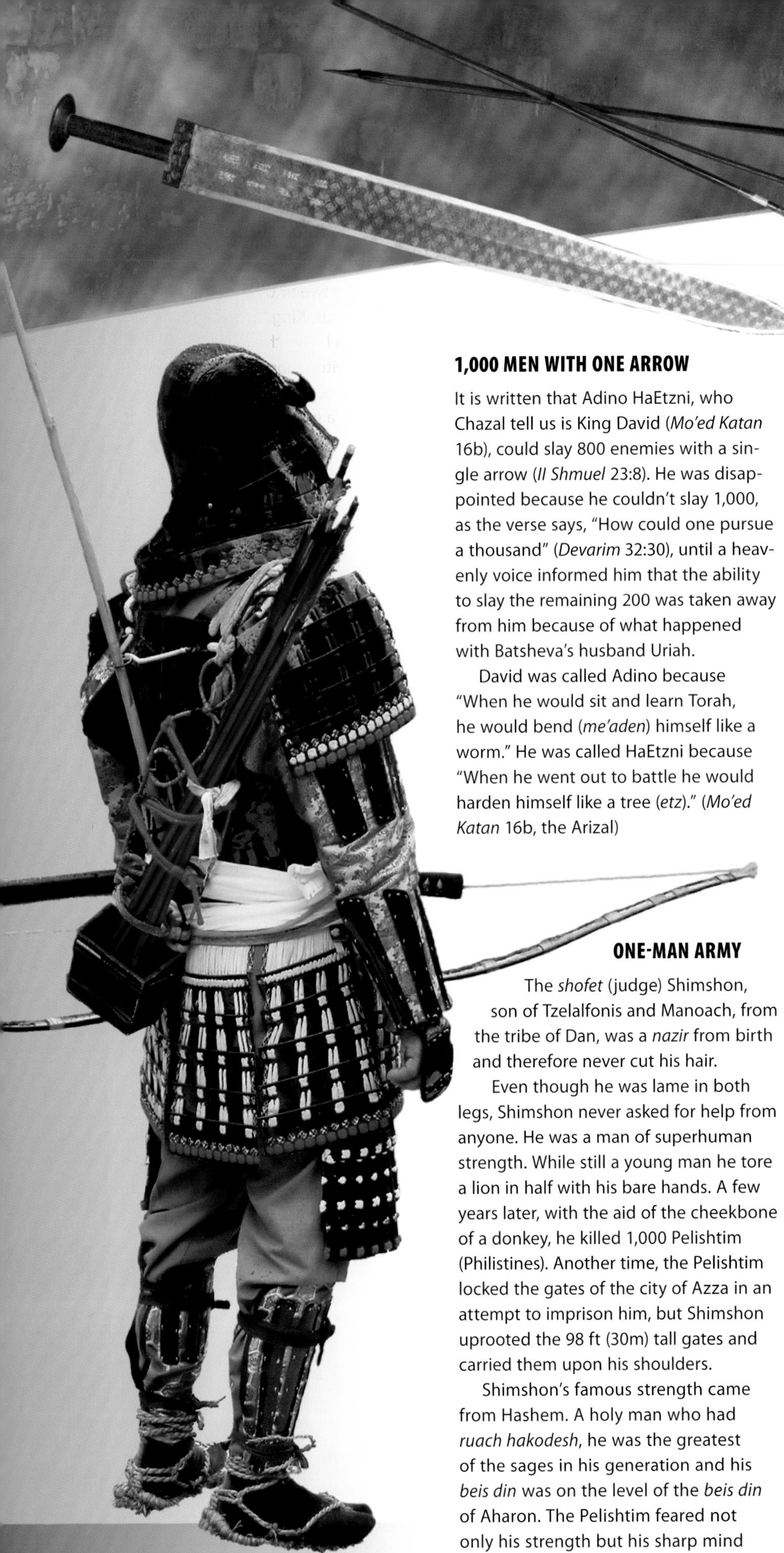

1,000 MEN WITH ONE ARROW

It is written that Adino HaEtzni, who Chazal tell us is King David (*Mo'ed Katan* 16b), could slay 800 enemies with a single arrow (*II Shmuel* 23:8). He was disappointed because he couldn't slay 1,000, as the verse says, "How could one pursue a thousand" (*Devarim* 32:30), until a heavenly voice informed him that the ability to slay the remaining 200 was taken away from him because of what happened with Batsheva's husband Uriah.

David was called Adino because "When he would sit and learn Torah, he would bend (*me'aden*) himself like a worm." He was called HaEtzni because "When he went out to battle he would harden himself like a tree (*etz*)." (*Mo'ed Katan* 16b, the Arizal)

ONE-MAN ARMY

The *shofet* (judge) Shimshon, son of Tzelalfonis and Manoach, from the tribe of Dan, was a *nazir* from birth and therefore never cut his hair.

Even though he was lame in both legs, Shimshon never asked for help from anyone. He was a man of superhuman strength. While still a young man he tore a lion in half with his bare hands. A few years later, with the aid of the cheekbone of a donkey, he killed 1,000 Pelishtim (Philistines). Another time, the Pelishtim locked the gates of the city of Azza in an attempt to imprison him, but Shimshon uprooted the 98 ft (30m) tall gates and carried them upon his shoulders.

Shimshon's famous strength came from Hashem. A holy man who had *ruach hakodesh*, he was the greatest of the sages in his generation and his *beis din* was on the level of the *beis din* of Aharon. The Pelishtim feared not only his strength but his sharp mind as well.

Shimshon instilled fear into the Pelishtim during the 20 years he served as *shofet* —and for another 20 years following his death, as the Pelishtim refused to believe that he had died. Surely he somehow managed to be saved and would one day return to take revenge on them.

ARMY WITHOUT WEAPONS

During the days of King Shaul, the Jewish people waged war without weapons. Their only weapon was their strong belief in Hashem. They would gather for war without a single sword.

Rav Huna said in the name of R' Yitzchak that an angel would bring one sword for King Shaul and one for his son Yehonasan, out of respect for their royal status. The Sages say that the swords were delivered by Hashem Himself. (*Midrash Rabbah, Bemidbar* 10:1)

LARGEST ARMY

The largest army in history was the army of Sancheriv which came to capture Yerushalayim. It is recorded that his army had "2.6 billion soldiers minus one." This included 185,000 officers. The camp was 1,000 mi (1,600 km) long. All the horses placed side by side extended 100 mi (160 km).

Why this odd description of the army — "2.6 billion minus one"? One opinion says that this shows how exact was the number — there was no exaggeration. Another opinion explains that Sancheriv's army was so strong, skilled, and well-armed that it was as if it contained 2.6 billion soldiers. The "One" that was missing was Hashem, the Unique One in the World.

Sancheriv's army was so large that when they reached a river, the first group would swim across. By the time the next group was ready the river was only a foot high, so they walked across. By the time the next group came they were walking on dry land and drinking water had to be brought in from elsewhere.

Greek historians relate that when Sancheriv's army would arrive at a lake, the soldiers would stop to give water to the animals. Within a matter of minutes the animals had drunk up all the water in the lake.

The Midrash teaches us that an army of this size waged war against Avraham Avinu — and that same army will fight against the Mashiach, speedily in our days. (*Sanhedrin* 95b, Maharal, *Ben Yehoyada*)

Warriors

EW AGAINST THE MANY

/hen Avraham Avinu found out that his ephew Lot had been taken into captivity, e took his servant Eliezer (some say he ook with him his 380 disciples all named vram) and went out to wage war against e 4 kings, whose army numbered "2.6 illion soldiers minus 1."

Rav Yehudah teaches that the dirt Avra-am threw at them turned into swords, hile the straw he threw turned into ar-ows.

Rav Nechemiah adds that this was 2-way miracle: the swords which the emy threw toward Avraham turned into rt and their arrows turned into straw. *a'anis* 21a, *Midrash Rabbah*, *Bereishis* 43)

FT-HANDED WARRIORS

e only left-handed person mentioned the Tanach by name is the *shofet* Ehud n Gera, who took advantage of this usual trait to attack Eglon king of oav and rescue the Jewish nation from s bondage.

In Yisrael's war against the tribe Binyamin following the incident of *'egesh baGiv'ah* (*Shoftim* 19–20), Bin-min's army numbered 700 left-handed ldiers, all expert marksmen who could gotiate a slingshot with incredible ac-racy (ibid., 20:16).

EROES OF THE FIRST BEIS AMIKDASH

ring the period of the first Beis Ha-kdash, there were warriors in Yerusha-im who killed many of the Kasdim diers who were trying to capture the city. One of these Jewish heroes, Avika ben Gevatri, would stand on top of the city wall and catch the stones which the Kasdim tried to catapult over the wall. He would then throw them back at the Kas-dim. However, war cannot be won by might alone, and due to the Jews' many sins, a strong wind came and knocked Avika off the wall, killing him. It was at that moment that the walls of Yerusha-layim were breached and the soldiers of the Kasdim were able to enter.

HIGHEST NUMBER OF PEACE TREATIES

King Shlomo signed peace treaties with all the nations and principalities of his time, managing to bring peace to the entire world. In an effort to strengthen the treaties, they were brokered through marriage between the rulers or with their children. Thus, King Shlomo took 1,000 wives, each being the daughter of a king or prince with whom he signed a peace treaty. This custom of intermarrying for the sake of a peace treaty was prevalent throughout the world until the late 1700s.

CONQUERING THE WORLD

Sisera, the mighty chief-of-staff of Yavin, king of Canaan, would go out to battle with a chariot harnessed with 900 horses. At the age of 30 he conquered the entire world. There was not a single city left standing whose walls he did not knock down with the sound of his voice. How-ever, his strength was human and not Divine, and he met his end at the hands of a woman — Yael, the daughter of Chever the Keini.

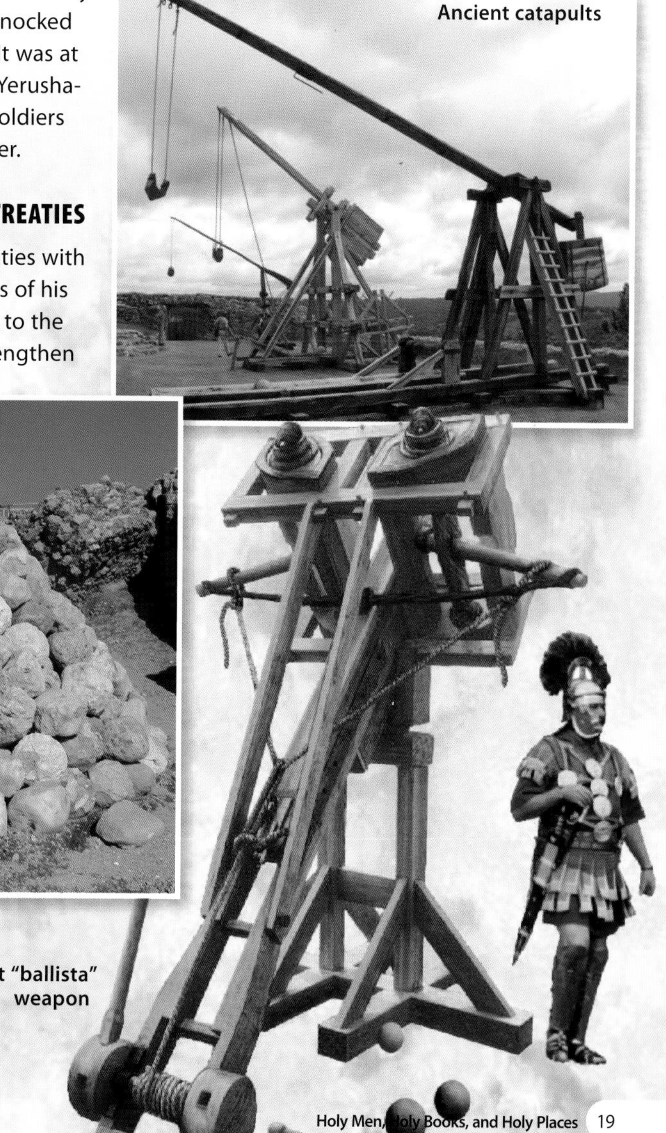

Ancient catapults

Catapult stones

Ancient "ballista" weapon

TALLEST PERSON IN HISTORY

Og, king of Bashan, descended from Shimchazai and Aza'el, giants (*nefilim*) who lived before the Flood. During the Flood, Og managed to save himself by tightly grasping the ark. He then swore to Noach that he would become a lifelong servant to him and his descendants.

When the Children of Israel left Egypt, however, Og lifted up an entire mountain, intending to fling it on them. Moshe Rabbeinu, a "mere" 10 *amos* (approximately 14.5 ft or 4.5 m) tall, jumped 10 *amos* into the air and struck Og's ankle with the aid of a stick 10 *amos* long.

If we assume that the distance from the ground to a person's ankle is approximately one-tenth of his full height, then Og must have been 300 *amos* (437 ft or 133 m) tall!

It was said that Og would eat 1,000 oxen in a single meal. (*Berachos* 54b)

SHORTEST PERSON IN HISTORY

The shortest person in history was the wicked Nebuchadnezzar, whose height was only a *tefach* (approximately 3 in., or 8 cm). Pharaoh, king of Egypt, was over 5 times taller: 1 *amah* (approximately 17 in. or 44 cm) tall. Pharaoh was a strange-looking creature because he was also 1 *amah* wide and his beard was 1 *amah* long. (*Yalkut Shimoni* 4:1062)

LONGEST STRIDES

Chazal say that when Avraham Avinu was pursuing the 4 kings who captured Sodom and took his nephew Lot into captivity, his strides were 1.9 mi (3 km) long. He merited *kefitzas haderech* (covering a vast distance in an impossibly short period of time), where both his legs and his body would stretch to accommodate the distances he need to cover in a short period of time.

An average person runs at 5 strides per second, approximately 18,000 per hour. If we calculate Avraham Avinu's strides this way, then he pursued the kings at a speed of 33,500 mph (54,000 km/h), 16 times faster than the fastest jet, and even faster than a spaceship.

SCIENTIFIC KEFITZAS HADERECH

For many years, scientists have been exploring the possibility of instant travel to distant worlds. The theoretical paths taken are referred to as "Black Holes." What is a Blac Hole?

All elements in the universe have their own gravitational pull. The sun, for example, has such a powerful force of attrac tion that all of its layers are pulled toward its center. However, Hashem designed the immense heat emitted by the sun to exer an opposing pressure, which maintains the delicate balance and insures that the sun keeps its circular shape. If the gas would somehow become depleted, then the sun's layers would immediately collapse one on top of the other and be sucked into a small hole This hole would have such an incredibly strong grav tational pull that the entire body, even the rays, would be swallowe up. With

Facts and Feats in Tanach

hese rays gone it would be impossible for he human eye to see such a body — thus he name Black Hole.

There have been theories over the ears that a Black Hole creates an openng beyond our notion of space and time nd which is connected to the universe hrough some sort of "tunnel." Thus, a tunel can supposedly connect two points housands of miles away.

These "tunnels" are created, expand, nd disappear at a speed of a billionth of a illionth of a second. Scientists claim that if nly they would be able to "catch" one of hem, people would be able to enter space nd travel to areas millions of light years way in a very short time. However, the unnel's opening would have such a strong ravitational pull that it would destroy ny living being that enters it. Researchers dmit that in order to survive this passage, he amount of opposing energy required o offset the gravitational pull would be so reat that it is beyond their ability to calcuate or even to comprehend.

Perhaps the answer to this is not to try o *offset* the pressure, but rather to *negate* he forces in a spiritual manner. Does this ound like science fiction? Chazal often bring stories of *tzaddikim* who would journey beyond our concept of space.

Midrash Rabbah on *Eichah* 3:9 comments that during the time of the Beis HaMikdash there were tunnels which would take people to Yerushalayim for the Festivals from distant places in a very short time. They say that the women of Lod were able to knead their dough, travel to Yerushalayim to pray in the Beis HaMikdash, and return home before the dough would have a chance to sour. (Keep in mind that in those days, it took an entire day to travel from Lod to Yerushalayim.)

In the city of Migdal near Tiveriah, the shul attendant (*shamash*) would prepare the shul's Shabbos candles close to twilight, travel to the Beis HaMikdash, learn that week's Torah portion, pray the Minchah service, and return home in time to light the candles before Shabbos. And then there's the man who did not even mean to travel so far — he was innocently plowing his field in Eretz Yisrael when his cow broke loose and escaped. He ran after the cow and suddenly found himself in Bavel. We find similar stories about the Arizal and the Ba'al Shem Tov and his disciples.

LARGEST GROUP-KEFITZAS HADERECH

The exodus from Egypt numbered 600,000 males between the ages of 20 and 60. They were accompanied by their wives and at least another 3 million children, as well as tens of thousands of men above the age of 60. If we add the 1.2 million members of the *eirev rav* who accompanied the Jews out of Egypt (3.6 million according to R' Nasan), we arrive at a minimum of 5 million people who left Egypt. This entire multitude was transported on the wings of eagles to Ramses, some coming from a distance as far as 100 mi (160 km) away. A short time later they were transported once again on the wings of eagles to Sukkos, 75 mi (120 km) from Ramses. (Arizal)

FASTEST RUNNER

Naftali ben Yaakov Avinu was very fleet-footed. When Yaakov's children arrived at Me'aras HaMachpelah wishing to bury their father, the wicked Esav tried to stop them, claiming that Yaakov had already used his share of the cave to bury Leah and that the remaining portion was his. The brothers argued that he had sold the plot to Yaakov. They sent Naftali back to Goshen in Egypt to retrieve the bill of sale — a distance of approximately 326 mi (525 km) each way. If we assume that the matter was urgent and he was there and back in about an hour, Naftali must have traveled faster than a commercial jet plane. (*Pirkei d'Rabbi Eliezer* 38)

"LIGHTEST" RUNNER

Asa'el was the brother of Yoav and Avishai (King David's chiefs-of-staff). All three were nephews of David — their mother was Tzuriah, King David's sister. Asa'el was so light on his feet that he was able to pursue and overtake a deer. Chazal write that he had the ability to run on top of stalks of wheat without bending them. The Arizal says that this must be understood literally, for we are speaking of a man whose soul glowed so brightly that it lifted his body into the air. (*Midrash Rabbah, Koheles* 9:13)

The cave housing the tombs of the members of the Sanhedrin in Yerushalayim

FIRST TO STOP THE MOVEMENT OF THE SUN, MOON, AND STARS

From the day the heavens and earth were created, the sun, moon, and stars have been in almost constant motion — without stopping, interference, or changing direction. However, they did stop moving five times in history. The first time was during the Mabul, the Great Flood. Rav Yehoshua and Rav Yochanan say that during the Flood, the *mazalot* did not rule, and the sun and moon did not illuminate for an entire year.

The first person who actually stopped the celestial movement — and the only one to have done it twice — was Moshe Rabbeinu. After the Jews left Egypt and Amalek attacked them, the Amalekites would use the sun, moon, and stars to calculate at what time they would be victorious. Therefore, Moshe prayed to Hashem to make the sun stand still, which jumbled the hours (Rashi, *Shemos* 17:12). In other words, time stopped. Forty years later, Moshe again caused the sun to stand still, on the day of the battle against Og (Rashi, *Devarim* 2:25).

The next time this happened was during the days of Yehoshua bin Nun, when the Jewish nation battled to conquer Eretz Yisrael. It was Erev Shabbos, and Yehoshua saw that the Jews were upset that they might have to fight on Shabbos. Yehoshua spread his hands to the light of the sun and the light of the moon, pronounced the *Shem HaMeforash*, and the sun and the moon each stayed in a fixed position for thirty-six hours, until *motza'ei Shabbos*.

Rashi (*Bereishis* 28:11) also says that the sun set early for Yaakov, in order that he would sleep on the site of the future Beis HaMikdash.

In the time of the Prophets, the sun sped forward 10 degrees — i.e., the day was made shorter — when the wicked King Achaz died, so there wouldn't be time to say a *hesped* for him. Then, in the time of his son, King Chizkiyahu, the sun moved back 10 degrees — i.e., the day became longer — in order to "make up" the loss (Rashi, *II Melachim* 20:8–11).

The Gemara in *Ta'anis* 20a says that the sun also stopped for Nakdimon ben Gurion.

GOOD THINGS COME IN GROUPS OF 8

The entire Jewish nation would gather annually in the Beis HaMikdash on the Festival of Sukkos to celebrate *Simchas Beis HaSho'evah*. Chazal write, "Whoever did not see the celebration of *Simchas Beis HaSho'evah* never saw rejoicing in his life."

When Rabban Shimon ben Gamliel, the nasi of his generation, rejoiced at *Simchas Beis HaSho'evah* he would take 8 flaming torches and juggle them, without their touching each other.

The *amora* Levi ben Sissi would do the same thing with 8 knives in front of his *rebbi*, Rabbi Yehudah HaNasi.

Shmuel, the leading *amora* in Bavel, would juggle 8 full glasses of wine in front of the Persian king Shavur Malka without any of them touching each other and without spilling a single drop of wine.

EARLIEST RECALL

R' Yehoshua ben Levi could remember things that happened immediately following his birth. Years later he was able to recognize women who had come to wish his mother *mazal tov* after he was born. R' Yehoshua ben Levi lived at the end of the period of the *tanna'im* and thus some consider him a *tanna* while others consider him an *amora*. As mentioned above, he was one of the 10 people who entered Gan Eden during his lifetime.

The *amora* Shmuel was also born with the intellectual faculties of an adult and he could even remember his midwife. He lived during the first generation of *amora'im* and served as rosh yeshiva of Nehardea. He was called Yarchina (from the word *yerach*, meaning month) because he was an expert in the *sod haibur* (intercalation) and testified regarding himself, "The paths of Heaven are as clear to me as the paths of Nehardea." (*Yerushalmi Kesubos* 5:30)

22,273 LEVI'IM ON A SINGLE DAY

On Rosh Chodesh Nisan, the day the Mishkan was put up for the 1st time, Aharon HaKohen was commanded to lift and wave all 22,273 Levi'im, which breaks down to 928 per hour or 4 Levi'im per second for an entire day. The Levi'im assigned to transport the boards of the Mishkan were presumably taller and heavier than the average person. Even if we were to assume that each Levi weighed an average of 176 lb (80 kg), Aharon HaKohen would have had to wave a total of 3,920,048 lb (1,781,840 kg).

R' Yehudah asked R' Abba why it was necessary for Aharon to wave the Levi'im. R' Abba explained that the Levi'im represented the Divine Attribute of Strength (*middas hagevurah*), which seeks to exact judgment and destroy the world. Just as one who wishes to quiet a crying baby rocks it, so too, Aharon HaKohen —who was the epitome of *chesed* — had to wave the Levi'im in order to "quiet" their aspect of strength. This would prevent harsh judgment from being exacted in the world (Zohar 3, p. 303). (*Bemidbar* 8:1)

MOST LAVISH MEALS

King Shlomo would prepare a lavish meal for the entire nation every day. It required 2,928 gal (12,899 liters) of fine flour, 5,857 gal (25,798 liters) of flour, 20 bulls (approximately 13,200 lb or 6,000 kg of meat) and 100 sheep (approximately 12,100 lb or 5,500 kg), in addition to gazelle, deer, *yachmur* (a species of deer), and fattened fowl.

Facts and Feats in Tanach

LARGEST MEAL EATEN BY ONE PERSON

Yochanan ben Narbai was said to have polished off 300 calves and drunk 300 kegs of wine in a single meal. He then ate 40 *se'ah* (88 gal or 332 liters) of young fowl for dessert. Rashi explains that he used to host many Kohanim at his table, while others claim that he ate these large quantities in order to prevent the meat of the sacrifices from remaining overnight and becoming *nosar*. He ate purely *leShem Shamayim*.

Pekach ben Remalyahu, king of Yisrael, was also said to have consumed 40 *se'ah* of young fowl for dessert. However, he ate purely to satisfy his desires. Chazal say about him: "The stomach of the wicked will always lack" (*Mishlei* 13:25). (*Sanhedrin* 94b)

MOST EXPERT CRAFTSMEN

During the period of the first Beis HaMikdash there were families of master craftsmen, the likes of which the world has never seen. The Garmu family was able to bake the *lechem hapanim* and remove it from the oven in such a way that it would neither break nor become moldy.

The Avtinas family was expert in the burning of the *ketores* such that the smoke would rise like a stick.

When Hugras the Levi wanted to project his voice with sweetness, he would insert his thumb in his mouth and place his finger between the hairs of his mustache until his brethren the Kohanim would vault over backwards in reaction to the powerful sound.

These experts did not wish to impart their secrets unto others, lest an unsuitable person learn it and use it for idol worship. The Sages praised them for this.

One of these impressive craftsmen was a *sofer* named Ben Kamtzar, who would tie four quills between the fingers of his right hand and write four different letters of a word at the same time. Ben Kamtzar had no answer to the Sages' question of why he did not wish to teach his secrets to others. After all, there was no fear of it being used for *avodah zarah*, because writing in Hebrew was of no value to the other nations. The Sages were therefore unhappy with his decision. (*Yoma* 38a)

FLUENT IN THE MOST LANGUAGES

To reach the throne of the wicked Egyptian king Pharaoh, one had to climb 70 steps, about the height of a 4–story building. Each step corresponded to a different language that Pharaoh knew. The night before Yosef HaTzaddik's meeting with Pharaoh, the angel Gavriel arrived and taught Yosef all 70 languages, in order for Yosef to be able to reach the top step and stand opposite Pharaoh. Pharaoh did not know Hebrew and Yosef swore that he would never teach it to him.

The halachah requires a Sanhedrin to have at least 1 member who understands 70 languages and 1 who is able to both understand and speak all of them (*Sanhedrin* 17b, Rashi).

PERSON TODAY FLUENT IN THE MOST LANGUAGES

Hungarian translator Istvan Dabi (born 1943) became famous at age 18 by corresponding with 80 people in 50 different countries in 18 languages.

He is completely fluent in 10 languages: Hungarian, Russian, Polish, Czech, Slovak, German, Bulgarian, English, Lithuanian, and French. With a little practice and effort he can add the following 14 languages to that list: Ukrainian, Belarusian, Croatian, Macedonian, Serbian, Sorbian (Wendish), Latvian, Spanish, Portuguese, Italian, Danish, Swedish, Dutch, and Norwegian.

Over the years, Dabi developed a method of learning languages which he used to acquire expertise in another 79 languages, bringing the sum total of languages he is familiar with to 103. Many of these languages are from the same family as the 70 languages spoken by Chazal — which encompassed all the languages of the world.

Dabi can translate these 103 languages into Russian, Polish, and of course his mother tongue, Hungarian.

Population 26
Names 30
Healer of All Flesh 34
Mail and Communication 38
Inventions 44

Mankind

The Rabbis taught: If one sees a large gathering of Jews, He says "Blessed are You, Hashem ... the Knower of the Secrets," for their minds are not similar to each other and their faces are not similar to each other.

Ben Zoma saw a large gathering of Jews on a step of *Har HaBayis*. He recited the blessing: "Blessed are You...Knower of the Secrets and Who created all these to serve Me."

He used to say, "How hard did Adam HaRishon work until he had bread to eat — he plowed, he sowed, he reaped, he gathered, he threshed, he winnowed, he selected, he ground, he sifted, he kneaded, and he baked. Only afterwards was he able to eat his bread. But I wake up early in the morning and find that all these tasks have already been performed for me and that my bread is ready for me to eat.

"How hard did Adam HaRishon work until he had clothing to wear — he sheared, he cleaned, he disentangled, he spun, he wove, and only afterwards did he have clothing to wear.

"But I wake up early in the morning and find that all these tasks have already been performed for me and that my clothes are ready for me to wear."

Berachos 58a

"You shall see what the land is like" (*Bemidbar* 13:18). Moshe instructed the spies, "Observe the land: Some lands raise mighty warriors, while others raise weaker people; some lands cause their population to increase, while others cause their population to decrease."
(*Tanchuma, Shelach* 6)

WORLD POPULATION

According to the American Central Intelligence Agency (CIA), the number of people living on planet Earth in the year 2010 reached 6.81 billion. The approximate breakdown according to age-bracket is as follows:

Age	Percent of Population
0–14	27.8
15–64	64.9
65 and up	7.3

The number of male births is greater than the female birthrate, with 106 boys born for every 100 girls.

CHART OF WORLD POPULATION
(in millions of people)

YEAR	MILLIONS	YEAR	MILLIONS
1	200	1930	2070
1000	275	1950	2550
1250	400	1980	4410
1500	460	1990	5300
1700	680	2000	6122
1800	990	2009	6800
1900	1600	2025 (est.)	8000

WORLD POPULATION GROWTH

The chart above tracks world population growth throughout the years. In the year 1968, the United Nations predicted that by the year 2050 the world population would be greater than 12 billion. They have since adjusted their estimate many times. The current estimate, assuming no major cataclysmic changes, is that the world population will reach 9 billion by the year 2050.

COUNTRY WITH THE LARGEST POPULATION

The country boasting the highest number of residents is China. In the year 2010, the number of people living in China was approximately 1.338 billion. This means that 1 out of every 5 people in the world is Chinese. Forty-six thousand babies are born in China every day, amounting to more than 17 million per year (2.5 times the entire population of Israel). A staff of 5.1 million workers completed the latest population census in China in 10 days.

DID YOU KNOW?

If the entire population of China were to walk past you single-file at a rate of 1 person per second, it would take 41.6 years to complete the procession. As a matter of fact, this procession would never end, because in the meantime 698.464 million new Chinese will have been born, who would take an additional 22 years to walk by you.

SMALLEST POPULATION

The independent state with the smallest population is the Vatican, located in Italy. Its population is a mere 830 people, with zero natural population growth.

BIRTHS AND DEATHS

The world population grows by approximately 1.14% per year. The average number of births per 1,000 people is 20.4, while the average number of deaths per 1,000 people is 8.8. The average age is 27.6 years.

STAND UP FOR SENIORS!

The number of people in the world above the age of 60 stands at 245 million. The United Nations predicts a steady growth in the number of senior citizens and expects that number to reach 2 billion by the year 2070.

GREATEST PERCENTAGE OF CHILDREN

The country with the highest percentage of children is Uganda — approximately 50.4% of the population. The main reason for this is that is the average life expectancy in Uganda is only 41 years.

RESIDENTS IN ERETZ YISRAEL

In the year 2010 the population of Israel numbered 7.374 million, with 5,569,200 Jewish residents (75.5%). Of the Jewish population, 67% were born in Israel and 33% in the Diaspora. Israel is 97th in the world in population.

POPULATION BREAKDOWN IN ISRAEL

The population of Israel is relatively younger than the average Western country, with 28.5% of the general population (42% among the Muslims) age 14 and under, compared to 16% in the West on average.

Regarding senior citizens, 11% of Israel's population is 65 and older — 11.6% of Jews are in this age bracket, as opposed to only 2.7% of Muslims.

DEVELOPED AND DEVELOPING COUNTRIES

Israel has climbed 12 places in the UN Development Project's Human Development Index (HDI), reaching 15th place in the 2010 Index. The HDI includes 169 countries. The top 10 in the 2010 Index are: Norway, Australia, New Zealand, the United States, Ireland, Lichtenstein, the Netherlands, Canada, Sweden, and Germany. At the bottom of the rankings are Mali, Burkina Faso, Liberia, Chad, Buinea-Bissau, Mozambique, Burundi, Niger, the Democratic Republic of the Congo, and—in last place—Zimbabwe.

DID YOU KNOW?

You share your birthday with an additional 9 million people in the world.

LOWEST LIFE EXPECTANCY IN THE WORLD

According to a study conducted by the World Health Organization (WHO), the average life expectancy in Zimbabwe is the lowest in the world. Women on the average live until the age of 34, while men live until 40. The study shows that the 10 countries with the lowest life expectancies are all on the continent of Africa.

"GIVE ME YOUR TIRED, YOUR POOR..."

As of the end of 2010, there are 310.3 million people living in the United States — 4.5% of the world's population, or approximately 1 out of every 20 people in the world. This makes them 3rd in the world in terms of population, after China (#1) and India (#2).

In 1790, there were just under 4 million people living in the United States. By 1900, there were close to 76 million. Only twenty years later, there were over 105.7 million, and by 1970 the United States counted 203.3 million residents. It took only 36 more years for the United States to reach the 300 million mark, in October 2006.

The United States Census Bureau estimates that by the year 2043, the American population will reach the 400 million mark. Each 100 million more residents takes less time to add. It took the United States over 100 years to reach the 100 million mark, from 1776 to 1915. It reached the 200 million mark 52 years later, in 1967. The next hundred million was added in only 39 years.

Throughout the years, immigration has always played a tremendous part in America's huge population growth.

"Medicine Man,"
Zimbabwe

SPARSEST POPULATION

The country with the sparsest population is Mongolia, with only 4.4 people per mi^2 (1.7/km^2).

METROPOLISES WITH THE HIGHEST POPULATION

The metropolitan areas (city plus suburbs) with the highest populations are Tokyo (35 million), Jakarta (Indonesia) (22 million), Mumbai (21.2 million), Delhi (21 million), and Manila (Philippines) (20.8 million). New York ranks 6th with 20.6 million, Los Angeles is 14th with 14.7 million, Chicago is 28th with 9 million, and Tel Aviv ranks 132nd with 2.6 million.

In the year 1900, the only cities in the world with a population greater than 1 million were New York, Chicago, Philadelphia, London, Berlin, Paris, Moscow, Vienna, Tokyo, and St. Petersburg.

Mumbai, India

MEGALOPOLIS

The term "megalopolis" refers to the fusion of a number of metropolises whose borders have become blurred, giving it the feeling of one large city. The area of a megalopolis can be hundreds of miles, with tens of millions of residents. The world's largest megalopolis is the Taiheiyō Belt (Pacific megalopolis) in Japan, which includes the cities and suburbs of Tokyo, Shizuoka, Nagoya, Osaka, Okayama, Hiroshima, and Fukuoka. There are almost 83 million people living in this megalopolis.

The largest megalopolis in the United States is the northeast corridor between Washington and Boston. This area includes the cities and suburbs of Boston, MA, Hartford, CT, New York State, New Jersey State, Philadelphia, PA, Baltimore, MD, and Washington, DC. It has a population of over 50 million. Its density is well over 900 people per mi^2 (360/km^2), while the U.S. average is 82 people per mi^2 (31/km^2).

DENSEST POPULATION

The country with the densest population is Monaco, located on the southern coast of France. It has a population of 33,000 in an area of .75 mi^2 (1.95 km^2). This means there are 16,923 people per km^2.

Israel has 881 people per mi^2 (340/km^2).

HOME

There are 100 million people in the world who do not have a roof over their heads, while over a billion people live in temporary housing.

LARGEST CITY IN ERETZ YISRAEL

Since 1975, the largest city in Israel both in size and in population has been Yerushalayim. In the year 2010, Yerushalayim had a population of 769,400 — approximately 10% of the population of the entire country. The next largest city is Tel Aviv with 393,200 residents, followed by Haifa with a population of 265,300.

DIVORCE RATE

The highest divorce rate is in Belarus in the northwestern Russian Federation, where 68% of marriages end in divorce. This is followed by the country of Russia, where the rate is 65%, followed by the United States at 43%. The divorce rate in Israel is 28%.

RELIGION IN ISRAEL

According to a study by the Israel Institute for Democracy, those considering themselves secular Jews make up the smallest percentage of the population (27%), with that number shrinking all the time. *Dati* and *chareidi* Jews comprise 28% of the population, while those considering themselves traditional make up 44%. The following chart indicates the religious breakdown in various cities:

CATEGORY	YERUSHALAYIM	TEL AVIV	ASHDOD	HAIFA	RISHON LEZION
Chareidi	30.4%	0.9%	6.6%	2.6%	0.0
Religious – Traditional	26.7%	15.3%	24%	11.8%	15.5%
Traditional – Secular	21.1%	26.4%	37.3%	19.0%	35.5%
Secular	21.9%	57.5%	32.1%	66.6%	49.0%

OTHER RELIGIONS

We can only estimate the number of people belonging to other religious denominations, but Christianity is probably the most popular religion in the world.

It is estimated that the number of Christians in the world is 2.1 billion — about a third of the world's population. Approximately 95% of South Americans consider themselves Christians, as opposed to only 65% of Europeans.

The second-largest religion is Islam, which had an estimated 600 million followers in 2005. That number grew to 1.3 billion in 2010, comprising 20% of the world's population.

MEN'S NAMES	NUMBER	WOMEN'S NAMES	NUMBER
יוסף (Yosef)	60,775	רחל (Rachel)	49,608
דוד (David)	53,554	אסתר (Esther)	49,602
משה (Moshe)	49,969	מרים (Miriam)	39,336
יעקב (Yaakov)	48,375	שרה (Sarah)	38,301
אברהם (Avraham)	46,040	חנה (Chana)	32,091
יצחק (Yitzchak)	42,213	רבקה (Rivka)	26,042
מיכאל (Michael)	38,530	שושנה (Shoshana)	24,925
אלכסנדר (Alexander)	34,375	מיכל (Michal)	22,305
חיים (Chaim)	29,354	לאה (Leah)	21,483
שלמה (Shlomo)	27,891	ילנה (Yelena)	18,763

TEN MOST COMMON NAMES IN ISRAEL

There are 65,000 different first names among Israelis. This shows that Israel is home to Jewish people from all different parts of the world. Even taking this into account, as we can see from the chart to the right, the 10 most common names among Israeli residents above the age of 18 (in the year 2004) were almost all traditional Biblical names, specifically names related to leadership and redemption. These make up more than 10% of Israelis' names.

The name Chaim is not a Biblical name but is an ancient traditional name, related to the redemption — it is one of the names of the Mashiach.

The name Alexander has been given to Jewish boys since the period of the *tanna'im*. However, it is more popular among Russian immigrants. The same may be said for the woman's name Yelena.

Additional popular Hebrew names are Eliyahu, Meir, Shimon, Shmuel and Yehudah for men, and Yael, Ruth and Yehudit for women.

The Chida writes in his *Pesach Einayim* that when a person hates another he can't even mention his name, while when a person loves another he mentions his name over and over again.

When a person is given the name of a *tzaddik* who left this world, he inherits the light the *tzaddik* brings to this world from Heaven.

(*Noam Elimelech, parashas Bemidbar*)

MOST COMMON NAMES GIVEN TO BOYS IN ISRAEL

The 11 most popular names for newborn boys in Israel in 2009 were נועם (Noam), איתי (Itai), אורי (Uri or Ori), דניאל (Daniel), יהונתן (Yehonasan), דוד (David), עידו (Ido), משה (Moshe), יוסף (Yosef), יונתן (Yonasan), and אריאל (Ariel).

MOST COMMON NAMES GIVEN TO GIRLS IN ISRAEL

The 11 most popular girl's names in Israel are: נעה (Noa), שירה (Shira), יעל (Yael), תמר (Tamar), מאיה (Maya), טליה (Talya), שרה (Sarah), הילה (Hila), מיכל (Michal), עדי (Adi), and מעין (Ma'ayan).

The most popular names given to both boys and girls in Israel are שחר (Shachar), אליה (Elya), עומר (Omer), יהלי (Yahali), יובל (Yuval), מעין (Ma'ayan), עדי (Adi), דניאל (Daniel/Danielle), נעם (Noam), אריאל (Ariel), and עמית (Amit).

WORLD'S MOST POPULAR FIRST NAME

The most popular first name in the world is Li. There are approximately 100 million people in China with it, corresponding to 1.5% of the world population. This means that 1 out of every 67 people in the world is called Li. (The Chinese also have the world's most common last name — Chang.)

MOST POPULAR NAMES IN THE UNITED STATES

The following are the most popular American names as of the year 2008. Interestingly enough, Biblical names have topped the list for the previous 15 years: Jacob (יעקב), Michael (מיכאל), Ethan (איתן), Joshua (יהושע), and Daniel (דניאל).

DID YOU KNOW?

The most popular name given to newborns in England and Wales in the year 2009 was Mohammed — even more popular than Oliver, Jack, Harry and Alfie (in 2nd, 3rd, 4th and 5th places).

There are 13 ways to spell Mohammed in English. In total, 7,549 British baby boys received the name Mohammed in all of its spellings — 185 more than the name Oliver.

The most popular name given to Israeli Arabs is also Mohammed, with about 14% of newborn Arab boys being given the name per year. This is followed by Achmad (6%). The names Mohammed, Achmad, and together with Machmad and Machmud, account for more than 25% of the names given to newborn Muslim boys.

LEGAL REQUIREMENT FOR LAST NAMES

In the late 1700s and early 1800s, due to the great rise in population and to the centralizing of government authority, there arose a need to more easily identify people. This made it easier to collect taxes, draft men into the army, and conduct a population census. Many governments sent a directive that every resident was required to choose a last name by a certain date and register it in the appropriate office.

The first leader to require Jews to choose a family name was Emperor Josef II of the Austro-Hungarian Empire, who in the year 1787 instructed all Jews to choose a family name which sounds German. Although there was a certain degree of freedom of choice, they were not permitted to choose names of well-known families or Biblical names. Those who bribed the authorities were able to choose more distinguished names, such as Kluger (meaning wise) or Reich (rich). Many were called by their profession: Baker, Schuster (shoemaker), Schneider (tailor). Those who refused to bribe the authorities were given more degrading names.

Although many North African Jewish families had been using family names for generations such as Ben Attar, Chayun, and Azulai, the majority of the population adopted last names only when required by the country of which they were a colony (France, Italy, or England).

Emperor Josef II

RARE NAMES

There are hundreds of Israeli names which are so rare that there is only one known person who carries that name. This list includes: Acharon, Avdon, Bagit, Biladi, Bul, Chevrona, Dagim, Dagul, Dala'at, Gadot, Gershonit, Giladit, Jeddi, Katom, Vashti, and Vilhalmos.

Studies have shown that children bearing less accepted names do not perform as well in school.

LAST NAMES IN ISRAEL

The diversity of Israel's population is also apparent in the large number of different last names. The Diaspora Museum in Tel Aviv has approximately 20,000 family names on record, with this list growing daily.

CITY WITH THE MOST NAMES

There is no city in the world with as many names as Yerushalayim. We find in *Midrash HaGadol* that Yerushalayim has 70 names. However, more names can be found in other sources, bringing the total number of names for Yerushalayim to 105. Among the less well-known names are:

Beis Tefillah (*Yeshayahu* 56:7)
Carmel (*Yeshayahu* 32:16)
Chaim (*Yeshayahu* 4:3; *Yechezkel* 32:25)
Daltos HaAmim (*Yechezkel* 26:2)
Ir HaEmes (*Zechariah* 8:3)
Netzach (*I Divrei HaYamim* 29:11)
Saf Ra'al (*Zechariah* 12:2)

LAWS REGARDING CHOOSING NAMES

- Since 1901, Sweden has required all its citizens to have last names. In 1982 a more detailed law was passed which limited the choice of names, aimed at disqualifying degrading ones.
- Until the year 2002, parents in Norway were required to choose from a list of names. Later, this law was repealed on the condition that the names given were not curses, negative names, or names of diseases.
- In Denmark as well, until 2005 parents were given a list of names to choose from. Foreign names, such as American ones, were strictly forbidden.
- In the past, names in Portugal were chosen by the local priest. In the year 1911 a law was passed which permitted people to choose non-Catholic names on condition that it was in keeping with the tradition of the particular family. Any uncertainties were decided by a professor from Lisbon University, who with the aid of a dictionary would decide whether to allow the name. Today, the Portuguese Ministry of Justice has a list of permitted and forbidden names. Among the forbidden names are Mardona and Mona Lisa.
- In April 1998 a new law was passed in Peru forbidding boys' names to be given to girls and girls' names to boys. It is forbidden to use names which are considered absurd, insulting, or anti-religious. A child may not be given more than two names because it is too difficult to keep track of it. Government spokespeople claim that the law was necessary to combat names such as "boiling" and the chemical composition of water — H_2O. Government employees check each name given and determine whether or not it is within the boundaries of the law.
- In Iran, the government must approve all names given to children. Any names which have no connection to Islam are strictly forbidden.

PLACE WITH THE SHORTEST NAME

There are many cities in the world whose names comprise two letters and only one syllable. There are few cities in the world whose name contains only one letter. One of these is a fishing town in Norway, which is called simply Å. The name Å was given because it is the last of the Lupton Islands in the southern portion of Norway — Å is the last letter in the Norwegian alphabet.

There is a small town in Northern France near the Somme River called Y.

LONGEST NAME IN THE WORLD

The man with the longest name in the world was known simply as Hubert Wolfe. He was born on February 29, 1904, in Bergedorf, a borough of Hamburg, Germany. His full given name was Adolph Blaine Charles David Earl Frederick Gerald Hubert Irvin John Kenneth Lloyd Martin Nero Oliver Paul Quincy Randolph Sherman Thomas Uncas Victor William Xerxes Yancy Zeus — twenty six names in all, in alphabetical order.

Hubert's last name was 590 letters long:

Wolfeschlegelsteinhausenbergerdorffvoralternwarengewissenhaftschaferswesenchafewarenwohlgepflegeundsorgfaltigkeitbeschutzenvonangereifenduchihrraubgiriigfeindewelchevoralternzwolftausendjahresvorandieerscheinenbandererdeemmeshedrraumsciffgebrauchlichtalsseinursprunfvonkraftgestartseinlangefahrthinzwischensternartigraumaufdersuchenachdiesternwelshegehabtbewohnbarplaneetenkreisedrehensichundwohinderneurassevanverstandigmenshlichkeittkonntevortpflanzenundsicherfreunanlebenslamdlichfreudeundruhemitnichteinfurchtvorangreifenvonandereintlligentgeschopfsvonhinzwischensternartigraum..

Hubert would sign only his eighth and second given names and the first 35 letters of his last name: Hubert Blaine Wolfeschlegelsteinhausenbergerdorff, Sr.

The "senior" at the end of the name implies that his son was called by the same name. When Hubert moved to Philadelphia in the United States, he shortened his name to "Wolfe + 585 Sr."

COUNTRY WITH THE LONGEST NAME

England, whose formal name is United Kingdom of Great Britain and Northern Ireland, is the longest name of any country in the world, with 8 words and 45 letters. Libya, whose original, official name is Great Socialist People's Libyan Arab Jamahiriya, comes in second, with 6 words and 41 letters.

Passport from Montenegro, 1887

Passport from China, 1898

Passport from Persia, 1892

Train station at the village with the world's longest name

PLACE WITH THE LONGEST NAME

The place with the longest name (58 letters) is a village in northern Wales called Llanfairpwllgwyngyllgogerychwyrndrobwllllantysiliogogogoch. The name was given to this village at the turn of the 20th century as a public relations ploy and as a means of attracting tourists.

FEAR OF LONG WORDS

The name given to the psychological condition of fear of long words is 36 letters long: Take deep breath and don't be afraid to read it: Hippopotomonstrosesquippedaliophobia.

MOST POPULAR STREET NAME IN ERETZ YISRAEL

The most popular of the 12,000 names of streets throughout Eretz Yisrael is Rechov HaZayit — "Olive Street" — with 112 streets throughout Israel bearing that name.

Rechov HaZayit in Jerusalem

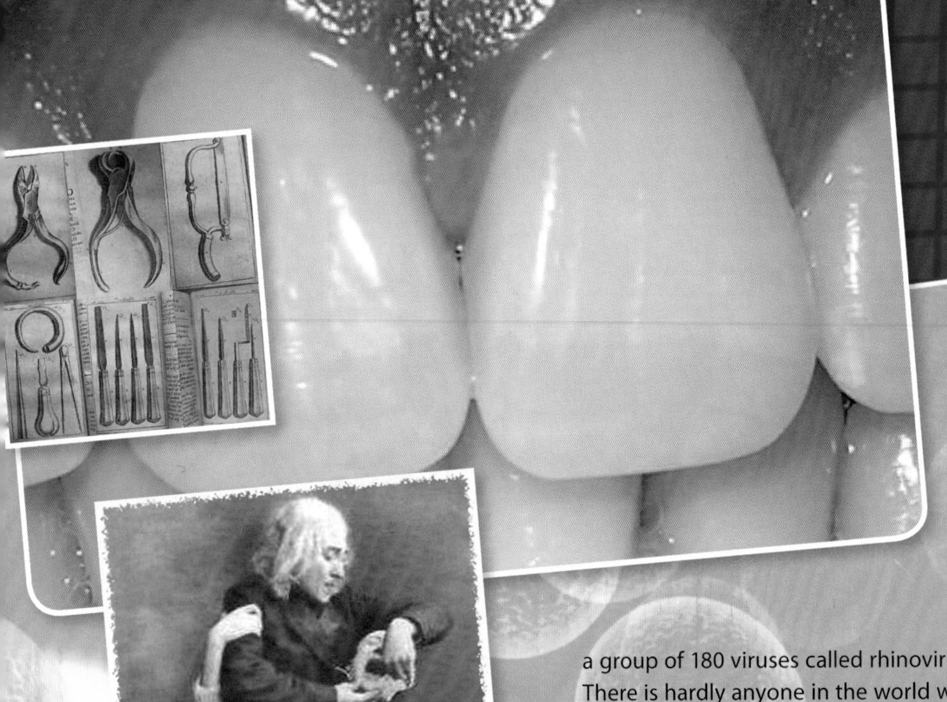

Dentist of old

> **DID YOU KNOW?**
> The electric chair was invented by a dentist named Alfred P. Southwick from Buffalo, NY.

MOST COMMON ILLNESS

The most common non-contagious illness is tooth decay. At least 90% of the world population suffers from it. Tooth decay is caused by bacteria, mainly those of "Streptococcus mutans" which lie permanently on the teeth. The bacteria break down the sugars in foods, and convert them to acids which slowly eat away at the outer layer of the teeth (the enamel). The decay spreads to the nerve at the root of the tooth and causes toothaches.

HIGHEST NUMBER OF DENTISTS

Israel has the highest number of dentists per capita in the world, with 1 dentist for every 783 people. Germany has 1 dentist for every 1,430 people, France has 1 per 1,494, the United States has 1 per 1,882, and Britain has 1 per 2,500. In Israel, 63% of senior citizens above the age of 65 have lost all their teeth, while in the rest of the Western world that figure stands at between 28% and 50%.

MOST COMMON CONTAGIOUS DISEASE

The most common contagious disease is a cold and a runny nose. It is caused by a group of 180 viruses called rhinovirus. There is hardly anyone in the world who has not caught a cold, with the exception of those in a few remote places in the world such as Antarctica where these viruses have yet to reach. The average adult catches between 2 and 4 colds per year, with children catching much more.

COLDS AND ANTIBIOTICS

According to a study published in the last decade, colds account for 100 million annual doctor's visits, reaching a total cost of $7.7 billion. One-third of the patients are given a prescription for antibiotics, even though most cases are viral – in which case antibiotics have no effect whatsoever. The 41 million prescriptions given in one year cost $1.1 billion.

MOST COMMON SKIN CONDITION

The most common skin condition is tinea pedis (athlete's foot). This fungus strikes 70% of the population. The heat and moisture of the soles of the feet provide the perfect environment for development of the fungus.

FIRST ILLNESS SUCCESSFULLY ERADICATED

Smallpox, a disease which claimed so many lives, is the first, and in the meantime, the only disease which mankind has managed to eradicate. The last known case of smallpox that was contracted naturally was a hospital worker in Somalia, Africa, in 1977, who eventually recovered. However, the last known case of smallpox took place in Birmingham, England, in 1978. It was caused by an unauthorized experiment on the smallpox virus by microbiologist Henry Bedson. A small amount of the virus leaked through the ventilation system, infecting a medical photographer.

In December 1979, nearly 200 years since Edward Jenner invented the first vaccination, it was announced that there was not even a single case of smallpox in the entire world. The World Health Organization (WHO) then attested to the fact that smallpox had been eradicated from the world.

The last smallpox vaccination of civilians was given in 1980, and a few years later they stopped vaccinating military personnel.

LARGEST NUMBER OF PSYCHIATRISTS

The United States has the largest number of psychiatrists (and psychologists), and as a result the largest number of patients receiving counseling, guidance, and therapy on a regular basis. The American Association of Psychiatrists lists more than 62,000 psychiatrists. In addition, there are many private therapists, holistic and other non-conventional doctors who are not registered in the association.

LEAST COMMON ILLNESS

Koro disease is the least common illness today. The symptoms of the illness, also referred to as the "laughing disease," are shivers, pain in the joints, and uncontrollable laughter. The illness strikes only those of the Fore tribe living in the eastern part of New Guinea in East Asia.

Tribesman in New Guinea

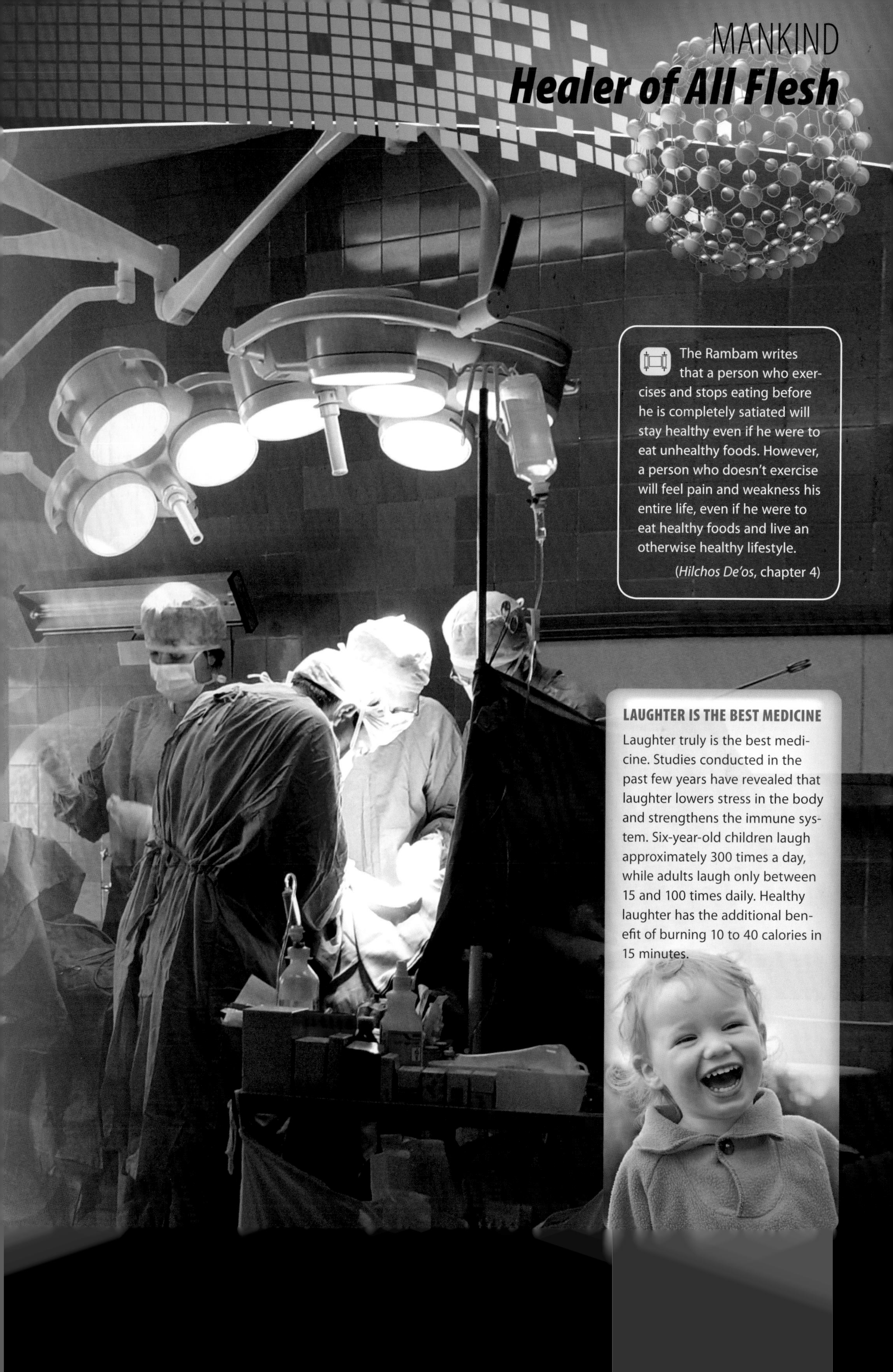

Healer of All Flesh

The Rambam writes that a person who exercises and stops eating before he is completely satiated will stay healthy even if he were to eat unhealthy foods. However, a person who doesn't exercise will feel pain and weakness his entire life, even if he were to eat healthy foods and live an otherwise healthy lifestyle.

(*Hilchos De'os*, chapter 4)

LAUGHTER IS THE BEST MEDICINE

Laughter truly is the best medicine. Studies conducted in the past few years have revealed that laughter lowers stress in the body and strengthens the immune system. Six-year-old children laugh approximately 300 times a day, while adults laugh only between 15 and 100 times daily. Healthy laughter has the additional benefit of burning 10 to 40 calories in 15 minutes.

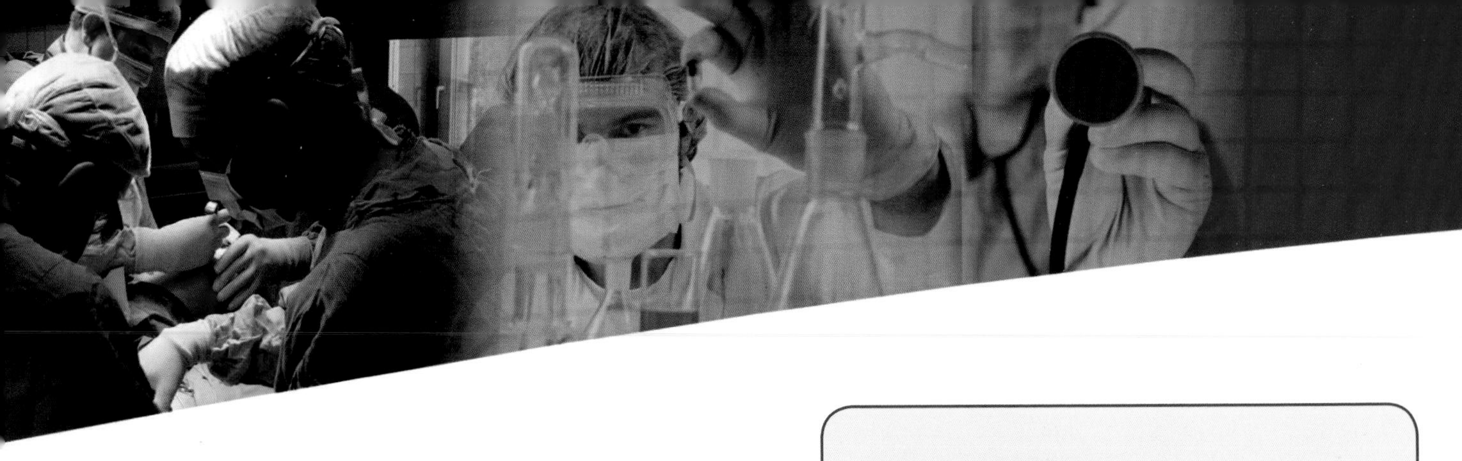

MOST SOLD MEDICINE

The medicine which is sold the most in the world, including Israel, is acetaminophen (paracetamol). In the United States it is most commonly bought as Tylenol, and in Israel as Acamol. It is hard to find a house without acetaminophen in the medicine cabinet. It is important to know that taking it at too-high dosages can lead to permanent liver damage.

HIGHEST RECORDED BODY TEMPERATURE

Willie Jones was hospitalized in 1980 in Atlanta, GA (USA), with a fever of 115.7° F (46.5° C), when he was 52 years old. In general a body temperature higher than 107.6° F (42° C) can prove fatal. Three weeks later Jones was back to his old self.

LOWEST RECORDED BODY TEMPERATURE

In 1994, 2-year-old Karlee Kosolofski was left outside her house in Canada for 6 hours while the outside temperature dipped to -7.6° F (-22° C). She was admitted to the hospital with a body temperature of only 57.74° F (14.3° C). After a few days, Karlee had completely recovered.

MOST USED MEDICINE

The most consumed medicine in the world is aspirin. Aspirin is used mainly for headaches, blood-thinning, and blood flow. Constant usage of this medication can cause unwanted side effects. Interestingly, placing an aspirin in a flower vase can keep the flowers fresh for much longer.

CAUSES OF DEATH IN ISRAEL

In the year 2009, the main cause of death was cancer (24.6% of deaths), followed by heart-related diseases (18.4%), and diseases related to blood vessels in the brain (6.3%). Haifa had the highest number of incidents of cancer (424 new cases per 100,000 men and 410 per 100,000 women). The area with the lowest incidents was Yerushalayim (266 per 100,000 men and 269 per 100,000 women).

FIRST VACCINATION

In 1796, the British physician Edward Jenner developed the first vaccination against a viral illness, when he invented the smallpox vaccination. Jenner developed the vaccination after discovering that milkmaids suffering from cowpox did not contract smallpox. Therefore, he "built" the components of the vaccine with the viruses which caused cowpox. In fact, the word "vaccination" is derived from the Latin word "vacca," meaning "cow."

People mocked Jenner, saying that he was trying to turn people into cows. It was only after Louis Pasteur further developed Jenner's method that vaccinations became routine.

NUMBER OF DOCTORS PER CAPITA

The smallest number of doctors per capita in the world is in the country of Malawi in eastern Africa — 1 doctor for every 50,000 people. The other extreme is Monaco, where there are the highest number of doctors per capita — 1 for every 170 people. In Israel the ratio is 1 doctor for every 255 citizens.

"I have a tradition from my mother, who received it from her ancestors, that if a person develops some new weakness he shouldn't reveal it to anyone for a while. This is a tried and tested *segulah* for it to go away by itself." (*Shomer Emunim*)

One of the three things that King Chizkiyahu did that the Sages approved of was his hiding the *Sefer HaRefuos* (Book of Remedies) written by King Shlomo. Chizkiyahu wanted people to pray to Hashem for mercy rather than rely on these cures (see *Berachos* 10b, Rashi).

LARGEST HOSPITAL IN THE WORLD

Chris Hani Baragwanath Hospital is the largest in the world. It occupies a sprawling 173 acres, and has 3,200 beds and 6,760 staff members. The hospital is in the Soweto area of Johannesburg, South Africa. It is a teaching hospital for the University of the Witwatersrand Medical School.

More than 2,000 patients check into the hospital daily.

LARGEST HOSPITALS IN THE UNITED STATES

The 10 largest hospitals in the United States are: Johns Hopkins Hospital, Baltimore, MD; the Mayo Clinic, Rochester, MN; the Ronald Reagan UCLA Medical Center, Los Angeles, CA; the Cleveland Clinic, Cleveland, OH; Massachusetts General Hospital, Boston, MA; New York-Presbyterian University Hospital of Columbia and Cornell, New York, NY; UCSF Medical Center, San Francisco, CA; Barnes Jewish Hospital/Washington University, St. Louis, MO; the Hospital of the University of Pennsylvania, Philadelphia, PA; and Duke University Medical Center, Durham, NC.

LARGEST HOSPITAL IN ISRAEL

In January 1996, the two hospitals Beilinson and HaSharon merged into what is now the largest medical center in Israel. The hospital has 1,250 beds and 4,520 staff members. The emergency room treats 150,000 people per year, with 34,000 operations being performed per year in the 37 operating rooms — 1,300 of which are heart operations (the largest number of heart operations in Israel).

GLASSES WITH THE WRONG PRESCRIPTION

Many people think that wearing glasses with the wrong prescription is bad for the eyes, causing eye strain which results in headaches and fatigue. However, no discernible damage is caused to the eye.

Reading with poor lighting, even in semi-darkness, will not cause someone with healthy eyes to need glasses. The only side effect is the feeling of tiredness resulting from the strain and effort on the eyes.

SENSITIVE EYES

Although in the winter the sun is hidden by the clouds, the level of radiation is the same and can damage sensitive eyes. It is therefore important to protect the eyes by not looking directly at the sun, even on a cold, wintry day. Light-colored eyes (blue or green) contain a slightly higher amount of pigment than darker eyes and therefore are more sensitive to sunlight and require greater protection.

EYE EXERCISES

The idea that not wearing glasses strengthens the eye muscles and prevents the need for a higher prescription is incorrect. In most cases, the glasses prescription is determined by that particular eye's structure, with exercise having no effect. However, for someone with weak eye muscles, exercises aimed at strengthening them can improve eyesight.

LEADING CAUSE OF BLINDNESS

Diabetes is the leading cause of blindness in the western world. Imbalance in sugar level causes irreversible damage to the small blood vessels in the eye, cutting off its oxygen supply. This eventually leads to blindness.

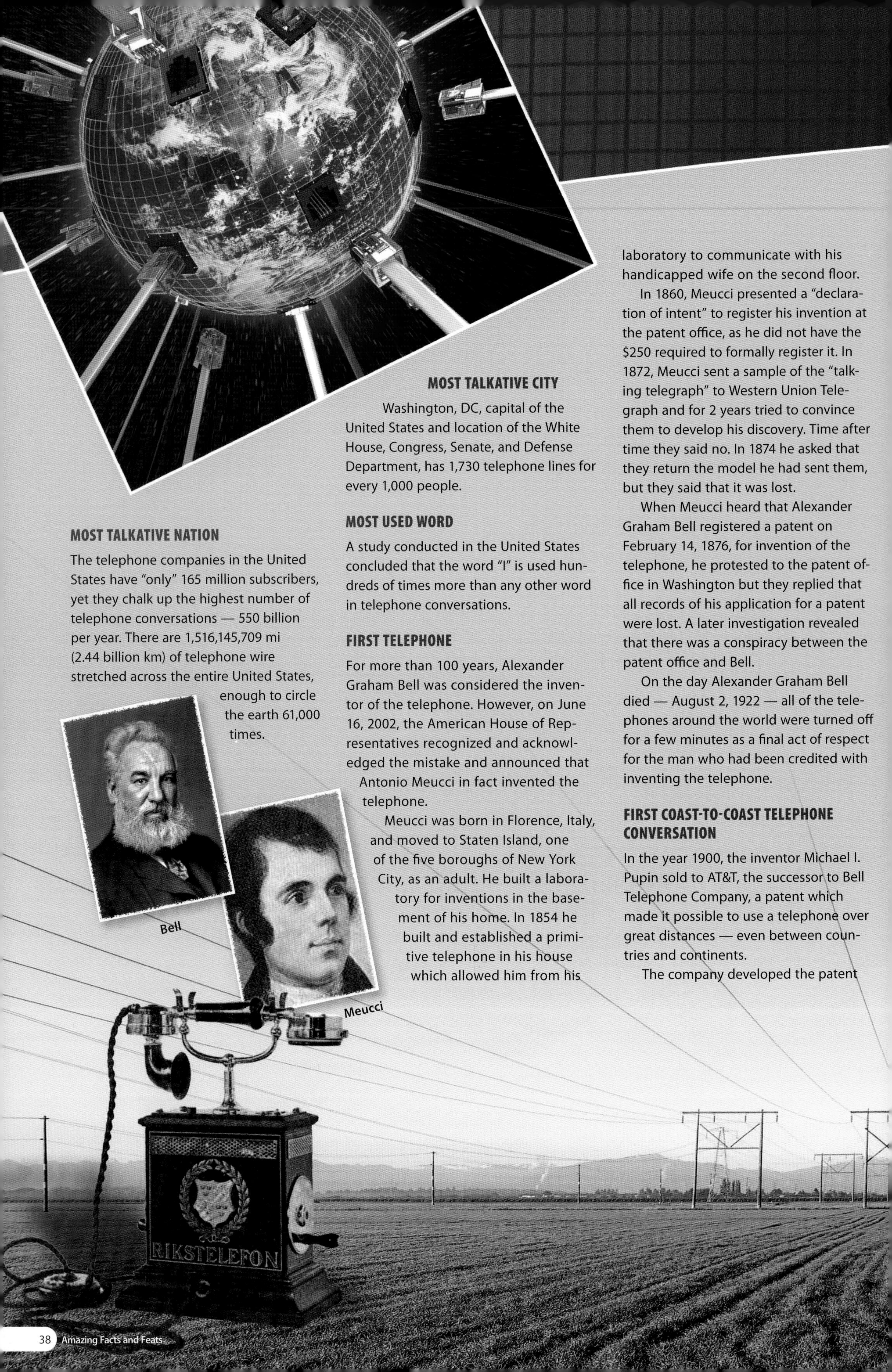

MOST TALKATIVE NATION

The telephone companies in the United States have "only" 165 million subscribers, yet they chalk up the highest number of telephone conversations — 550 billion per year. There are 1,516,145,709 mi (2.44 billion km) of telephone wire stretched across the entire United States, enough to circle the earth 61,000 times.

MOST TALKATIVE CITY

Washington, DC, capital of the United States and location of the White House, Congress, Senate, and Defense Department, has 1,730 telephone lines for every 1,000 people.

MOST USED WORD

A study conducted in the United States concluded that the word "I" is used hundreds of times more than any other word in telephone conversations.

FIRST TELEPHONE

For more than 100 years, Alexander Graham Bell was considered the inventor of the telephone. However, on June 16, 2002, the American House of Representatives recognized and acknowledged the mistake and announced that Antonio Meucci in fact invented the telephone.

Meucci was born in Florence, Italy, and moved to Staten Island, one of the five boroughs of New York City, as an adult. He built a laboratory for inventions in the basement of his home. In 1854 he built and established a primitive telephone in his house which allowed him from his laboratory to communicate with his handicapped wife on the second floor.

In 1860, Meucci presented a "declaration of intent" to register his invention at the patent office, as he did not have the $250 required to formally register it. In 1872, Meucci sent a sample of the "talking telegraph" to Western Union Telegraph and for 2 years tried to convince them to develop his discovery. Time after time they said no. In 1874 he asked that they return the model he had sent them, but they said that it was lost.

When Meucci heard that Alexander Graham Bell registered a patent on February 14, 1876, for invention of the telephone, he protested to the patent office in Washington but they replied that all records of his application for a patent were lost. A later investigation revealed that there was a conspiracy between the patent office and Bell.

On the day Alexander Graham Bell died — August 2, 1922 — all of the telephones around the world were turned off for a few minutes as a final act of respect for the man who had been credited with inventing the telephone.

FIRST COAST-TO-COAST TELEPHONE CONVERSATION

In the year 1900, the inventor Michael I. Pupin sold to AT&T, the successor to Bell Telephone Company, a patent which made it possible to use a telephone over great distances — even between countries and continents.

The company developed the patent

Mail and Communication

Model of Bell's telephone

and in the year 1915, 39 years after the initial conversation on Bell's telephone, Bell successfully called from New York his assistant Thomas Watson in San Francisco, CA, 3,000 mi (5,000 km) away.

Twelve years later, in the year 1927, the first conversation between New York and London took place.

One of the first telephones

Bell launching the 1st telephone call between New York and Chicago

An old-fashioned switchboard

FIRST DIAL PHONE

The first models of telephones did not have dials. The owner would lift up the receiver and automatically be connected to a switchboard operator, who would connect 2 wires in the switchboard. This established a connection between 2 telephone owners, allowing them to speak to each other.

An American undertaker named Almon Strowger was not happy with this system. He was angry at his local switchboard operators, claiming that they would chatter nonstop when they were supposed to be working. Even worse, claimed Strowger, whenever a resident of the city died, one of the switchboard operators — whose husband was also an undertaker — would connect the deceased's relatives with his competitor.

Strowger invented an automated switchboard connecting subscribers to each other without the need for an operator, resulting in a great increase in telephone usage and making the telephone one of the most widely used instruments today.

Almon Strowger

DID YOU KNOW?

On the same day that Bell applied for a patent for his invention, Elisha Gray, who had been working for Western Union Telegraph, applied for a patent for a machine which transfers sounds based on the same principles as Bell's invention. Gray registered his patent 2 hours after Bell had done so. As Chazal say, *"Zerizin makdimin."*

The AT&T building Los Angeles, CA

FIRST CELLULAR PHONE

In 1968 Bell Laboratories and AT&T came up with the idea of using radio broadcasting stations for cellular telephones. Should a user pass from an area covered by one station to an area covered by another, he would be transferred automatically to the second station, insuring the continuity of the reception.

Two companies, Bell Laboratories and Motorola, worked on further developing this idea, and in 1973 Motorola presented a model of the first cellular telephone. However, it was Bell Laboratories who in 1979 presented the first prototype of cellular communication, and the first experiment was carried out in 1980 in the Chicago area with 2,000 participants.

A year later, in Tokyo, Japan, the first commercial cellular communications company was established. Only in 1982 did the Federal Communications Commission (FCC) permit establishment of the first commercial cellular communications company in the United States. It was established in the year 1983 — 15 years after the idea was first suggested.

LARGEST CELLULAR TELEPHONE MANUFACTURER

The largest manufacturer of cellular telephones in the world is Nokia (with about 30% of the market), followed by Motorola, Samsung, LG, Simmons, and Sony-Erikson.

In 2003, 520 million cellular telephones were sold throughout the world. In 2009, 1.2 billion were sold worldwide, and projected sales for the year 2010 are 1.3 billion.

CELLULAR TELEPHONE COMPANY WITH THE MOST SUBSCRIBERS

In 2009, China Mobile boasted 508,370,000 subscribers, followed by the British company Vodafone with 472,900,000 subscribers throughout the world.

LARGEST CELLULAR PHONE COMPANY IN ISRAEL

Cellcom is the largest cellular communications company in Israel. In 2009 Cellcom had 3.2 million subscribers. In the past few years the company's income has exceeded NIS 5 billion per year. Cellcom is the only cellular communications company in Israel with its own transmission, giving it the best potential reception of all the companies.

LARGEST NUMBER OF TELEPHONE LINES

In 2009 there were 365.6 million domestic telephone lines in China, more than any other country in the world. China is also the country with the highest number of cellular telephone subscribers — 634 million.

SMALLEST CELLULAR TELEPHONE

The smallest cellular telephone in the world is the IMoblie C1000 watch (Chinese, of course) with multimedia capabilities. Because of its small size, actions are done via a touch screen whose size is 1.5 in. (3.8 cm).

With this tiny screen it is possible to watch films, listen to MP3, and look at pictures. Earphones can also be used and Bluetooth technology permits speaking comfortably without having to use the watch's mouthpiece. The watch also contains a calendar, games, a radio, and more.

LARGEST CELLULAR TELEPHONE

The largest working cellular telephone in the world was placed in the middle of Rotmein, Germany, in June 2004. The telephone is made from wood, metal, and polyester. Its length is 6.7 ft (about 2 m), its width is 2.7 ft (83 cm), and it has a thickness of 147.6 ft (45 m). This telephone is able to send and receive written messages.

NOKIA

CONNECTING PEOPLE

FARTHEST COMMUNICATION EVER

At the end of 2006 the American unmanned spaceship Voyager I reached a distance of 9,010,300,000 mi (14,500,000,000 km) from Earth, as part of its mission to research the outer borders of the solar system and beyond. The radio signals that were sent from earth at the speed of light were received in the spaceship only 14 hours later.

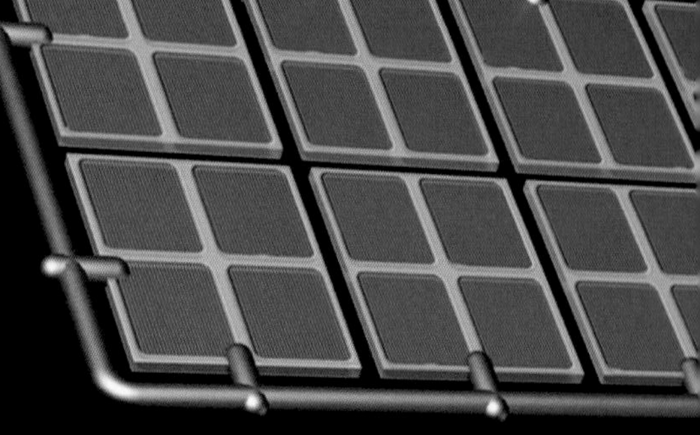

DID YOU KNOW?

A weekday edition of *The New York Times* contains more information than the average person living in England in the 17th century was exposed to his entire life.

STORAGE AND DELIVERY OF INFORMATION

In the year 2000, ten billion billion (10^{18}) bits of information were stored, an average of 1 gigabyte per person on the entire earth. This information includes films, computing output, music, and pictures. By now, that number is much, much, larger.

Only .003% of the information is ever printed on paper. To store all this information requires billions of CDs, which together would fill a tower 621.4 mi (1,000 km) high. With the aid of nanotechnology there are experiments aimed at developing methods which would allow 10 times that amount of information to be stored in something the size of a sugar cube.

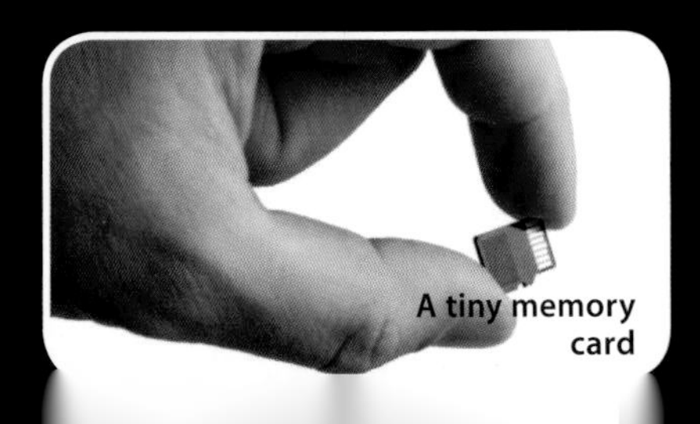
A tiny memory card

Mail and Communication

FIRST KOSHER CELL PHONE

The company to introduce the first kosher cellular phone was MIRS. In 2005, in response to the request of the *gedolei hador*, MIRS manufactured three *mehadrin* cellular telephones approved by the Rabbinical Committee for Communications as appropriate for the *chareidi* public. The phones were simple, meant to be used only for speaking, without any other services such as Internet or sending text messages.

DID YOU KNOW?

In the year 2005 there were 1,206,315,500 ordinary telephone lines in the world and 1,752,183,600 cellular telephone lines — almost 1.5 times the number of phone lines in homes. On the other hand, in that same year, almost half the world's population had never used a telephone even once. However, by 2008, there were 1.268 billion land lines and 4.017 billion cellular lines, and by now almost everyone on earth has used a telephone, either cellular or land.

INVENTOR OF THE STAMP

The idea of a purchasing a stamp and sticking it on a letter for the purpose of sending the letter was suggested in 1837 by Roland Hill in an attempt to improve the English postal system. Roland was knighted for this invention.

DID YOU KNOW?

England is the only county in the world which does not explicitly state its name on its stamps.

FIRST POSTAGE STAMP

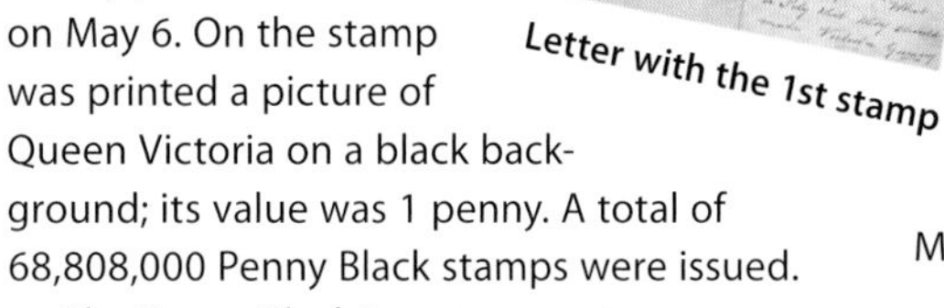

Letter with the 1st stamp

The first stamp, called the "Penny Black," was printed in England on May 1, 1840, and approved for use on May 6. On the stamp was printed a picture of Queen Victoria on a black background; its value was 1 penny. A total of 68,808,000 Penny Black stamps were issued.

The Penny Black is not a rare stamp. This is because at the time it was used, envelopes were not used to send letters. Rather, a letter was written on a piece of paper, folded, and glued shut. The address was written on the outside of the letter and a stamp was pasted next to it. Letters, unlike envelopes, are saved; therefore, many stamps were preserved. However, due to the historical significance of the Penny Black, it is in great demand. The asking price for a used stamp is $210 and an unused stamp in good condition sells for $3,000.

FIRST ISRAELI STAMP

The first stamp of the State of Israel was issued on May 16, 1948. Printed on the stamp was a picture of an old coin from the period of the second Beis HaMikdash. The words דאר עברי ("Jewish Post") were printed on the stamp. The stamp was worth 50 mil (at the time 1,000 mil equaled one lira). The stamps were designed by Otto Walish, one of three graphic artists who were asked to design the first series of stamps of the "Jewish Post." Walish suggested printing pictures of coins minted in Eretz Yisrael 2,000 years previously, highlighting two Jewish revolts — the Great Revolt (67–73 C.E.) and the Bar Kochva Revolt (132–135 C.E.), expressing the Jewish nation's desire for freedom.

Today the "Jewish Post" series is one of the most valuable stamp series in Israel. Postal articles of that time are sold today for thousands of shekels. "Jewish Post" stamps were used in Israel until the year 1950.

LARGEST STAMP

The largest commercial stamp was issued in 1979 in the Marshall Islands, with a width of 4.33 in. (11 cm) and a length of 6.3 in. (16 cm). The largest non-commercial stamp is 6.9 ft (2.1 m) long and 4.6 ft (1.4 m) wide. It was designed and manufactured by Amnon Shalmon from Kiryat Ono. On the stamp is printed a picture of the famous Jewish artist Marcel Janko.

LARGEST POSTAL SERVICE

The largest postal system in the world is that of the United States. In the year 2008 the US Postal service delivered 203 billion pieces of mail — 46% of the world's volume. This translates to 7,700 pieces processed per second! The number of employees in the postal service stands at 656,000 — the 2nd largest civilian employer (after Wal-Mart) in the United States. The postal service has the largest civilian fleet of cars and trucks in the world — 221,000. This requires over 120 million gal of fuel per year.

THE STORY BEHIND THE STAMP

One of the factors which raise the value of a stamp in the eyes of collectors is the story behind the stamp or postal article. The following is the story behind the 1¢ stamp of British Guiana in South America, issued in 1856.

One day there were no stamps left at the post office and the local manager decided to print two stamps on his own and stamp them by hand. A few years later, one of these stamps fell into the hands of a young man, who then sold it to a collector for a very low price. From there it was sold from one collector to another, until it was purchased by an American Jew named Arthur Hind in 1922 for $7,500.

At around the same time a sailor who was also a stamp collector discovered the other stamp on one of his journeys. The stamp held by Arthur Hind was known throughout the world of stamp collectors for its value and rarity, and the sailor therefore offered Hind the 2nd stamp for a very handsome price. Hind agreed, purchased the stamp, and immediately burned it, insu ing that his stamp would be the only remai ing copy in the world and therefore worth fortune.

Following Hind's death, the stamp was sold at public auction for $1 million.

COUNTRY WITH THE MOST UNUSUAL STAMPS

The small country of Bhutan, located in the upper Himalayas (see picture on opposite page), issued 10 series of unconventional stamps beginning in 1962.

On the 40th anniversary of the king's rule, and after the country was refused a loan by the World Bank, it was decided to i sue unusual stamps to generate income fo building schools, roads, and hospitals. The 1st series consisted of round stamps printe on gold-plated sheets, with a picture of th king in the center of the stamp. These soo to-be world-famous stamps were the first their kind. They were bought by many collectors and the country of Bhutan realized that this had potential to be a money-mak ing business. The next series were triangul stamps with an illustration of the legendar snowman from the Himalayan Mountains. This stamp too brought in large profits.

In 1967 Bhutan issued their outer space series, which amazed the international stamp-collecting community. The stamps were printed using a special method whic produced a 3-dimensional picture. Hundreds of thousands of stamps were sold to excited collectors from all over the world. The next series were plastic stamps which gave the appearance of oil paintings printe on iron and silk, followed by flower stamps which emitted the scent of the flower prin ed on the stamp. In 1973 they manufactured a series of stamps shaped like record which could be placed on a phonograph t play the Bhutan national anthem and loca folk songs.

Although Bhutan achieved great success in the unconventional stamp business among stamp collectors, their stamps are not displayed in the professional philatelic community or in international exhibits. They are even banned by some, with the claim that they were never intended to be used as real postage stamps.

Bhutan's phon stamp

'here was a change of government in 1973, at which point Bhutan returned to issuing ordi-ıary stamps.

ıOST FAMOUS STAMP

ı the year 1857, the most famous stamp ı the world, the "Treskilling Yellow," was ›rinted in Sweden ("tre" is 3 and a skilling ; a Swedish coin). Three-skilling stamps vere green, while 6-skilling stamps were 'ellow. However, on one occasion, while ›rinting 6-skilling stamps, the plate or the 3-skilling stamp was ac-identally inserted. The result vas a yellow rather than a green -skilling stamp.

It was only 30 years later that his stamp was accidentally discov-ered by a Swedish child on a letter e found in his grandfather's ouse. This is the only known opy in the world oday, and in 1996 : was sold for 2.3 million.

MISTAKES WORTH MILLIONS

Many stamp collectors specialize in stamps with printing errors. For example, there was a stamp printed in Italy with a picture of a traffic light. The only problem was that the red light was printed on the bottom rather than on the top where it belongs.

A rare American stamp has a picture of a train traveling with its steam blowing in one direction and the flags at the train station blowing in the opposite direction.

"Upside Down Jenny" or "Inverted Jenny" is the name of an American stamp printed in 1918 in which the picture of a Curtiss JN-4 airplane appears upside-down. The Upside Down Jenny is one of the most sought-after stamps in the world, with only 100 known copies in existence. In 2005 a sheet of 4 of these stamps sold for $2.7 million, and in 2007 one was sold for $977,500.

"Upside Down Jenny"

A village in Bhutan

hutan's scented stamp

The world's 1st round stamp, Bhutan

Paper being manufactured by hand

FIRST PRODUCTION OF PAPER

The Chinese began producing paper in the beginning of the 2nd century. The secret of how to make paper was discovered by the Arabs, who revealed it to the Europeans only 1,200 years later.

Until the late 1700s paper was manufactured by hand, making it a very rare and expensive item. In 1799 the first paper-manufacturing machine was invented by a Frenchman named Louis Robert. From that time on, the production of paper underwent many drastic changes and improvements.

Old-time paper-manufacturing machine in Holland

THE BALLPOINT PEN

In 1944, Argentine Laszki Biro invented a revolutionary pen which became known as "the pen which could be used underwater." At the end of this pen was a small ball that would turn around while being used and transfer the ink from the ink cartridge to the page.

The invention of the ballpoint pen was of especially major significance for left-handed people and for right-handed people writing in Hebrew. In each of these cases, the hand goes over what has just been freshly written before the ink has had a chance to dry, thus smearing the letters. The ink used for a ballpoint pen is thicker than ink used for a fountain pen, permitting writing without smearing.

Because the principle behind the ballpoint pen involves gravity, it does not work in outer space. The space agency NASA therefore developed a ballpoint pen which is usable in outer space. The Russian cosmonauts simply wrote in pencil.

Ballpoint pen

FIRST ERASER

Throughout the continent of Europe, small cubes of rubber, brought from South America, were used for erasing lead pencil markings from paper. However, rubber in its raw state wears out quickly and leaves black markings on the paper. In 1839, the inventor Charles Goodyear discovered a way to transform rubber into a more durable and hard-wearing product, making it more effective and cleaner for erasing.

THE MATCH

In 1680, an Irishman named Robert Boyle discovered that rubbing sulfur with phosphorous causes a burst of flame. In 1827, an English pharmacist named John Walker developed "sticks from sulfur peroxide" which were 12.2 in. (31 cm) long. Small sulfur matches were first marketed in Germany in the year 1832, though they had a terrible smell and were very dangerous. Onl in the year 1845 was the problem solved when Carl Lindstrom of Sweden presente the first "safe" matches as we know them today made from red phosphorous.

FIRST PENCIL

The pencil, made from lead, was first used for writing on papyrus. This heavy lead was soon replaced with softer graphite after vast deposits were discovered in 1564 in Cambria, England. Graphite in its natural state is pure and solid, making it easy to mold into stick-like shapes in any size.

Mass production of pencils began in Germany in approximately 1600. In 1858 someone tried to register a patent for attaching an eraser on the edge of a pencil, but the patent was rejected with the claim that this was not considered a new invention but simply attaching 2 existing products.

FIRST TRAFFIC LIGHT

The world's first traffic light was introduced outside the British Parliament on December 10, 1868. It was identical to the train signals of the time — flags on top of a metal housing with gas lights colored green and red to be lit up at night. A handle operated by a policeman directing traffic was used to change the flags. It blew up shortly thereafter in January 1869, injuring its operator.

The modern traffic light as we know it was invented in 1912 in the United States by a policeman named Lester Wire in Salt Lake City, UT. On August 5, 1914, the first traffic light, designed by James Hoge, was introduced in Cleveland, OH.

The first 3-color traffic light was invented by a policeman named Lester Potts in Detroit, MI, in 1920.

DID YOU KNOW?

The word plastic is derived from the Greek word *plastikos*, implying "something which can be molded into any shape." Over the years plastic has been replacing other natural raw materials — Perspex is taking the place of glass, nylon and rayon are used to manufacture clothing, Teflon and Bakelite are replacing metal and othe materials used for cleaning and adhering. In fact, plastic is being used in food additives and food coloring.

GUNPOWDER

Gunpowder was invented in China in the year 1040. At first gunpowder was used to create fireworks, but soon after the Chinese began using it to send small missiles, bombs, and cannons. Arab merchants brought gunpowder to the Middle East in 1304 and from there it made its way to Europe. In 1846 an Italian chemist named Ascanio Sombrero made gunpowder even more effective by using 2 parts sulfuric acid and 1 part nitric acid. Sombrero also invented nitroglycerin, which has far greater explosive capability than gunpowder and is of course far more dangerous.

Ivory gunpowder container

DYNAMITE

In 1867 the Swedish chemist Alfred Nobel discovered that mixing nitroglycerine with diatomaceous earth made explosives safer and easier to use. He called his new invention dynamite and patented it. This explosive was used by civilians for, among other things, excavating roads, tunnels, and mines.

DID YOU KNOW?

From the year 1893, Alfred Nobel suffered from chronic heart-related chest pain known as angina and from heart attacks. His suffering was eased after he began medicating himself with nitroglycerine. The biochemical effect of nitroglycerine was only discovered a few decades ago and it is still used today as medication for angina.

THE "FATHER" OF EXPLOSIVES

In 1837, when Alfred Nobel was nine years old, his father established an ammunitions factory. In 1859 Nobel went to Paris to study chemistry, and upon his return to Sweden decided to devote his time to researching the manufacture of explosives. This was a very dangerous occupation and on one occasion there was an explosion in the family factory, killing several employees — among them his younger brother. In 1867 Nobel registered his patent for a more effective and safe use of gunpowder, called dynamite. He continued developing explosives with greater explosive potential but which were safer to use. Altogether, Nobel registered 355 patents and amassed great wealth from the explosives in Sweden and 20 other countries.

Nobel suffered a stroke and died on December 10, 1896. He never married and therefore had no descendants. In his will he bequeathed his wealth, which has now grown to over $262 billion, to a fund which would award 5 annual prizes each for research in physics, chemistry, physiology, medicine, literature, and peace. The first prize was awarded in 1901. Today the fund still awards prizes to scientists and other people who the committee feels have contributed greatly to science and to mankind.

In 1969 the Nobel Prize for economics was added to the list, but since this was not included in Nobel's will, the prize is sponsored by the Bank of Sweden.

Alfred Nobel

The Stockholm (Sweden) Concert Hall, where Nobel Prizes are awarded

FIRST PURELY SYNTHETIC MATERIAL

The first purely synthetic material was nylon, invented in 1935 by the American engineer Dr. Wallace H. Carothers. He was working in the laboratories of the Dupont company in the United States. Research and development was kept secret, and the material was meant to replace the silk manufactured by the Japanese. Dupont invested $27 million — an astronomical amount in those days — in nylon's development. The company had planned to use nylon mainly for manufacturing socks. After more than 12 years of development, the product was presented in the 1939 New York World's Fair. The first product to use nylon was the toothbrush.

Nylonmania swept the world until 1941. Production was halted when the United States entered World War II, at which point Dupont concentrated on manufacturing parachutes for the army. After the war, Dupont renewed production of nylon. The product was so popular that endless lines appeared at stores selling Dupont's nylon products.

According to legend, the name nylon was coined by one of the scientists who were present when the advantages of nylon over silk were discovered. He said: "Now You Lose, Old Nippons" ("Nippon" is another word for Japanese).

FIRST PLASTIC — CELLULOID

In 1850, inventors began searching for synthetic materials which would replace ivory and other valuable natural raw materials. The first one to develop "synthetic ivory" was the English inventor Alexander Parkes, who used cellulose, the main element found in the walls of plant cells, to develop a material called Parkesine. The problem with Parkesine was that it tore and broke after only a short use. The American John Wesley Hyatt discovered how to improve the cellulose, and in 1863 introduced a new type of plastic and called it celluloid.

One of the first products made from this new material was false teeth. They could only be used for eating cold food because celluloid melts when heated and loses its shape. However, celluloid was used to make waterproof clothing. Hyatt sold the clothes for an astronomical sum of money.

With time, however, celluloid would turn yellow and become breakable. Worst of all, the process Hyatt employed to improve cellulose involved nitric acid, one of the main ingredients used in the manufacture of gunpowder. Celluloid clothing was therefore flammable and explosive, endangering those wearing it.

Nations of the World 48

Governments 54

A Common Language and a Shared Purpose 58

Lawbreakers 62

Nations and Governments

Our Sages taught that man should naturally desire government. This is because it is almost essential for humans to live together for their sustenance and survival. For this reason, it is appropriate for those gathered in one state or area, or even the entire world, to have some semblance of order to preserve righteousness and remove injustice, and to insure that no altercations result from any dealings and negotiations between men.

Sefer Halkarim, First Essay, chapter 5

LARGEST COUNTRY

Prior to its breakup, the Soviet Union encompassed an area of 8,649,545 mi^2 (22,402,220 km^2). Even today, the country of Russia still has the largest area — 6,601,668 mi^2 (17,098,242 km^2) — 11.5% of the land on earth.

Russia is followed by:

Canada — 3,855,100 mi^2 (9,984,670 km^2)
The United States — 3,717, 813 mi^2 (9,629,091 km^2)
China — 3,705,407 mi^2 (9,596,961 km^2)
Brazil — 3,287,612 mi^2 (8,514,877 km^2)

Israel is the 151st largest country, with an area of 8,765 mi^2 (22,700 km^2).

Six percent of Eretz Yisrael is forest, while 27% is designated for agriculture.

LARGEST EMPIRE

In 1900 the British Empire, at the height of its growth and power, ruled over an area greater than 15,057,984 mi^2 (39,000,000 km^2), 1/6 of the combined area of all the countries in the world. More than 1/4 of the entire world population at the time resided within the British Empire. The British Empire encompassed such a large area that there was a famous saying: "The sun never sets on the British Empire" — in other words, every minute of the day the sun was shining in at least one area under British rule.

SMALLEST UNOFFICIAL COUNTRY

The principality of Sealand lies on a floating port whose area is only 5,920 ft^2 (550 m^2): 180.4 ft x 32.8 ft (55m x 10m). It is located approximately 6 mi (10 km) west of the English coast. The port is referred to as "Rough Tower" and served the British during World War II until it was abandoned in 1956. In 1967 it was taken over by Paddy Roy Bates, a 55-year-old former major in the British army, who proclaimed the establishment of the Principality of Sealand and crowned himself "Prince Roy."

Not long afterwards, a British ship turned up with the intent of evacuating the inhabitants of Sealand, and Bates' son Michael fired toward it. A British court declared that since Sealand was outside British territorial waters, it was beyond their jurisdiction; therefore, they could not judge the case.

In 1978 Sealand's prime minister, Alexander G. Achenbach, took advantage of Prince Roy's absence from Sealand, and with the aid of a few German and Dutch citizens tried to take control over the floating dock with the intent of using it as a tax haven, taking Bates' son as their prisoner. Prince Roy, however, managed to regain control over Sealand with the aid of mercenaries, and imprisoned all the intruders.

Germany sent a representative to negotiate with Bates for the release of the prisoners, which Bates saw as recognition of Sealand's sovereignty. However, Alexander G. Achenbach, the rebel prime minister, established a "government-in-exile" which exists in Germany to this day.

Unfortunately, forged passports of the principality were used to carry out crimes all over the world. Therefore, in 1997, Sealand announced that it was declaring all 150 passports it issued as null and void.

In 2007, the Bates family put the country of Sealand up for sale the price of $2 billion.

Sealand is basically a platform on top of poles in the North Sea. The official language of Sealand is English. It has a population of 27, and the official currency is the Sealand Dollar.

Nations of the World

tellite photo of Israel

ONLY COUNTRY WITH AN UNDEFINED AREA

The only country in the world whose area and borders are undefined is the State of Israel. Israel annexed the Golan Heights and East Jerusalem, yet the nations of the world refuse to recognize this annexation. Even the border with the Palestinian Authority remains undefined and unrecognized by any political body.

> Eretz Yisrael is referred to as *Eretz HaTzvi* — land of the deer. Rabbi Chanina explained, Just as a deer whose skin is not large enough to accommodate its flesh, so is the case with Eretz Yisrael: When people live there, it expands to accommodate them, but when people do not live there it contracts.
>
> (*Gittin* 57a)

SMALLEST MEMBER OF THE UNITED NATIONS

The smallest member of the United Nations is Monaco, located within the territory of France with an area of only 0.75 mi² (1.95 km²). Monaco's length extends 3.5 mi (5.61 km) along the coast, with a width of less than 1,640 ft (.5 km) — the smallest coastline. Monaco also has the distinction of having the highest ratio of bank accounts to population, with an average of 12 bank accounts per person.

SMALLEST NATION IN THE WORLD

The smallest independent state (i.e., not an official country) in the world is the Vatican, located in the middle of Rome, Italy, and covering an area of only 109 acres — less than 0.17 mi² (less than .5 km²).

LARGEST POLITICAL ALLIANCE IN THE WORLD

The largest political alliance in the world is the British Commonwealth of Nations, known today simply as "The Commonwealth." The British Commonwealth combines 54 independent countries and 27 countries which do not have independent sovereignty. If we add the other areas under British protection, they form a combined area of 1,511,590 mi² (3,915,000 km²), with a total population exceeding 2 billion people — almost 1/3 of the world's population. Ninety-four percent of these people live in Asia and Africa combined; 1.17 billion alone live in India. All member states recognize the queen of England, Queen Elizabeth II, as head of the Commonwealth.

TIME TO BUY A NEW MAP

Since 1990, 33 new countries have been created — most due to the dissolution of the USSR and Yugoslavia.

Out of the former USSR, 15 countries were created: Armenia, Azerbaijan, Belarus, Estonia, Georgia, Kazakhstan, Kyrgyzstan, Latvia, Lithuania, Moldova, Russia, Tajikistan, Turkmenistan, Ukraine, and Uzbekistan. Five countries were carved out of the former Yugoslavia: Bosnia and Herzegovina; Croatia; Macedonia; Serbia and Montenegro (also known as Yugoslavia); and Slovenia.

Another 13 countries have declared their independence since 1990: Namibia became independent of the Republic of South Africa; North Yemen and South Yemen merged to become Yemen; East Germany and West Germany merged to become Germany; the Marshall Islands and the Republic of Palau, which were part of the Trust Territory administered by the United States, both gained independence; Micronesia (previously called the Caroline Islands) became independent of the United States; the Czech Republic and Slovakia became separate nations when Czechoslovakia dissolved; Eritrea seceded from Ethiopia; East Timor (Timor-Leste) became independent of Indonesia; Montenegro and Serbia split, becoming two independent countries; and Kosovo unilaterally declared independence from Serbia.

Photos of East Timor (Timor-Leste)

COUNTRY WITH THE MOST BORDERS

China has the largest number of countries bordering it (16). They are: Mongolia, Russia, North Korea, Hong Kong, Macau, Vietnam, Laos, Myanmar (formerly Burma), India, Bhutan, Nepal, Kyrgyzstan, Pakistan, Afghanistan, Tajikistan, and Kazakhstan.

Indonesia shares 19 bodies of water with neighboring countries.

LONGEST DRY LAND BORDER

China's 16 borders reach a total length of 13,743 mi (22,117 km), the shortest border being the 1,116 ft (.34 km) border with Macau (which is under administrative control of China). China's coastline is spread over 9,010 mi (14,500 km).

LONGEST BORDER BETWEEN TWO COUNTRIES

The border between the United States and Canada is the longest in the world — 5,526 mi (8,893 km). This consists of 3,987 mi (6,416 km) dividing the northern portion of the United States and southern Canada, and an additional 1,539 mi (2,477 km) separating northern Canada from Alaska.

The Rock of Gibralta

COUNTRY WITHOUT A CAPITAL

The Republic of Nauru in the South Pacific is the only country in the world without an official capital.

NATION OF IMMIGRANTS

Between the years 1820 and 2004 the United States absorbed 69,869,450 legal immigrants, and approximately 27 million illegal immigrants. There are between 11 million and 13 million illegal immigrants living in the United States today. This means that approximately 1 out of every 24 residents of the United States is an illegal immigrant.

There are over 39 million European immigrants living in the United States today. The largest group is from Germany (7.24 million).

There are over 10 million Asian immigrants living in the United States. The majority are from China (over 1.5 million).

MOST CROSSED BORDER

The most crossed border in the world is the border between the United States and Mexico. More than 120 million people, largely smugglers and illegal immigrants, cross this border every year.

Sign at the United States–Mexico borde

Nations of the World

SMALLEST INTERNATIONAL BORDER

The smallest border between two countries is the land border between Gibraltar and Spain — only 0.75 mi (1.2 km). The Straits of Gibraltar, 984 ft (300 m) deep and only 8.1 mi (13 km) wide at its narrowest point, serves as the only sailing route between the Atlantic Ocean and the Mediterranean Sea.

SRAELIS IN AMERICA

)fficial statistics list 195,725 emigrants rom the State of Israel to the United tates. However, the Israeli Foreign Office stimates that there are no less than million illegal Israelis living in the "land f the free." In Los Angeles alone there reide an estimated 500,000 Israelis.

ID YOU KNOW?

1 2009 there were approximately 40 illion Spanish-speaking immigrants ving in the United States, comprisng 13% of the general population. ccording to conservative estimates, panish will soon become the second nguage in the United States, a couny in which there are 300 different other tongues spoken.

RESIDENTS OF ISRAEL ACCORDING TO ORIGIN

The following lists the five most popular countries of origin in Israel as of 2009: the total number of people whose roots can be traced to that country, as well as the number among them who are Israeli-born children of immigrants.

COUNTRY OF ORIGIN	NUMBER OF PEOPLE	ISRAELI BORN
Russia	1,173,000	242,000
Morocco	495,000	337,000
Iraq	242,000	170,000
Rumania	235,000	122,000
Poland	214,000	150,000

IMMIGRANTS IN ISRAEL BY CONTINENT

In 2009, 3.7 million residents of Israel were Israeli-born, comprising 67% of the population. The following chart lists their ancestors' continents of origin.

CONTINENT OF ORIGIN	NUMBER	PERCENT OF POPULATION
North America and Europe	2,200,000	39
Africa	867,000	15.6
Asia	695,400	2.6

Out of those of African origin, the highest representation was from Ethiopia, numbering 105,000 (approximately 12% of those from Africa).

SECOND GENERATION

Thirty-two percent of the general population is made up of Israeli-born residents born to families who have been living in Israel for at least two generations.

MOST POPULAR FLAG COLOR

The most popular color for a flag is red. The reason is that red represents bravery and battle for independence, which generally involves the spilling of blood.

MOST POPULAR FLAG COLOR COMBINATION

Most of the world's flags are comprised of three color stripes one next to the other, either horizontal or vertical. The most popular color combination is blue, white, and red — the colors of the French Revolution, the symbol of democracy.

Flags bearing these colors belong to France, the United States, the Netherlands, Russia, Chile, Britain, and New Zealand, among others.

MOST BORING FLAG

The Libyan flag, which became official in 1977, is the only flag in the world sporting just one color — and nothing else. It is completely green, without any symbol or even a shade of another color. The color green is the traditional color of Islam, the national religion of Libya. It represents the "Green Revolution" of the Libyan ruler Muammar al-Gaddafi.

NON-RECTANGULAR FLAG

The flag of Nepal, which became official on December 6, 1962, is the only non-rectangular national flag in the world. The flag, which consists of two right triangles one on top of the other, is a combination of two of the flags of previous rulers from the Rana dynasty. The two royal symbols (containing the sun and the moon) were symbols of hope that Nepal would last at least as long as the sun and the moon.

IDENTICAL FLAGS

At the Berlin Olympics of 1936, participants from the State of Liechtenstein noticed that their flag was almost completely identical to that of Haiti. Therefore, in 1937, a crown was added to Liechtenstein's flag.

HEAVIEST INTERNATIONAL FLAG

The Great American Flag, which was hoisted in Indiana in 1980, is the world's heaviest flag weighing 7 tons. It is 420 ft (128 m) long and 223 ft (68 m) wide. The flag was presented a gift to the White House.

LARGEST FLAG

The world's largest flag is a flag of the city of Jerusalem. It was unfurled on September 17, 2009, in Jerusalem's Teddy Stadium. It is 473,612 ft^2 (44,404 m^2) and weighs 9.5 tons. It took 6 people to make the flag in 120 days at a cost of $120,000. The flag is 4 times larg than the stadium, so spectators could see o the Jerusalem lion emblem in the center.

The flag was the brainchild of a Philippin businesswoman, who in 2007 financed what was then the world's largest flag: that of Isra

HIGHEST FLAGPOLES

In Panmunjeom, South Korea, the national f was hoisted upon the world's highest supported flagpole — 525 ft (160 m).

In Aqaba, Jordan, a flag was hoisted on t highest non-supported flagpole — 417 ft (127 m).

FLAGS OF THE TRIBES OF ISRAEL

"Hashem said to the nations of the world, 'There are many flags, but the flags that are dearest to Me are those of the children of Yaakov.' When Hashem revealed Himself at Mt. Sinai, 22 groups of 10,000 angels descended — each in the guise of flags. When the Jewish people saw that the angels were made of flags, they too yearned to become flags, saying, 'If only we could become flags like them!' Hashem responded, 'Do you really wish to become flags? I will grant your wish.' Hashem then instructed Moshe, 'Go make the Jewish people flags as they desire.'"

(*Bemidbar Rabbah* 2:3)

DID YOU KNOW?

The study of flags is called vexillology, which is a combination of the Latin word *vexillum* (flag or placard) and the suffix *logy* (which means discipline or study of). A look at the various world flags shows that neighboring countries or those based on common religion or culture share similar flag colors:

Blue is popular in the flags of North and Central American countries, while green is widely used in flags of Islamic countries in the Middle East as well as in Asian and African nations.

Arab countries often include black in their flags.

Many African countries, as well as countries which were established by freed slaves such as Jamaica and Brazil, have flags of red, yellow, and green.

Aqaba flagpole

Panmur flagp

ITE FLAG

e white flag is the international symbol nifying surrender or ceasefire. A white g carried by a messenger indicates at the messenger is unarmed and wish- to enter into negotiations. According the Geneva Convention, it is forbidden harm anyone carrying a white flag. sely displaying a white flag in ler to be able to make a surprise ack is a violation of the rules of r and considered a war crime.

erman soldier carries the white flag in World War II

ALLEST FLAG

o electronic engineering students in llas, TX (USA), managed, with the aid of ionic beam (which is the microscopic uivalent of a laser beam), to draw an nerican flag 1/10 the thickness of a hu- an hair. Of course, the flag can be seen ly with an electronic microscope.

NGEST AND SHORTEST NATIONAL THEMS

e average national anthem is approxi- ately 1 minute long. The Greek anthem the longest, with 158 stanzas. Each anza contains four lines, totaling 632 es. The Japanese, experts at minimiz- g, are proud to have the world's shortest them: 4 lines. The following is a free nslation of it:

"The emperor's reign will last 1,000 nerations, 8,000 generations until little ones will turn into a large boulder and covered with hyssop."

We will leave the Greek anthem for an- her time.

DEST ANTHEMS

e Japanese anthem is also the oldest in rms of words. It was composed in the h century, during the reign of the Heian nperors, which lasted from the year 794 til 1185.

The oldest melody for a national an- em is that of the Dutch anthem, "Het ilhelmus," which was composed during e Eighty Years War (1568–1648). The text as written between the years 1569 and 72 in honor of Willem of Orange.

The words of the song were recognized the national anthem on May 10, 1932.

ANTHEM WITHOUT WORDS

The Spanish anthem, known as "Royal March," was composed in 1761 and was established as the national anthem by King Carlos at the end of the 18th century. In 1942 General Franco declared it the official anthem. Over 200 years have passed since its composition, yet the Spaniards have still not managed to find words for the song.

ANTHEM COMPRISED OF 5 LANGUAGES

In 1994, the blacks in South Africa protested against "Die Stem van Suid Afrika" (The Voice of South Africa), which had served as the white anthem during the period of apartheid. At that time there were 2 official anthems, the "white" anthem and the competing black anthem known as "Nkosi Sikelel' iAfrika" (G-d bless Africa). With the encouragement of President Nelson Mandela, the 2 anthems were combined into 1.

The anthem comprises the 5 most widely spoken of South Africa's 11 official languages. It opens in Xhosa (pronounced Koza) — 1st stanza, 1st 2 lines; continues in Zulu (1st stanza, last 2 lines); then segues into Sesotho (2nd stanza); Afrikaans (3rd stanza); and finally, English (4th stanza).

ANTHEM CHANGED THE MOST NUMBER OF TIMES

Between 1791 and 1833, the unofficial Russian national anthem was "Let the Thunder of Victory Be Heard." After the second Russian-Turkish war in 1833, it was officially changed to "G-d Save the Czar." Following the Bolshevik Revolution, which brought down the czarist government in 1917, the French anthem "La Marsellaise" served as the Russian anthem for a short time.

In 1922, "International," the international workers' anthem, whose origin is also French, became the official anthem of the Soviet Union as well. In 1944, Stalin replaced the "International" with a song praising himself. From the day of his death on March 5, 1953, until 1977, the melody was sung without the words.

In 1993, a patriotic melody without words from the opera *A Life for the Czar* was adopted as the official national anthem of Russia. In 1999, there was a competition for adding words to it, but the text never became official because Russian president Vladimir Putin did not wish to change the anthem yet another time.

In 2001, the old melody from 1944 was restored and the text was rewritten.

DID YOU KNOW?

Anthems, such as the British anthem, used to be songs of praise for the kings and emperors. However, in the early 1800s, inspired by the French Revolution, the anthems became national songs of praise which speak of war and freedom, accompanied in general by marching tunes.

CRUELEST ANTHEM

The French national anthem, "La Marsellaise," which served as inspiration for many other anthems, is one of the most well-known anthems in the world — and one of the cruelest. Here's a sample:

Arise, children of the fatherland
The day of glory has arrived.
Against us, tyranny's
Bloody flag is raised….
They are coming into our midst
To cut the throats of your sons and friends.

Grab your weapons, citizens!
Form your battalions!
March, march!
Let impure blood
Water our fields….

Tremble, tyrants; and you, traitors,
The disgrace of all groups,
Tremble! Your parricidal plans
Will receive their just reward.
We are all soldiers against you,
If our young heroes fall,
France will make more,
Ready to fight you….

[Don't spare] these bloodthirsty despots…
All these animals who pitilessly
Tear their mothers to pieces….

Drive on, sacred patriotism,
Support our avenging arms….
Join the struggle with [liberty's] defenders…
May your dying enemies
See your triumph and our glory!

In the early 2000s the French government attempted to soften the words, but due to public protest the words remained. In 2007 the French parliament established a law requiring schools to teach the words of the anthem, beginning in nursery school.

MOST PRACTICAL ANTHEM

The Egyptian national anthem reserves a place for the name of the president. Therefore, the anthem changes every time there is a new president.

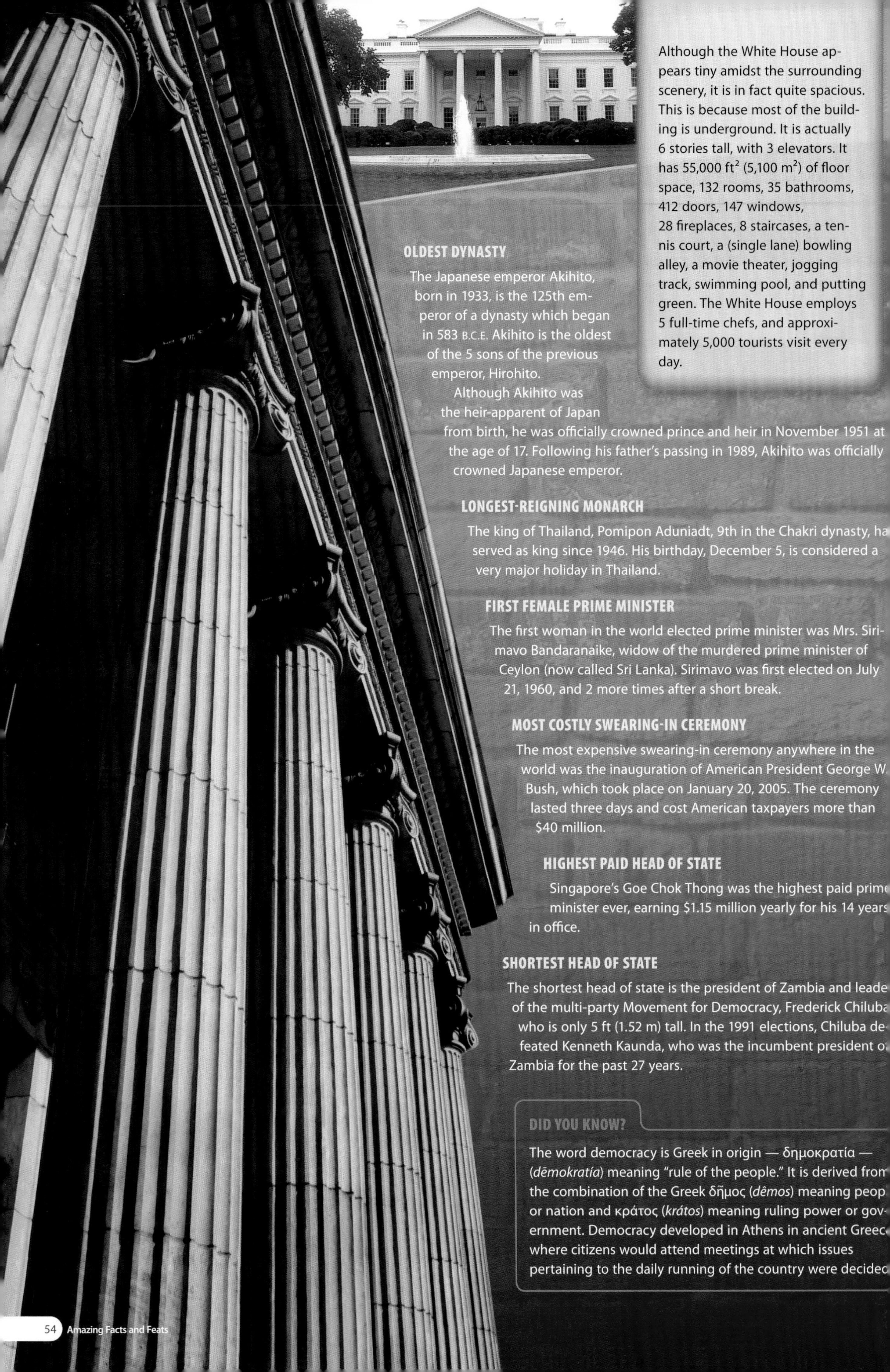

Although the White House appears tiny amidst the surrounding scenery, it is in fact quite spacious. This is because most of the building is underground. It is actually 6 stories tall, with 3 elevators. It has 55,000 ft^2 (5,100 m^2) of floor space, 132 rooms, 35 bathrooms, 412 doors, 147 windows, 28 fireplaces, 8 staircases, a tennis court, a (single lane) bowling alley, a movie theater, jogging track, swimming pool, and putting green. The White House employs 5 full-time chefs, and approximately 5,000 tourists visit every day.

OLDEST DYNASTY

The Japanese emperor Akihito, born in 1933, is the 125th emperor of a dynasty which began in 583 B.C.E. Akihito is the oldest of the 5 sons of the previous emperor, Hirohito.

Although Akihito was the heir-apparent of Japan from birth, he was officially crowned prince and heir in November 1951 at the age of 17. Following his father's passing in 1989, Akihito was officially crowned Japanese emperor.

LONGEST-REIGNING MONARCH

The king of Thailand, Pomipon Aduniadt, 9th in the Chakri dynasty, ha served as king since 1946. His birthday, December 5, is considered a very major holiday in Thailand.

FIRST FEMALE PRIME MINISTER

The first woman in the world elected prime minister was Mrs. Sirimavo Bandaranaike, widow of the murdered prime minister of Ceylon (now called Sri Lanka). Sirimavo was first elected on July 21, 1960, and 2 more times after a short break.

MOST COSTLY SWEARING-IN CEREMONY

The most expensive swearing-in ceremony anywhere in the world was the inauguration of American President George W. Bush, which took place on January 20, 2005. The ceremony lasted three days and cost American taxpayers more than $40 million.

HIGHEST PAID HEAD OF STATE

Singapore's Goe Chok Thong was the highest paid prime minister ever, earning $1.15 million yearly for his 14 years in office.

SHORTEST HEAD OF STATE

The shortest head of state is the president of Zambia and leade of the multi-party Movement for Democracy, Frederick Chiluba who is only 5 ft (1.52 m) tall. In the 1991 elections, Chiluba defeated Kenneth Kaunda, who was the incumbent president o Zambia for the past 27 years.

DID YOU KNOW?

The word democracy is Greek in origin — δημοκρατία — (*dēmokratía*) meaning "rule of the people." It is derived from the combination of the Greek δῆμος (*dêmos*) meaning peop or nation and κράτος (*krátos*) meaning ruling power or government. Democracy developed in Athens in ancient Greec where citizens would attend meetings at which issues pertaining to the daily running of the country were decided

Governments

HIGHEST MAJORITY IN AN ELECTION

Boris Nikolayevich Yeltsin (1931–2007), the first democratically elected president of Russia, was elected by the biggest landslide in history following the collapse of the Soviet Union in March 1989. He received 5,118,745 out of 5,722,937 votes. Yeltsin was among the key players in the dismantling of the Soviet Union.

YOUNGEST MAYOR

In the elections of November 2005, Michael Sessions, still in school and only 18 years and 2 months old, defeated the previous mayor of Hillsdale, MI (USA).

Sessions' name did not appear on the ballots. Voters had to remember his name and cast their votes as a write-in. In spite of this obstacle, Sessions defeated his opponent by only 2 votes and became the world's youngest mayor.

MONKEY SEE, MONKEY DO

In 1988, the anti-establishment Banana Party in Brazil nominated a chimpanzee as their candidate for mayor of Rio de Janeiro. More than 400,000 citizens voted for the chimpanzee, placing him 3rd among the 12 mayoral candidates.

LARGEST PARLIAMENT

The largest legislature in the world is the Chinese National Congress, whose first session took place in March 1993. At this session there were 2,977 elected representatives from 22 districts. They each have a 5-year term.

LARGEST NUMBER OF CHANGING PRESIDENTS

In December 2001, in response to the violent riots which took place because of the economic recession, there were 5 different presidents of Argentina in a space of only 3 weeks.

VOTERS IN ISRAEL

There were 5,278,985 eligible voters in the 2009 Knesset elections.

LARGEST NUMBER OF REVOLUTIONS

The country of Bolivia in South America was part of the Inca kingdom. In 1825 it gained independence and was named Bolivia after Simon Bolivar, who freed Panama, Venezuela, Colombia, Ecuador, Peru, and Bolivia from Spanish rule. In the first 150 years of Bolivia's existence there were 192 changes of government and 23 successful revolution attempts. In 6 of these revolutions the president was assassinated in the middle of his term, and 11 new constitutions were legislated.

New and old Supreme Court buildings, Singapore

MOST EXPENSIVE VOTE

In the New York City mayoral election of 2009, Mayor Michael Bloomberg spent $114 million for the 688,750 votes he received — an average of $209 per vote. Bloomberg is listed as one of the world's richest men, with total assets of $18 billion.

GREATEST GOVERNMENT SPENDING

The expenditures of the United States government amount to more than $2 trillion per year.

WOMEN IN GOVERNMENT

In almost every country in the world, there are many more men than women in government. In Israel, for example, women have made up between 6% and 10% of the members of Knesset in the past 20 years. Since the founding of the State in 1948, there have been only 11 female government ministers. In contrast to this, in Western Europe and North America, women make up more than 20% of government representatives. In Scandinavia, the figure ranges between 40% and 50%.

The highest percentage of female members of Parliament is in Rwanda, in central Africa, where 44 out of 80 seats are occupied by women.

Francis Wheatley painting of the Irish House of Commons, 1780

The Singapore River, with the Parliament building in the front

North Carolina: Don't use these to plow your cotton field!

STRANGE AND UNUSUAL LAWS STILL ON THE BOOKS

- Denmark — "It is permitted to try to escape from jail, but if the captor is caught then he will be required to serve the remainder of his sentence."
- Alabama — "It is forbidden to walk around with an ice cream cone in the back pocket of your pants."
- California — "It is forbidden to hunt moths which are flying under streetlights."
- Thailand — "It is strictly forbidden to step on state-manufactured money under any circumstance." A picture of the king of Thailand is printed on the money, and stepping on it is considered disgracing the king. Violation results in severe punishment.
- Singapore — "Someone who neglects to flush a public toilet will be fined 500 Singapore dollars."
- Singapore — "One who throws garbage in a public area, destroys public property, or even draws on it, will be fined 2,000 Singapore dollars, or will be forced to clean the street or park while wearing an orange or phosphorus vest on which it is written: 'dummy who litters,' at times while being filmed for television." Such scenes are often broadcast on television or printed in the newspaper.
- Alaska — "It is forbidden to wake up bears hibernating in the winter and it is forbidden to shoot at a sleeping bear."
- North Carolina — "It is forbidden to use an elephant to plow a cotton field."
- Kentucky — "Every citizen is required to shower at least once a year."
- Oklahoma — "Hunting whales is forbidden in all areas of the state." (Keep in mind that Oklahoma is nowhere near any water. It would therefore stand to reason that 100% of the residents obey this law.)

MOST PRESIDENTIAL HOMES

Saddam Hussein, former President of Iraq, had a total of 1,061 presidential residences throughout Iraq — 8 primary palaces, and more than 1,000 additional residences. The fanciest palace, located in the city of Babylon, was built near the remains of Nebuchadnezzar's palace. On each and every brick in the palace is the "modest" inscription: "In the era of Saddam Hussein, protector of Iraq, who rebuilt civilization and rebuilt Babylon."

Alaska: Don't shoot or awaken sleeping bears!

IOST ASSASSINATION TTEMPTS

Fidel Castro

s of 2010 there have been recorded 638 assassination ttempts on the life of Cuban ictator Fidel Castro, leader f Cuba since 1959. Attempts nclude an exploding cigar, a oisoned wetsuit, and a acteria-infected handkerchief. he majority of the assassina- on attempts were carried out y the government of the United States.

At least 9 American Presidents have attempted to verthrow Castro's government in any way possible. This ncluded many attempts on his life. Castro moves from lace to place and his precise location is a military secret.

Charles de Gaulle, president of France during World Var II and the first president of the 5th French Republic, urvived 31 assassination attempts during his 22 years in ffice.

ONGEST JAIL TERM FOR A FUTURE PRESIDENT

elson Rolihlahla Mandela (born 1918), former president South Africa, was imprisoned from 1964 until 1990. Iandela was accused of treason during the apartheid egime. Four years after his release, Mandela was chosen s the new South Africa's first democratically elected resident. Many South Africans consider him "the father f the nation."

MOST CORRUPT REGIME

An organization called Transparency International assesses the corruption level of 180 nations. In 2009, Somalia was found to have the most corrupt government. Israel was the 32nd least corrupt country in the world, with a Corruption Perception Index (CPI) of 6.1 out of a possible score of 10. Compared to its neighbors, however, Israel fared quite well, with Jordan having a CPI of 5 (ranked 49), Egypt — 2.8 (ranked 111), Syria — 2.6 (ranked 126), Lebanon — 2.5 (ranked 130), and Iran — 1.8 (ranked 168).

LEAST CORRUPT GOVERNMENTS

The governments with the highest CPI in 2009, indicating that they are the least corrupt, were New Zealand, with a CPI of 9.4, Denmark — 9.3, and Singapore and Sweden tying at 9.2. The United States was given a CPI of 7.5, the 19th least corrupt country in the world.

GREATEST AMOUNT OF BRIBERY

Another index published by Transparency International is the bribing of companies doing business abroad. Out of the 22 nations assessed in 2008, the last year recorded, Belgium and Canada shared 1st place for "cleanest" countries, with a score of 8.8 out of 10. Mexico, China, and Russia were at the bottom of the list, with scores of 6.6, 6.5, and 5.9, respectively.

THE POT CALLS THE KETTLE BLACK

The evil kingdom of the Soviet Union is responsible for approximately 43 million deaths. Joseph Stalin, *yemach shemo*, killed 23 million people while he was the leader of the USSR. In addition to this, 14.5 million people starved to death, 1 million were executed for political "offenses," and 5 million never returned from exile to the "Gulag Archipelago."

Nevertheless, the USSR had the audacity to accuse the government of China of carrying out the greatest massacre ever attributed to any nation.

During the 16-year reign of Mao Tse-tung (1949–1965), 26.4 million Chinese were murdered. In a period of one month, over 2.3 million people were killed in the eastern China provinces of Anhui and Shandong, and the southern regions — an average of more than 3,200 people per hour murdered by the Chinese government.

Western sources estimate that the numbers are actually much higher. Research conducted in the United States determined that since 1948, more than 62 million people have been murdered by the Chinese.

The first massacre in China's history took place during the two Mongolian invasions into Northern China during the years 1210–1219 and 1311–1340. The Mongolians slaughtered more than 35 million Chinese. During the rule of Chang Hsien-chung (known as the "Yellow Leopard") between the years 1643 and 1647, more than 40 million Chinese were murdered in the Szechwan area alone.

Joseph Stalin (right) with the famous Russian writer Maxim Gorky

The Chinese communists enter Beijing, June 1949

LANGUAGE MOST UNDERSTOOD

The language understood by the most people in the world is English — it is the mother tongue of 355 million people and a second language for 1.5 billion others. This means that almost 1/3 of the world population understands English.

The Mandarin dialect of Chinese is understood by 1.1 billion people.

LARGEST VOCABULARY

The English language contains the largest number of words. It is difficult to give the precise number, as new words are constantly being added to the English lexicon. It is estimated that the English language consists of more than 600,000 words. This number, however, has little effect on the average English speaker, who manages with the same number of words as those who speak any other language.

LANGUAGES MOST SPOKEN

The following chart lists the most common mother tongues. As you can see, the Mandarin dialect of Chinese serves as a mother tongue far more than any other language.

LANGUAGE	MOTHER TONGUE TO:
Mandarin Chinese	918 million
English	355 million
Spanish	325 million
Hindu	300 million
Arabic	272 million
Russian	165 million
Japanese	127 million
German	107 million

IT'S ALL GREEK — OR MAYBE CHINESE — TO ME

"It's all Chinese to me" is an expression used in many languages to indicate that the person being spoken to does not understand what is being said to him; it's a more refined way of saying, "I have no idea what you are talking about." In France and Finland the expression is, "It's all Hebrew to me."

HEBREW

The Hebrew language is the 90th most spoken language, being spoken by slightly more than 7 million people — 0.01% of the world population. Many Jews in the Diaspora study Hebrew in school and reach a proficient level of speech and communication.

DID YOU KNOW?

Twenty-eight percent of English words are Latin-based, 28% are French-based, 25% are derived from German, Dutch, and Scandinavian languages, 5% are from Greek, 1% are from other languages, 9% are new words, and 4% are of unknown origin.

HEBREW VOCABULARY

Spoken Hebrew consists of a total of 125,000 words. This includes words borrowed from other languages and international terms and expressions. The Tanach lexicon consists of approximately 1,898 different words. This, of course, is only a small portion of ancient *lashon hakodesh*, which also includes the additional 7,878 words found in the writings of Chazal.

SPEAKERS OF YIDDISH AND LADINO

There are an estimated 3 million Yiddish speakers in the world, 235,000 of whom live in Israel. The number of Ladino speakers in the world, which had been the Yiddish equivalent in Sephardic countries, is less and getting smaller all the time. There are 100,000 Ladino speakers living in Israel, 8,000 in Turkey, and 1,000 in Greece.

THE ONLY WESTERN LANGUAGE TO BE RESURRECTED

Cornish, a member of the Celtic language family, became extinct in the year 1777, when the last person to speak it as a mother tongue died. In the 20th century, it was revitalized, and today approximately 3,500 people speak it in Cornwall, on the southwest coast of England.

THE ONLY COUNTRY WHOSE CONSTITUTION IS WRITTEN IN A "DEAD" LANGUAGE

In May 1814, after 250 years of unification with Denmark, Norway became independent and wrote its constitution in…Danish! Now, 300 years later, the Danish language has changed completely — and so has Norwegian — but Norway still insists on keeping its constitution in Old Danish. Legislators must write all new laws and amendments in that language, which no one knows how to write and very few people understand.

A Common Language and a Shared Purpose

WHISTLING LANGUAGE

Silbo Gomero (Spanish for "Gomeran Whistle"), also known as El Silbo, is a whistled language used by the inhabitants of La Gomera, a small island in the heart of the Canary Islands. The language developed as a means of "conversing" across distances of several miles over the island's long ravines and valleys. An El Silbo "speaker" places a finger in his mouth, forming a U shape, and blows. The other hand assists by moving the hand in the mouth, thereby varying the sounds and tones. This enables "speaking" complete and complex sentences over a distance of more than 3 mi (5 km).

By 1970 only a few individuals were familiar with the whistling language. In order to preserve their tradition, the residents of La Gomera decided to teach the language in schools. The elders of the island taught a number of people to become whistling teachers. Hundreds of children now whistle in class.

LOST LANGUAGES

Even languages can die. The number of spoken languages in the world is shrinking daily. According to the world's leading linguists, by the year 2100, half of the world's 6,000 languages will disappear.

Most of the world's languages — 53% — are spoken by less than 10,000 people, and 28% of these languages are spoken by less than 1,000 people.

An example of the demise of languages is the fact that more than 200 of the 250 once-spoken languages in Australia have been completely forgotten.

Many languages are spoken by only a small number of elderly people. An example of this is Kuskokwim, formerly the language of central Alaska. It is now remembered by only 3 families.

Penutian, once frequently heard in the states of Washington, Oregon, and California, remains spoken by only a few elderly people residing in the Lake Klamath region of Oregon. When these people will leave this world, the language will disappear as well.

Occupation by other countries and the resulting assimilation into that culture has in the past been the main cause for a language becoming extinct. Today, an additional factor is the world media, which broadcasts in a limited number of languages. The younger generation feels that in order to succeed in today's world a person must be familiar with the language used by the media (mainly English), and they therefore see no practical value in acquiring knowledge of other languages.

Kuskokwim tribesman

LARGEST FAMILY OF LANGUAGES

Austronesian comprises 1,268 languages, the largest family of languages — 1/5 of the languages spoken in the world. An estimated 300 million people in Southeast Asia, Okiana, and East Africa speak an Austronesian language.

Javan, spoken by 80 million people — almost 1/3 of them living in the island of Java in Indonesia — is the most spoken of all Austronesian languages. However, the majority of Austronesian languages are spoken by only a few hundred people living in the Pacific islands.

LARGEST VARIETY OF LANGUAGES

The largest variety of languages is spoken in Papua New Guinea, located in the eastern portion of the island of New Guinea, which is north of Australia. A population of 6.5 million speaks 860 different languages. English, Tok Pisin, and Hiri Motu are considered Papua New Guinea's official languages, even though only a small number of people consider the latter 2 their mother tongue.

Ludwig Zamenhof

United Nations General Assembly hall

A Solomon Islands dwelling

NEWEST LANGUAGE

The Esperanto language was invented in 1887 by a Jew named Ludwig Zamenhof. It was intended to become an international language aimed at easing communication between people of different cultures. The language was named after the pen name of its inventor, Doktoro Esperanto, meaning "Doctor Hopeful." Zamenhof hoped that an international language would help bring peace to the world.

The advantage of Esperanto is its simplicity. Its vocabulary, which consists of only 10,000 roots, is smaller than the vocabulary of many other well-known languages. There are very few rules of grammar and pronunciation, with absolutely no exceptions to any rules. A few thousand families view Esperanto as their mother tongue and an additional 1.5 million people throughout the world are able to communicate in it.

MOST TRANSLATED DOCUMENT

The Universal Declaration of Human Rights, published by the United Nations in 1948, has been translated into 322 languages.

WORLD LITERACY

Approximately 77% of the people in the world are able to read and write — 83% of the world's men and 71% of the world's women. Most of Western civilization boasts a near 100% literacy rate. The African nations south of the Sahara have the lowest literacy rate:

Ethiopia — 28%
Sierra Leone — 21%
Eritrea — 20%
Burkina Faso — 18%

LONGEST ALPHABET

The Cambodian language has the longest alphabet — 74 letters. But what about Chinese? There are no letters in Chinese, only symbols; every word consists of a symbol. The Chinese dictionary published in 1990 contains 54,678 symbols. However, even the most educated Chinese can manage with only 5,000 symbols, and the modern Chinese dictionary consists of only 7,000 symbols. You can imagine what a Chinese keyboard must look like.

SHORTEST ALPHABET

Rotokas, mother tongue in the Solomon Islands (Southwestern Pacific), consists of only 11 letters.

LONGEST ENGLISH WORD

The longest non-technical word in the English language contains 29 letters and means "something of no value": floccinaucinihilipilification.

LONGEST HEBREW WORD

The longest word in spoken Hebrew contains 17 letters: ולכשהתפוצצויותיהם.

DID YOU KNOW?

Although we associate shaking the head from side to side to imply "no" and nodding up and down to imply "yes," in Bulgaria the exact opposite is the case — shaking means "yes" and nodding means "no." In Greece throwing the head upwards (generally accompanied by a sound) indicates "no," while tilting the head to the side and downwards and closing the eyes indicates "yes." The Turks raise their chins and eyebrows (accompanied by a sound) to indicate "no," while sharply lowering the head to indicate "yes." The Eskimos nod as we do to indicate agreement, but for a "no" they blink.

EASY AS ABC

Kiribati is a Micronesian language consisting of 13 letters, spoken in Kiribati, Fiji, Nauru, the Solomon Islands, Tuvalu and Vanuatu by about 70,000 people. All of these island nations are in the Pacific Ocean, between Hawaii and Australia.

Kiribati was only spoken and not written until 1857, when a missionary arrived in Kiribati (then called the Gilbert Islands) and devised a way of writing Kiribati using 13 English letters. He used these few letters to produce a translation of the Bible. Other missionaries devised different spelling systems.

The Kiribati Alphabet: letters and pronunciation

A	B	E	I	K	M	N	NG	O	R	T	U	W
ah	bee	eh	ee	kee	mm	nn	ngg	oh	ree	see	oo	wee

A Common Language and a Shared Purpose

LONGEST ENGLISH WORD IN DICTIONARY

The longest English word that appears in a dictionary is the name of a lung disease cause by inhaling volcanic dust following the eruption of volcano. This 46–letter word is pneaumonaultramicroscopicsilico-volcanoconiosis.

READING WITH HANDS

Braille permits a blind person to read using his sense of touch. In 1847 a Frenchman named William Moon developed raised letters, making it possible to read with the fingertips. Louis Braille was one of his students. Braille had become blind at the age of 3 when he accidentally poked himself in the eye with one of his father's workshop tools. The injury wasn't thought to be serious until it got infected. Braille's other eye went blind as a result of sympathetic opthalmia. Braille developed Moon's idea further, and the language for the blind was ultimately named for him.

The original system involved combinations of 12 dots. Braille eventually lowered this to 6 dots.

Today there are typewriters and printers and even a Braille keyboard for the computer. Many companies write Braille on the packages of their products, and in most modern buildings the floor numbers on the elevators are also written in Braille.

LONGEST NAME FOR A LIVING ORGANISM

The germ which infects tobacco leaves, as listed in American Chemical Society Chemical Abstracts, is comprised of 1,185 letters.

methi-nylglutaminylarginyltyr-sylglutamy
lserylleucylphenylalanylalanylglutaminyll
eucyllysylglutamylarginyllysylglutamylgl
ycylalanylphenylalanylvalylpr-lylphenylal
anylvalylthre-nylleucylglycylaspartylpr-
lylglycylis-leucylglutamylglutaminylseryl
leucyllysylis-leucylaspartylthre-nylleucylis-
leucylglutamylalanylglycylalanylaspa
rtylalanylleucylglutamylleucylglycylis-
leucylpr-lylphenylalanylserylaspartylpr-ly
lleucylalanylaspartylglycylpr-lylthre-nylis-
leucylglutaminylasparaginylalanylthre
-nylleucylarginylalanylphenylalanylalany
lalanylglycylvalylthre-nylpr-lylalanylglu
taminylcysteinylphenylalanylglutamylmet
hi-nylleucylalanylleucylis-leucylarginylgl
utaminyllysylhistidylpr-lylthre-nylis-
leucylpr-lylis-leucylglycylleucylleucylmeth
i-nyltyr-sylalanylasparaginylleucylvalylphen
ylalanylasparaginyllysylglycylis-leuc ylaspar
tylglutamylphenylalanyltyr-sylalanylglutami
nylcysteinylglutamyllysylvalylg lycylvalylas
partylserylvalylleucylvalylalanylaspartylvalyl
pr-lylvalylglutaminylgl utamylserylalanylpr-
lylphenylalanylarginylglutaminylalanyl
alanylleucylarginylhist idylasparaginylv
alylalanylpr-lylis-leucylphenylalanylis-
leucylcysteinylpr-lylpr-l ylaspartylalanylaspa
rtylaspartylaspartylleucylleucylarginylglutam
inylis-leucylala nylseryltyr-sylglycylarginylg
lycyltyr-sylthre-nyltyr-sylleucylleucylserylar
ginyla lanylglycylvalylthre-nylglycylalanylgl
utamylasparaginylarginylalanylalanylleucylp
r-lylleucylasparaginylhistidylleucylvalyl
alanyllysylleucyllysylglutamyltyr-sylasp
araginylalanylalanylpr-lylpr-lylleucylglu
taminylglycylphenylalanylglycylis-leucyl
serylalanylpr-lylaspartylglutaminylvalyl
lysylalanylalanylis-leucylaspartylalanylg
lycylalanylalanylglycylalanylis-leucylse
rylglycylserylalanylis-leucylvalyllysylis
-leucylis-leucylglutamylglutaminylhistid
ylasparaginylis-leucylglutamylpr-lylgluta
myllysylmethi-nylleucylalanylalanylleucylly
-sylvalylphenylalanylvalylglutaminylpr
lylmethi-nyllysylalanylalanylthre-
nylarginylserine

LONGEST NAME FOR A CHEMICAL COMPOUND

The chemical name for titin, the largest known protein, consists of 189,819 letters.

ACETYLSERYLTYR-SYLSERYLIS-
LEUCYL-THRE-NYLSERYLPR-
LYLSERYLGLUTAMINYL-PHENYL
ALANYLVALYLPHENYLALANYLLE
UCYL-SERYLSERYLVALYLTRYPT-
PHYLALANYL-ASPARTYLPR-LYLIS-
LEUCYLGLUTAMYLLEUCYL-LEUCYLASPARA
GINYLVALYLCYSTEINYL-THRE-NYLSERYLS
ERYLLEUCYLGLYCYL-ASPARAGINYLGLUTA
MINYLPHENYLALANYL-GLUTAMINYLTHRE-
NYLGLUTAMINYLGLUTAMINYL-
ALANYLARGINYLTHRE-NYLTHRE-NYL-G
LUTAMINYLVALYLGLUTAMINYLGLUT
AMINYL-PHENYLALANYLSERYLGLUT
AMINYLVALYL-TRYPT-PHYLLYSYLPR-
LYLPHENYLALANYL-PR-LYLGLUTAMINYLSERYLTHRE-
-NYLVALYL-ARGINYLPHENYLALANYLPR-LYLGLYCYL
ASPARTYLVALYLTYR-
SYLLYSYLVALYLTYR-SYL-ARGINYLTYR-
SYLASPARAGINYLALANYLVALYL
-LEUCYLASPARTYLPR-LYLLEUCYLIS-
LEUCYL-THRE-NYLALANYLLEUCYLL
EUCYLGLYCYL-THRE-NYLPHENYLAL
ANYLASPARTYLTHRE-NYL-ARGINYL
ASPARAGINYLARGINYLIS-LEUCYL-IS-
LEUCYLGLUTAMYLVALYLGLUTAMYL-
ASPARAGINYLGLUTAMINYLGLUTAM
INYLSERYL-PR-LYLTHRE-NYLTHRE-
NYLALANYLGLUTAMYL-THRE-NYLLEU
CYLASPARTYLALANYLTHRE-NYL-ARGI
NYLARGINYLVALYLASPARTYLASPARTY
L-ALANYLTHRE-NYLVALYLALANYLIS-
LEUCYL-ARGINYLSERYLALANYLA
SPARAGINYLIS-LEUCYL-ASPARAGI
NYLLEUCYLVALYLASPARAGINYL-
GLUTAMYLLEUCYLVALYLARGINYLGL
YCYL-THRE-NYLGLYCYLLEUCYLTYR-
SYLASPARAGINYL-GLUTAMINYLAS
PARAGINYLTHRE-NYL-PHENYLALA
NYLGLUTAMYLSERYLMETHI-NYL-
SERYLGLYCYLLEUCYLVALYLTRYPT-
PHYL-THRE-NYLSERYLALANYLPR-
LYLALANYLSERINE

LARGEST RANSOM

The largest ransom in history was paid in Peru in 1532 by the Inca Indians to the Spanish conqueror Francisco Pizarro for the return of their kidnapped King Atahualpa. The Indians filled an entire hall with gold, which today would be worth $200 million. Although the Spaniards took the gold, they still killed Atahualpa, the last of the Incan kings.

LARGEST RANSOM PAID TO AIRPLANE HIJACKERS

The government of Japan paid $6 million to a group of terrorists who hijacked a DC-8 Japanese International Airline jet, holding 38 people hostage. The transfer of the money took place in October 1977 at the Dhaka Airport in Bangladesh. The government of Bangladesh refused to get involved in the incident.

MOST EXPENSIVE ITEM STOLEN

The most expensive item ever stolen was the painting Mona Lisa, taken from the Louvre Museum in Paris in 1911. The painting depicts Lisa del Giocondo, the wife of a wealthy silk merchant from Florence, Italy. In 1503 he commissioned the portrait from the famous Italian artist Leonardo da Vinci. The merchant was not happy with the finished product, however, and refused to purchase it. After Leonardo died, the French King Francois I purchased the painting, which eventually made its way to the Louvre.

On August 21, 1911, one of the museum's maintenance men, an Italian named Vincenzo Peruggia, took advantage of the lax security and stole the painting with the intent of returning it to its rightful owners — the Italian people. Peruggia demanded .5 million Italian liras to cover the cost of the "operation."

Peruggia was eventually caught by the Italian police and after the portrait was displayed all over Italy, the Italian government agreed to return it to the Louvre.

Due to great public support for Peruggia's attempt to return the painting to its birthplace, he was sentenced to only 1 year in prison (but he served even less time behind bars). Today, after other attempts at vandalism and robbery, the Mona Lisa stands behind bullet-proof glass embedded with alarm sensors.

Vincenzo Peruggia's trial

Lawbreakers

LARGEST COUNTERFEIT SCHEME EVER

Operation Bernhard was carried out by the Third Reich in the years 1940–1941. The Germans counterfeited English monetary notes of 5, 10, 20, and 50 pounds sterling, totaling £132 million. Today, this would have a value of $6 billion. The counterfeiting operation took place in the Saxenhausen concentration camp, about 15 mi (25 km) north of Berlin. The operation was named after S.S. officer Bernhard Krueger, who masterminded the operation and forced 142 prisoners, some of them Jews, to work for him.

The Nazis wanted to hurt the British economy by dropping the forged bills from airplanes flying over English cities. Things did not go as planned, because in 1943 the Nazis needed the counterfeit notes to pay for the import of strategic raw materials and to pay Nazi secret agents. However, the International Bank of England was forced to change the look of all English banknotes of £5 denomination and higher.

When the Allies were on the way to Saxenhausen, the counterfeit staff was moved to the Mauthausen concentration camp in Austria. Realizing they were about to be defeated, the Nazis planned to kill the entire staff. However, as the Allies approached the Nazis fled, and the counterfeiters were liberated by the American army on May 5, 1945.

Krueger was eventually caught by the French government, who hired him to counterfeit documents for the French secret service. In 1950 he was returned to Germany and placed on trial. However, he was acquitted after some of the survivors testified that he had actually saved their lives. Krueger died in 1989 in Frankfurt. The irony of it all was that after his trial and for the rest of his life, he was employed by the company that had supplied the Nazis with the paper used to counterfeit the notes.

Before they were defeated, the Nazis threw all the evidence — the templates, type, and counterfeit notes — into Lake Toplitz in the Austrian Alps. Together with this they threw several cartons of gold which they had embezzled from the countries they had occupied.

In 1959, a search team managed to remove cartons containing £72 million in counterfeit money.

Since 2005, American treasure hunters have been searching the lake hoping to discover the gold.

DID YOU KNOW?

There are over 10 million incarcerated people in the world. In Israel in 2009 there were 22,725 people in prison, 501 of whom were women and 8,130 of whom were political prisoners.

MOST EXPENSIVE FUGITIVE HUNT

It is impossible to even estimate how many tens of millions of dollars were spent by the American and other governments in their pursuit of the ever-elusive, arch-terrorist Osama Bin Laden, *yimach shemo*, leader of the Islamic terror organization Al-Qaeda. On top of this, the American government promised $25 million in reward money for those who would provide "actionable information" that would lead to Bin Laden's capture — dead or alive.

On May 1, 2011, American Navy SEAL forces in Pakistan killed Bin Laden in his compound about 35 mi (56 km) outside of the capital city of Islamabad. Thus ended the 10-year search for one of history's most evil men.

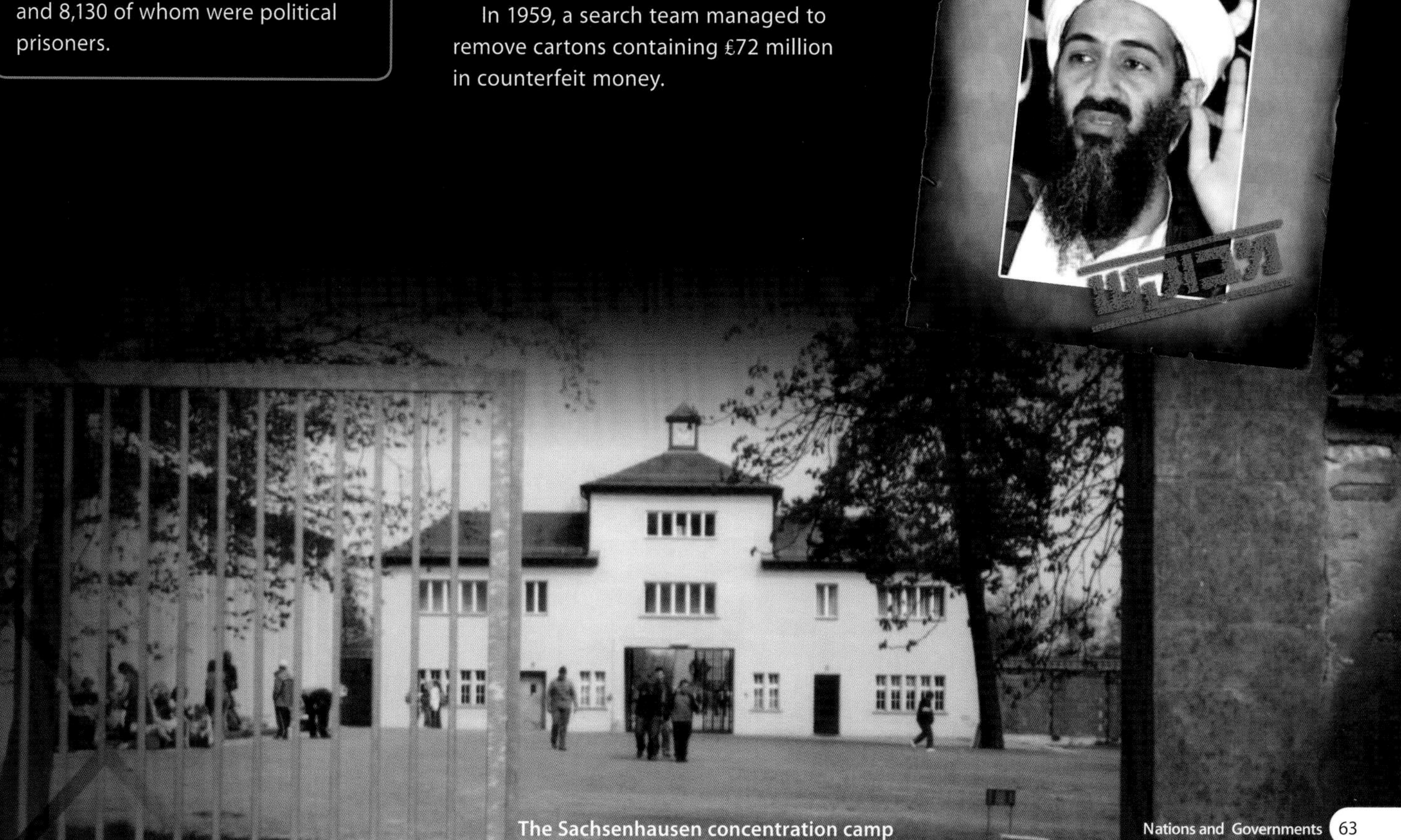

The Sachsenhausen concentration camp

PRISON FROM WHICH NO ONE EVER ESCAPED

The federal prison on the island of Alcatraz in the San Francisco (CA) Bay was the most secure prison in the world. Only 36 people were involved in 14 separate attempts to escape. Twenty-three were caught, 6 were shot and killed, 2 drowned, and 5 others were reported missing and assumed to have drowned. In December 1962, 3 months before the prison closed, a prisoner managed to reach the shore alive. After having overcome so many obstacles to reach the shore, he was caught and returned to his prison cell.

Alcatraz began holding Indian prisoners in 1873, and held prisoners on and off until it officially opened its doors as a federal prison in 1934.

Devil's Island was France's largest penal colony situated not far from the coast of French Guiana in South America. The last of its prisoners was returned to France in 1953. Estimates claim that only 2,000 out of 70,000 of those imprisoned in Devil's Island during its 99-year operation ever escaped.

MOST SECURE PRISON

The Supermax prison located east of Pueblo, CO (USA), is equipped with sensors that detect movement, 1,400 steel doors which are controlled from a distance by laser beams, and attack dogs.

Among the more well-known prisoners serving time there are Timothy McVeigh, who is responsible for the Oklahoma City bombing, Theodore Kaczynski, the "Unabomber," and the infamous Mafioso John Gotti.

THE GREAT ESCAPE

Arthur Simons, a retired United States army colonel, led a group of 14 people who broke into a Tehran prison with the intent of freeing 2 American prisoners in February 1979. Approximately 11,000 additional inmates took advantage of the commotion and managed to escape as well.

COUNTRY WITH THE MOST PRISONERS

The United States, land of freedom and liberty, has over 2.3 million people in prison — one out of every 134 citizens. Seven percent of these are women. There is a man in an Illinois state prison who has been there since 1946 — the longest of anyone currently in prison.

California has the most prisoners (175,000), while North Dakota has the least (1,300).

China has 1.57 million sentenced prisoners, and Russia has 890,000. If you add the people in China who are being held in "administrative detention," the number for that country goes up to 2.4 million.

ABOLISHING THE DEATH PENALTY

Venezuela was the first country to abolish its death penalty, in 1863. It was followed by San Marino (1865), Portugal (1867), and Costa Rica (1877).

Israel abolished the death penalty in 1954, except for crimes against humanity, high treason, genocide, and crimes against the Jewish people. Only 2 executions have taken place there: for accused traitor Meir Tobianski, in 1948 (who was posthumously acquitted a year later), and for high-ranking Nazi Adolf Eichmann, in 1962.

The micronation of San Marino in Europe has gone the longest without a state execution: since 1468. Next comes another European micronation, Liechtenstein, whose last execution was in 1785. Iceland is in 3rd place; it hasn't invoked the death penalty since 1830. There are 11 countries that have never used the death penalty, and another 19 that haven't used it since gaining independence from another country.

Lawbreakers

EXECUTION BY ELEPHANT

For 4,000 years, the most common method of execution in South and Southeast Asia was being crushed by an elephant. The elephant was generally trained to place his huge leg gently above the head of the prisoner. Witnesses were then called to identify the accused, who would beg them to retract their accusation. The witnesses rarely changed their testimony because the penalty for lying under oath was punishable by death — the witnesses would then simply switch places with the accused. Following this positive identification, the driver of the elephant would command the elephant to step on the person's head.

In British-controlled India, execution by elephant was in force until as late as April 1947. The last such execution took place in the city of Bikaner by an elephant named Hawai (sic) who weighed over 8 tons and who during his career under British rule crushed more than 10 robbers and murderers to death.

The Mughal emperor, Jalaluddin Muhammad Akbar (1542–1605), would use his favorite elephant as his judge. Jalaluddin believed that a royal elephant has the ability to distinguish between the innocent and the guilty. During his 15-year rule in the city of Agra, thousands of suspects, even those accused of minor crimes, must have trembled as the elephant would debate whether or not to trample them to death. The majority of suspects were indeed crushed to death, but there were cases in which the elephant absolutely refused. Jalaluddin claimed that this was clear proof that the person was innocent, at which point he would immediately be released.

Sefer HaChashmonaim (3:5–6) relates how Ptolemy Philopator wished to execute a large group of Jews at a horse racing track near the city of Alexandria, Egypt. The executions were scheduled to be carried out by 500 warrior elephants that had been intoxicated with wine and were wearing cast iron. The executions were delayed twice, and at the last minute before the 3rd attempt, 2 angels descended and prevented the elephants from trampling the Jews. At that point Ptolemy decided to grant them clemency.

Execution by elephant

DID YOU KNOW?

In the entire history of the State of Israel, only two people were ever executed. The first was Captain Meir Tobianski, the officer in charge of the Jerusalem airstrips. He was falsely accused of transferring secret information to the enemy. He was arrested, given a field trial, found guilty, and executed, all on June 30, 1948.

Several months later, an Israeli Arab by the name of Ali Qasim, who spied for Israeli Intelligence, was found dead in a forest in the Carmel region near Haifa. He had been working as a double agent and it was discovered that it was he who had passed on the information which Tobianski had been accused of passing.

A year following the sentencing, on July 1, 1949, Prime Minister Ben Gurion sent a letter to Tobianski's widow stating, "Your husband was free of guilt and the judgment and sentencing were a grave mistake." Tobianski was acquitted of all wrongdoing and was posthumously awarded the rank of Major. On July 7, 1949, he was buried in a temporary grave in Givat Ram, Jerusalem, and finally on June 21, 1951, he was honored with burial in the military cemetery on Mt. Herzl in Jerusalem.

The second execution took place on May 31, 1962, with the hanging of Adolf Eichmann, the "Architect of the Holocaust." After he was declared dead, his body was cremated and the ashes were scattered in the sea outside Israeli territory.

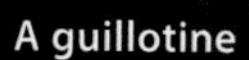
A guillotine

THE DEATH PENALTY

The death penalty exists in some form in 67 countries. China has the distinction of being the country which executed the most people in 2009.

COUNTRY	EXECUTIONS IN 2009
China	Unknown; believed to be in the thousands
Iran	388+
Iraq	120+
Saudi Arabia	69+
United States	52
Yemen	30+

DESTRUCTIVE SANHEDRIN

"A Sanhedrin which executes once in 7 years is called a destructive Sanhedrin. Rabbi Elazar ben Azaryah says: once in 70 years. Rabbi Tarfon and Rabbi Akiva say: Had we been on a Sanhedrin, no person would ever have been executed. [The Gemara explains that they would have the witnesses undergo such thorough interrogations that they would find a way to disqualify them.] Rabban Shimon ben Gamliel [disagrees and] says, 'Such an approach increases the number of murders in the world.'" (Mishnah *Makkos* 1:10)

Energy 68

The Power of Nature 72

Tragedies 76

"If Hashem Will Not Protect" 78

The World

Hashem created His world and built it on the foundations of nature. He decreed that fire should burn and that water should extinguish a blaze…

There are a few human beings whom the King desires to honor due to their immense piety and cleaving to the ways of Hashem. These are great, pious men who were of tremendous renown such as the *Avos* and many of their descendants — Daniel, Chananyah, Mishael, and Azaryah. Hashem placed nature in their hands. At first, nature controlled them, but eventually, due to their greatness, they became masters over nature. We know that Avraham Avinu was thrown into the fiery furnace and emerged unscathed…

The majority of people, however, due to their sins, do not merit reaching such a level, and therefore the Torah commands us to safeguard our dwellings and locations. (*Sefer HaChinuch, Mitzvas Ma'akeh* 546)

In this world of nature and dealings with other people, man is convinced that he is leading his life in accordance with the laws of nature. However, a person with understanding and wisdom will realize after some contemplation that something supernatural is buried within nature. If not for Hashem's Divine Providence in every detail of this world, everything would cease to exist. (*Imrei Noam*)

CRUDE OIL

The real name for that colorless liquid which people refer to as crude oil is petroleum, or kerosene. In the past, kerosene was used for lighting oil lamps, for cooking on top of a "primus" stove, and for heating. Today its main use is for rocket and jet fuel. Petroleum is one of the main raw materials used for the production of ethylene and propylene, and for dissolving plastic-based materials such as PVC.

DIESEL OIL

Diesel oil is a liquid fuel which is produced during the purification process of crude oil at temperatures ranging from 400°F (200°C) to 650°F (350°C). Diesel has a higher energy capacity than gasoline (petrol). It is most commonly used to power diesel engines.

The original diesel engines were known to be less efficient, and for that reason even tanks were powered with gasoline, even though it is highly flammable and could easily cause a fire if the tank were hit. The newer diesel engines, however, conserve 40% more fuel than gasoline motors, with the same fuel capacity.

GASOLINE

Gasoline is a more volatile fuel than diesel and kerosene. The octane level of gasoline indicates the fuel's ability to protect itself against combustion, which affects the efficiency of the motor. In general, gasoline has a low octane level and combusts at a relatively low temperature and relatively low compression. Higher octane fuels require higher pressure and a higher temperature in order to ignite and to convert heat energy to power.

Lower octane fuel is therefore more appropriate for older cars, which work on lower compression. High octane fuel is more appropriate for newer cars, which have a higher compression level.

Many people mistakenly think that using higher octane gasoline will improve the effectiveness of their motor and lower fuel consumption. The fact is that engines are most efficient when using fuel with the octane level they were designed for.

In the 1920s, in an effort to lower the combustion level of gasoline, lead was added to it. However, in the 1980s it was discovered that lead was an environmental hazard, and they began producing and using unleaded

Off-shore oil-drilling barge

MOST IMPORTANT SOURCES OF ENERGY

The main energy source in the world is crude oil, which supplies approximately 37% of the energy consumed. Other common energy sources are coal and natural gas, which together supply approximately 48% of the world energy consumption. These three energy sources release 6 billion tons of carbon dioxide per year into the atmosphere. This is one of the main causes of what is known as global warming.

Energy resources are the most heavily traded natural resources in the world, and therefore have the greatest influence on world economy as well as diplomatic relations between

WORLD CRUDE OIL RESERVES

Geologists estimate that the amount of crude oil in the world once stood at 2,330 billion barrels and that 1/3 of that amount has already been consumed. These are only estimates, for the reserves of available crude oil increase as methods of searching and drilling become more sophisticated.

The world uses 85 million barrels of crude oil per day.

LARGEST CONSUMER OF CRUDE OIL

The 300 million residents of the United States, approximately 5% of the world population, consume more than ¼ of the crude oil drawn in the world — over 20 million barrels per day. Two-thirds of this amount is used for transportation. The average American car uses double the fuel of a Japanese or European car, due to the larger size of the car, the longer distances traveled, and the greater frequency of travel. American cars use approximately 43% of the oil used for all forms of transportation throughout the world.

DID YOU KNOW?

In 2006, the Israeli crude oil producer Genco reported successful drilling for crude oil in the Dead Sea area. These drillings produced 125 barrels of oil per day. Keep in mind that Saudi Arabia produces 125 barrels per second.

CRUDE OIL IN ISRAEL

The search for oil fields with commercially worthwhile quantities in Israel began during the period of the British Mandate. All oil drilling in Israel, whether on land or in the sea, was always carried out by one of the government oil companies. Large oil fields were discovered in 1968 in the Sinai Peninsula, and the production of crude oil grew significantly and reached a plateau of 310,000 tons per year. This area, however, together with its rich oil fields, was given to Egypt in 1977.

LARGEST OIL PRODUCER

At the top of the list of oil-producing nations is Saudi Arabia, with a production of 8.5 million barrels per day. At this rate Saudi Arabia's reserves will be fully depleted within 85 years. The United States is the next highest on the list, producing 3 million barrels per day. If the United States does not manage to discover new oil fields within its borders, all of its reserves will be depleted within a decade.

NEVER GIVE UP

Despite all the modern, advanced scientific methods that have been developed for locating oil deposits, 80% of the oil drilling is still in areas which do not produce sufficient oil for commercial purposes.

"GEYSER" OF OIL

The world's largest fountain of oil, known as an oil gusher, burst forth from the ground near Qum, Iran, on August 26, 1956. The uncontrolled oil gushed to a height of 170 ft (52 m) and filled 120,000 barrels per day.

Oil gushing from the drilling site

LARGEST CRUDE OIL RESERVES

Approximately 65% of the crude oil reserves and 35% of the natural gas reserves are found in the Middle East, mainly in Saudi Arabia, Iran, Iraq, Kuwait, and the United Arab Emirates. The following chart lists the countries with the largest declared reserves of crude oil (as of 2009):

COUNTRY	BILLIONS OF BARRELS OF CRUDE OIL
Saudi Arabia	266.7
Canada	178.59
Iran	138.4
Iraq	115
Kuwait	104
United Arab Emirates	97.8
Venezuela	87.03
Russia	60
Libya	41.5
Nigeria	36.2
Kazakhstan	30
United States	21.3

An ancient windmill and a modern nuclear reactor

ISRAEL'S FIRST NUCLEAR REACTOR

The first nuclear reactor in Israel was established in Nachal Sorek in 1958 by the Atomic Energy Commission. It was intended to advance the technological base for developing nuclear methods for use with electricity, industry, medicine, and agriculture in Israel.

In the Middle East, nuclear reactors are always suspected of being used for the development of nuclear bombs. However, Israel's first reactor was truly used only for research purposes and was not even kept secret. Today Israel no longer has a nuclear reactor for producing energy, and the research carried out in its reactors is in fact kept secret. All that is known about "our" reactors is only from what is reported in the foreign press throughout the world.

CENTER FOR NUCLEAR RESEARCH

The second nuclear reactor in Israel was established south of the town of Dimona with the aid of French engineers as part of the security aid which Israel received at the time. The reactor is located in the "Center for Nuclear Research," where most of Israel's nuclear activity takes place.

Israel at first denied the reactor's existence, claiming in June 1960 that the complex under construction was to be nothing more than an ordinary textile factory. However, in September of that year, rumors began circulating that the building under construction was a "station for meteorological research." Only a year later, on December 21, 1961, responding to a question he was asked in the Knesset, did Prime Minister David Ben-Gurion announce that Israel was in fact developing a "Nuclear Reactor for Research" for peaceful purposes. In the 1980s, approximately 2,700 people were employed there.

The Center for Nuclear Research near Dimona is one of the most protected and guarded places in Israel. On international flight maps, the complex is marked off as a permanent no-fly zone. On the first day of the Six Day War, an Israeli Dassault Ouragan jet returning after being hit during an attack on Jordan, flew back over the research center. The pilot, Yoram Harpaz, did not identify himself. His plane was shot down by the hawk missiles used to protect the reactor.

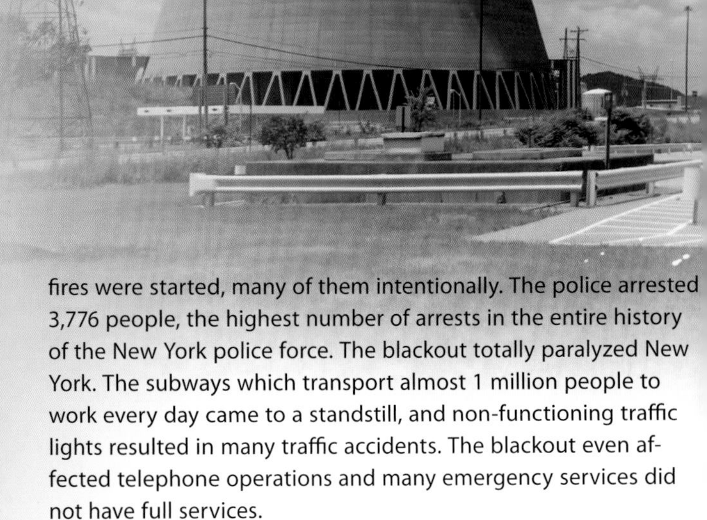

MOST EXTENSIVE DAMAGE FROM A POWER OUTAGE

On July 13, 1977, lighting struck the power station above the Hudson River in New York and caused damage estimated at $330 million. During the duration of the blackout, which lasted 25 hours, there was a wave of violence and destruction to stores, public buildings, and private houses: 1,617 stores were looted and 1,037 fires were started, many of them intentionally. The police arrested 3,776 people, the highest number of arrests in the entire history of the New York police force. The blackout totally paralyzed New York. The subways which transport almost 1 million people to work every day came to a standstill, and non-functioning traffic lights resulted in many traffic accidents. The blackout even affected telephone operations and many emergency services did not have full services.

HYDROELECTRIC ENERGY

A hydroelectric power station produces electricity from turbines that are turned by water which bursts from the opening of an artificial dam, or from a natural waterfall.

The largest hydroelectric power plant in the world is "Itaipu" on the Parana River near the Brazil-Paraguay border. The station officially began operating in 1984 using 20 huge turbines and producing approximately 12.6 million kW. The station produces 93% of Paraguay's and 20% of Brazil's electricity.

WER STATION — HIGH AND LOW TIDES

e Rance River Tidal Power Station is the world's st and largest power station powered by high d low river tides. It was dedicated in November 66, and is located in the estuary of the Rance ver in Brittany, France. The power station was ilt over a five-year period at a cost of ₣620 million out $120.3 million). During high tide, 590.5 mil- n ft³ (180 million m³) of sea water is collected in a ater reservoir created on the other side of a 2,265 (800 m) dam. As the waters flow into the reservoir ey pass through and turn 24 turbines for the pur- se of producing electricity. During low tide, grav- pulls the water back toward the sea, once again rning the turbines, and producing altogether 240 V of electricity. Unfortunately, it supplies only 2% of France's power demand.

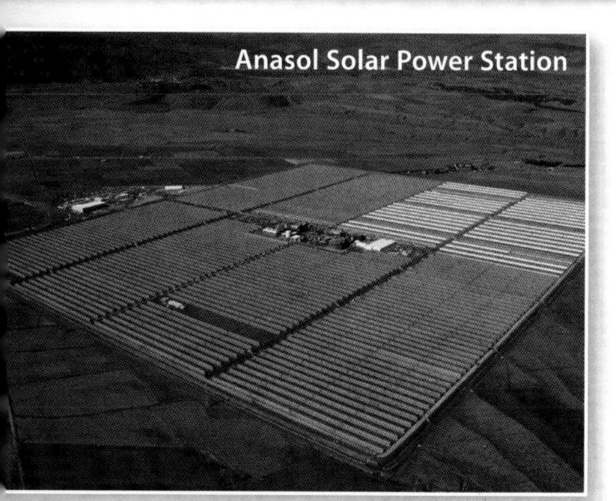
Anasol Solar Power Station

Nevada Solar One

Enercon E-126 wind turbine

LARGEST SOLAR ENERGY STATIONS

The world's largest solar energy station is the Solar Energy Generating Systems (SEGS), located in California's Mojave Desert. It consists of nine solar power plants, and together they generate 354 mW of electricity. The 2nd largest solar energy facility is the Andasol Solar Power Station in Granada, Spain. It has a capacity of 100 mW, and can supply solar electricity for up to 200,000 people. The 3rd largest solar energy station is Nevada Solar One, in Boulder City, NV (USA). It generates 64 mW.

All 3 facilities use parabolic troughs, and the electricity is generated by a turbine. Each parabolic trough uses glass mirrors to collect and transfer the sun's heat via tubes. The heat is then exchanged to water, which produces steam to drive the turbine. In the case of Nevada Solar One, 760 parabolic troughs use over 180,000 glass mirrors and 18,240 tubes. Each tube is 13 ft (4 m) long.

WIND ENERGY

At the beginning of 2010, worldwide capacity of wind-powered generators was 159.2 gW, producing about 2% of the world's electricity. Approximately 90% of the wind turbines in the world are located in California, although the country which has the highest production of wind energy is Denmark. Approximately 20% of Denmark's energy is produced by wind turbines.

The world's largest wind turbine is the Enercon E-126. Located in Emden, Germany, the turbine is 453 ft (138 m) high and has a rotor diameter of 413 ft (126 m). It produces over 7 mW of power — 20 million kWh per year. That's enough to supply 5,000 European households, or 1,776 American homes.

GAS ENERGY

The largest importer and consumer of gas energy in the world is Japan. Japan imports 40% of world gas energy production, which is 94.3 trillion ft³ (2.67 trillion m³) per year. Gas is a much cleaner and more environment-friendly source of energy than coal and crude oil.

LARGEST POWER OUTAGES

The power outage that affected the most people was the Java-Bali Blackout of 2005, in which 100 million people were left without electricity. The Southern Brazil Blackout of 1999 affected 75 million people, while a power outage 10 years later in Brazil and Paraguay affected 60 million people.

The year 2003 saw the next two largest power outages in terms of people affected: The Italy Blackout, in which the entire country plus a small part of Switzerland lost electricity, and the Northeast Blackout, which affected people in 8 northeastern and midwestern states plus parts of Canada. In each of these blackouts, 55 million people were without power.

The longest power outage occurred in 1998, when the entire central business district of Auckland, New Zealand, was without electricity for 5 weeks.

The longest blackout in Israel took place in 1991 and lasted 9.5 hours.

DID YOU KNOW?

Two billion people, 1/3 of the world's population, do not have daily access to electricity.

A tornado

LARGEST HURRICANE

The deadliest Atlantic hurricane in all of history was the great hurricane which struck the Martinique Islands, St. Eustatius, and Barbados on October 10–16, 1780. Approximately 22,000 people died in this storm and thousands more drowned at sea. Two additional hurricanes occurred that same month, each resulting in at least 1,000 deaths.

FIERCEST TORNADO

The fiercest tornado, named the "Tri-state Tornado," struck the United States on March 18, 1925, and resulted in 695 deaths and 2,000 injuries. Total damage from the tornado was estimated at $17 million.

The majority (90%) of tornadoes in the United States strike at an area referred to as "Tornado Alley," which is located in the plains between the Rocky Mountains and the Appalachian Mountains. It comprises the Texas Panhandle, Oklahoma, Kansas, eastern South Dakota, and the Colorado Eastern Plains. Texas records the most tornadoes in the United States, with Kansas 2nd and Oklahoma 3rd.

A tornado appears as a large pillar of air coming down from storm clouds. It is shaped like a narrow and moving funnel, with an average width on earth of 985 ft (300 m). The pillar of air usually advances at a speed of 9 mph (15 km/h), while spinning at the incredible speed of 310 mph (500 km/h). As the tornado moves it lifts heavy objects in its path, such as cars and boulders, and throws them a great distance. The tornado generally dies down after a few minutes.

In April 2006, a small land tornado was spotted in the Galil region of Israel. A sea tornado, which has the appearance of a wall of water descending from the clouds above the sea, is generally not as strong as a land tornado. Sea tornadoes appear regularly in many parts of the world, including the shores of Israel.

DEADLY CYCLONE

The deadliest cyclone in history struck the shores of eastern Pakistan and the islands of the Ganges Delta on November 12–13, 1970. The tidal waves crashing into the shores caused more than 241,000 deaths, with 100,000 additional people declared missing. Experts estimate that hunger and disease resulting from the storm took an additional 200,000 lives — a total of more than .5 million casualties.

A cyclone, like a hurricane, is a storm which moves from the ocean to the shore. While hurricanes originate in the center of the Atlantic Ocean and move to the eastern shores of the United States, cyclones originate in the Pacific Ocean and strike the eastern shores of Australia and Asia, or move from the Indian Ocean to the southern shores of Asia. In addition to strong winds, cyclones cause massive tides which destroy everything in their path.

DID YOU KNOW?

Each year more than 500,000 seismic fluctuations caused by the earth's vibration occur in the world, 400,000 of which can be detected only by scientific instruments. Approximately 100,000 can be felt and 1,000 of these result in damage or injury.

STORMY WINDS

Winds greater than 60 mph (100 km/h) are considered storms. Oklahoma University scientists measured 291 mph (468 km/h) winds at a height of 165 ft (50 m) above the ground near a tornado which struck Oklahoma on May 3, 1999. This was the highest recorded wind speed in history.

A ship pushed onto dry land by strong winds

DID YOU KNOW?

The Center for Research on the Epidemiology of Disasters (CRED) at Belgium's Catholic University of Louvain, the institute which collects data on natural disasters, reports that more than 64,000 natural disasters have occurred in the past 30 years. Natural disasters include earthquakes, tsunamis, volcanic eruptions, storms, floods, avalanches, and famines. The institute estimates that during the past 30 years, more than 5 billion people were injured and 182 million people lost their homes due to natural disasters, with the total damage estimated at $1.38 trillion. The scientists of the institute point out that in many places not all data was collected and therefore the numbers are actually much higher than reported. One such example is the great famine in Ethiopia in the years 1984–1985, which according to estimates took the lives of more than 1 million people.

ᴿM THAT CAUSED THE GREATEST ᴺOMIC DAMAGE

icane Katrina, which occurred on August
:005, was the storm that caused the highest
etary damage in history. Damages were esti-
ed at more than $100 billion (in 2010 dollars).
the 4 hurricanes which struck Florida in
caused a total estimated damage of "only"
billion.
onetary loss
des damage
ads, highways,
tric infrastruc-
and public
dings, as well as life and property insurance payments and the cost of rescue. Losses caused by businesses being unable to operate were estimated at $100 million per day.

The flooding from Katrina was the most severe in the history of the Western world, resulting in approximately 2,000 deaths and the flooding of more than 150,000 properties in New Orleans alone.

The only flood of similar proportions was the great storm which took place in Holland in 1953. Its giant waves flooded 47,000 properties and killed approximately 1,800 people. It took more than 6 months for the area to dry out.

Storm damage from Hurricane Katrina

A helicopter rescue

The flooded city after the storm

Katrina: the eye of the storm

MOST EXPENSIVE HEAT WAVE

In 1988 a massive heat wave struck the central-eastern United States, causing 8,000 deaths and damages estimated at $40 billion. However, a similar heat wave eight years earlier, while causing "only" $20 billion in damages, caused 10,000 deaths.

DEADLIEST HEAT WAVE

In August 2003, Europe was struck with a heat wave which broke all records of the previous 150 years. Deadly forest fires broke out throughout the continent, resulting in tens of thousands of deaths and the destruction of thousands of acres of agricultural produce. It is estimated that in France alone, more than 15,400 people died, mostly the sick and the elderly.

LONGEST HEAT WAVE

The longest heat wave struck western Australia on October 31, 1923, and lasted for 160 days. The average temperature during that period was above 98°F (37°C).

The world is run in 2 ways: The first is through the forces of nature…. This is what sustains the nations of the world. The Jewish people, however, are guided by a Higher Power, and their entire existence depends on this. But when they do not learn Torah, they are then guided by forces of nature and cease to have their own independent existence. (*Ohr Torah* 58)

DEADLIEST EARTHQUAKE

The deadliest earthquake in history took place on the morning of January 23, 1556, striking more than 97 provinces in the counties of Shaanxi, Shanxi, Henan, Gansu, Hebei, Shandong, Hubei, Hunan, Jiangsu, and Anhui in China. The earthquake is estimated to have measured 8 on the Richter scale, and it resulted in more than 830,000 deaths. In some of the countries, more than 60% of the population lost their lives. Most of the population in the area at the time lived in yaodongs (artificial loess caves on high cliffs), many of which collapsed during the catastrophe. An area of 520 mi^2 (840 km^2) was almost totally destroyed.

STRONGEST EARTHQUAKE

The strongest earthquake took place on May 22, 1960, in Chile. It measured 9.5 on the Richter scale and caused massive tsunami waves, which reached the shores of Japan and New Zealand on the other side of the Pacific Ocean. Approximately 2,000 people died in the quake and 3,000 more were injured.

MOST EXPENSIVE EARTHQUAKE

The earthquake resulting in the greatest monetary damage took place on January 17, 1995, in the cities of Osaka, Kiyoto, and Kobe in Japan. Measuring 7.2 on the Richter scale, 5,200 people were killed, 26,000 were injured, and thousands of buildings were destroyed. Damages were estimated at $100 billion.

AVALANCHE

More than 180,000 people were killed in an avalanche which took place in the Kan su area of China on December 16, 1920.

ATLANTIC OCEAN CURRENT

In 1983, the Atlantic current El Niño cause drastic weather changes in the United States and other parts of the world. The heat wave and dry spell that accompanied it lead to massive forest fires in Indonesia and in Australia and an estimated $8 billion of damage. In 1997 the phenomenon returned, causing even greater damage — this time estimated at $33 billion.

DEADLIEST RIVER

In the months of June, July, and August of 1931, the Yangtze River in China overflowed and caused 3.7 million deaths by drowning, disease, and starvation. In 1975 the tragedy recurred on a smaller scale: more than 63 dams along the river burst from the heavy water pressure and approximately 200,000 people drowned. In 1997, the river flooded the area again, leaving 3,000 people dead and 14 million homeless, with damage estimated at $20 billion.

The Yangtze River

Tsunami warning sign

A ship is grounded by the tsunami

The World

The Power of Nature

Tower Bridge in the city's famous fog

THE GREAT SMOG OF 1952

The heavy blanket of fog, smog and pollution that covered London from December 5 to 9, 1952, resulted in thousands of deaths. In most cases, these were due to respiratory tract infections from hypoxia (lack of oxygen), as well as mechanical obstruction of the air passages from lung infections caused by this thick layer of smog which covered the city.

The London Killer Fog was caused by a combination of cold weather, chimney smoke, coal, and other pollutants that formed a thick layer of smog. A layer of very cold air trapped under a layer of warm air, plus windless conditions, trapped the pollutants. At the time, it was estimated that 4,000 people died prematurely and 100,000 people fell ill as a result of the Great Smog. However, recent research puts the death toll at 12,000.

DID YOU KNOW?

An earthquake measuring 9 on the Richter scale is twice as powerful as an earthquake measuring 8.7.

FREQUENT TSUNAMIS

On December 26, 2004, at 7:58 A.M., an earthquake measuring 9.3 on the Richter scale struck the shores of Sumatra, an island in western Indonesia. The energy generated from an earthquake of that scale is the equivalent of 10,000 atom bomb explosions. The resulting tsunami which flooded twelve countries on the shores of Asia, Indonesia, and Africa caused 184,168 deaths (other estimates are as high as 283,000), with 42,883 people missing, 125,000 injured, and 1.69 million homeless. In addition, many people died of hunger and disease in the wake of the tsunami.

Three months later, on March 28, 2005, another earthquake measuring 8.7 occurred at precisely the same location. This time 1,313 people died, and there was additional economic damage. A year later, on May 26, 2006, a 3rd earthquake measuring 6.3 struck the area, causing 5,700 deaths and leaving an additional 135,000 people homeless.

Tsunami waves which struck Thailand in 2004

THE TRUTH ABOUT THE BERMUDA TRIANGLE

In 1964, American author Vincent Gaddis published a story called "The Bermuda Triangle" in the adventure-story periodical *Argosy*. Gaddis wrote that in a triangular area of the Atlantic Ocean whose vertices are Puerto Rico, Bermuda, and the eastern shore of Florida, a number of ships and planes mysteriously disappeared without leaving a trace. Other writers publicized their own versions of the legend with their own convincing explanations for the mystery: aliens, magnets, ancient cultures, black holes, and a wealth of other theoretical fantasies. The real mystery is how something so ludicrous became indisputable fact.

It was only in 1975 that journalist Larry Kusche decided to check out 50 of the more well-known "mysterious" disappearances. He discovered that most of them in fact took place outside this triangle. The debunked mysteries include a ship which disappeared in the Pacific Ocean and not the Atlantic Ocean, incidents which supposedly took place in calm weather that in fact took place during tropical storms, and reports of boats disappearing "without a trace" which turned out to be nothing but lies.

Kusche was able to find simple and logical explanations to all the other "mysterious disappearances," which he publicized in his book, *The Bermuda Triangle Mystery: Solved*. However, not surprisingly, these findings made no impression on fiction lovers, especially those who stood to profit from this non-existent phenomenon. The best proof that the stories surrounding the Bermuda Triangle are all fiction is that the triangle covers an area of approximately 386,000 mi^2 (1 million km^2) — larger than the combined area of Germany, France, and Britain — and has close to the highest sea and air traffic congestion in the world. The number of accidents that occur there, however, is not any higher than the international average, and insurance companies do not demand higher premiums from ships and planes passing through the area.

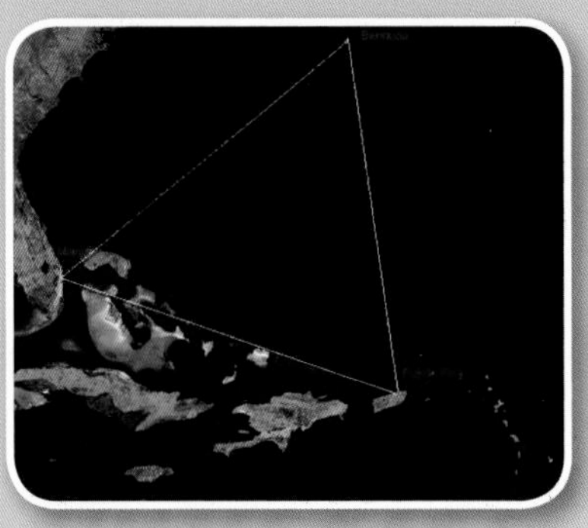

Area of the Bermuda Triangle

GREATEST NUCLEAR TRAGEDY

The "Lenin" nuclear reactor, located 10 mi (16 km) from the city of Chernobyl, was built between the years 1970 and 1983 and supplied 10% of the electricity consumed in the Ukraine. On the night between April 25 and April 26, 1986, an experiment was carried out on Reactor 4 aimed at testing the reactor's operation during a power outage. Due to operator mistakes, the reactor began producing a quantity of energy 10 times greater than normal production, resulting in a great explosion which destroyed the reactor's cover and spread radioactive material at a rate 30 times greater than the amount released when the first atom bombs were dropped on Hiroshima and Nagasaki in Japan.

The Soviet Union tried to cover up the incident, but the unusual levels of radiation reported in nearby Sweden and Norway forced the Soviet government to report the accident and to work toward saving the population. At the end of May 1986, a month after the accident, all 117,000 residents living in a 19 mi (30 km) radius were evacuated and an additional 300,000 people were relocated. Millions of people lived and continue to live in the contaminated area, whose mortality rate from illness and whose percentage of children born with defects is far above the average.

GREATEST EXPLOSIVE ACCIDENT

On the morning of December 6, 1917, a collision occurred at the entrance to the Halifax port in Nova Scotia, Canada, between the Norwegian ship *Imo* and the French ammunition ship *Mont Blanc*. The French ship was transporting 2,300 tons of picric acid, approximately 200 tons of TNT explosives, 35 tons of oil, and 10 tons of cotton for guns — all exceedingly flammable objects.

As a result of the accident, many spectators came to watch the *Mont Blanc* as it moved toward the platform. The port staff tried without success to warn onlookers of the danger of explosion. The port fire brigade arrived quickly, but the ship exploded 20 minutes after the collision. The great explosion razed more than 1 mi^2 (2.5 km^2) of the city of Halifax and smashed windows as far as 60 mi (100 km) away. The ship's anchor flew a distance of 3 mi (5 km) from the port. The tragedy, known as the greatest non-nuclear explosion in the history of the world, resulted in 1,635 deaths, 6,000 serious injuries, and an additional 3,000 other injuries.

Results of the Halifax Explosion

AIR ACCIDENTS

On March 27, 1977, there was a collision on the runway between a KLM (Holland) Boeing 747 and a Pan American (USA) plane in the city of Santa Cruz on the island of Tenerife in the Canary Islands. After waiting a long time for permission to take off, the captain of the KLM plane decided it was time to go, and he began inching toward the runway. At precisely the same moment, a Pan Am plane was moving in the opposite direction. The pilots' views were obstructed by fog. At the last moment, the Pan Am pilot noticed the lights of the KLM plane and tried to turn sharply, as the Dutch pilot attempted to take off above the American plane.

The two planes collided, and the resulting explosion and fire killed all 234 KLM passengers as well as the 14 crew members, and 335 out of the 396 people on board the Pan Am flight. The Pan Am flight crew members who were in the pilot's cabin at the time were saved. This accident is recorded as the worst air accident in history.

The worst accident involving one plane occurred when a Japan Airlines Boeing 747 crashed into a mountain on August 12, 1985, killing 15 crew members and 505 out of the 509 passengers on board.

WORST FIRE

One of the greatest catastrophes in the history of London was the great fire of September 2, 1666. The fire originated in the bakery of Thomas Farrinor, royal baker to King Charles II, and lasted for 3 days. The fire destroyed more than 13,500 homes, 87 churches, 6 chapels, 44 guild halls, St. Paul's Cathedral, a number of castles, 4 Thames River bridges, 3 of the city's gates, and over 80% of the buildings. The death toll from the fire is unknown, although it is estimated to be a few thousand.

SINKING OF SHIPS

On January 30, 1945, a Russian submarine torpedoed the German ship *Wilhelm Gustloff* in the Baltic Sea, opposite the shores of the German city of Danzig. On the ship were 173 crew, 373 nurses, 918 German army officers, 162 injured soldiers, and 8,956 German citizens. There were 10,582 passengers traveling on a ship designed to hold only 1,465. As a result, 9,343 drowned, including women and children. This is known as the worst sea tragedy in history.

Mecca

TRAGEDIES IN MECCA

Every year, approximately 2 million Moslems travel to Mecca, Saudi Arabia, from all over the world. Many of those making the yearly pilgrimage are trampled to death. The greatest of these catastrophes took place on July 2, 1990, when panic-stricken pilgrims fled into a 1,970 ft (600 m) long tunnel leading from the city of Mecca to the visitors' tents. This flight resulted in the deaths of no less than 1,426 Moslems.

On April 15, 1997, a fire and the resulting mass exodus resulted in 217 deaths and 1,300 injuries. This scenario was repeated on February 1, 2004, when 251 visitors were trampled to death in a panic flight which took place during the stone-throwing ceremony — considered one of the holiest and most significant Moslem ceremonies.

GREATEST PEACETIME CATASTROPHES

The greatest tragedy in the history of mankind was the Black Plague. The plague spread during a 15-year period in Europe and claimed the lives of more than 25 million people. The plague was "imported" by Tartar invaders arriving from the Mongolian desert who attacked the city of Caffa, Italy (now Feodosija, Ukraine), in 1346. The Tartars placed the bodies of soldiers stricken by the plague within the walls of the city — making them the first army to employ what is known as biological warfare. Those who escaped with their lives spread the plague throughout Europe, causing the deaths of more than 1/3 of the European population, mainly city dwellers. As usual the Jews were blamed. They were accused of poisoning the wells with sorcery and with deliberately infecting them. Many pogroms were carried out in retaliation.

In the months of April-November 1918 the flu epidemic claimed the lives of 21.5 million people throughout the world.

GREATEST ACT OF TERROR

On September 11, 2001, 2 passenger jets with full tanks of fuel deliberately crashed into the Twin Towers, prominent features of the New York City skyline, and completely destroyed them. Construction of the towers, completed in 1973, lasted 7 years at a cost of $750 million. The north tower — 6.5 ft (2 m) taller than the south tower — was 1,368 ft (417 m) high, at the time the tallest building in the world, surpassing New York's Empire State Building by a little over 100 ft (30 m).

Each building had 110 floors, 43,000 windows, and 103 elevators. Fifty thousand people worked in the buildings. At the top of the towers was an observation deck. Two hundred thousand people visited or passed through each day. Underneath the building was an enormous shopping mall and a large train station. The buildings were the commercial center of the world and symbolized the economic power of the United States.

Khalid Sheikh Mohammed, who was considered the brains behind the act, was apprehended by the United States in 2003 and explained that the original plan was to hijack 10 planes, 9 of which were supposed to be used to attack various targets throughout the United States, among them a nuclear power station. The 10th jet was supposed to be hijacked by Sheikh Mohammed himself and forced to land at an American airport where Sheikh Mohammed would deliver a speech denouncing the Western countries.

On the morning of September 11, 2001, the terrorists used utility knives to hijack 4 passenger jets. The 1st one, an American Airlines jet, was flown into the north tower, and 18 minutes later a United Airlines jet was flown into the south tower. At 10:05 one of the burning buildings collapsed, and a half hour later the 2nd one collapsed. The 3rd jet crashed into a wing of the Pentagon, while the 4th jet crashed into an open area in Pennsylvania after the passengers on the jet battled with the terrorists. In the collapse of the Twin Towers 2,605 people in the buildings were killed, as well as 127 passengers, 20 crew members, and the 10 hijackers of the 2 jets. The Pentagon incident claimed the lives of 125 people in the building as well those of the plane's 64 passengers. The 4th plane which crashed in Pennsylvania claimed 44 lives.

The total death toll from the terror acts of September 11 reached 2,985 people from 10 different countries. Identification of bodies continued for an additional 3.5 years, with the entire process being completed on February 23, 2005. The remaining body parts whose identities were not discovered were buried at the memorial site at the base of the towers, where new towers are being built.

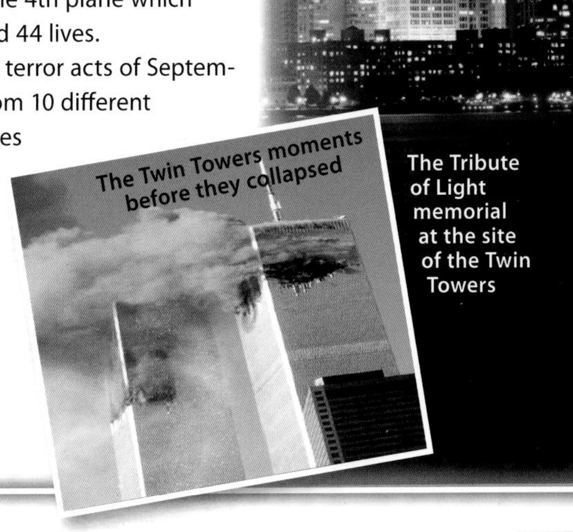

The Twin Towers moments before they collapsed

The Tribute of Light memorial at the site of the Twin Towers

FROM THE TIME atomic energy power was discovered, people assumed that the greatest threat to world survival were atomic and hydrogen bombs. However, in recent years we have discovered other ways in which man is capable of destroying the world with his own hands through irresponsible behavior. The main concern today is global warming, a phenomenon the consequences of which no one can predict.

We, however, are firm believers in the existence of a Creator Who guides this world, and just as He created the world out of nothing, He is able to sustain and protect it. In order to appreciate what it is that Hashem saves us from, we herewith present a number of "end of the world" scenarios.

"If Hashem Will Not Protect" (Tehillim 127:1)

THE LANDING OF AN ASTEROID

It is impossible to estimate the total number of asteroids because there are so many of them and because most of them are dark and small and therefore not easily seen. Estimates put them at more than 100,000. Approximately 5,500 of them were given a name and identification number based on the order in which they were discovered.

If an asteroid the size of the comet "Shoemaker-Levy 9" (which struck the planet Jupiter in 1994 and left scars visible even today) were to strike the earth, the results could be fatal. An asteroid can heat up the atmosphere to a temperature as high as 106,200°F (59,000°C) and burn everything underneath it, long before it even strikes the earth. Shockwaves from the asteroid would travel as fast as the speed of light and destroy everything within 185 mi (300 km) of the point it strikes. People living farther away would have to battle dust storms which would block the sun's light for a few months.

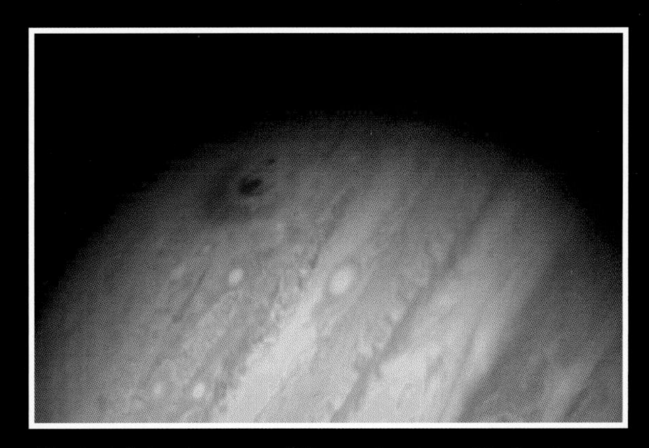

Marks left by the comet "Shoemaker-Levy 9" after having struck the planet Jupiter

GLOBAL WARMING

Although the issue of global warming is much disputed, the UN Panel on Climate Changes publicized that in approximately 100 years, the effects of warming will cause temperatures on earth to reach as high as 140°F (60°C) in the shade, and the Atlantic and Pacific oceans to rise to a level thousands of feet higher than they are today. The Greenland glaciers have receded by 9 mi (15 km) in the past few years, and many of the snow peaks, one of the identifying marks of Europe, have already begun melting in the summer months.

There is a long list of new and unusual climactic phenomena which have been recently discovered. Chazal, in fact, predicted thousands of years ago that in the future, Hashem will remove the sun from its case (see *Avodah Zarah* 3b).

MEGA TSUNAMI

A giant glacier breaking off the ice wall of Antarctica or a volcano erupting into the sea would create giant, mega-tsunami waves 820 ft (250 m) high which would travel at a speed of 460 mph (750 km/h), making the tsunami of 2004 appear like a minor storm.

EYJAFJALLAJÖKULL

There have been 4 recorded eruptions of the volcano Eyjafjallajökull (summit of 5,466 ft/1,666 m) — in the years 920, 1612, 1821–1823, and 2010.

Toward the end of 2009, seismic activity began, causing hundreds of small earthquakes measuring less than 2.0 on the Richter scale. By the beginning of March 2010, close to 3,000 earthquakes at the epicenter of the volcano were measured during a 3–day period. A small eruption is said to have started on March 20.

On April 14, the volcano itself erupted, melting a gigantic glacier in the center of the mountain which caused a tremendous flood. Cold water from melted ice chilled the lava quickly and fragmented it into glass. These glass shards were carried into the eruption plume, producing volcanic dust which caused damage to aircraft. The dust spread eastward toward northwestern Europe, shutting down all European airports. For 6 days Europe's skies were closed to flights, with the exception of the more southern regions such as the city of Rome.

The economic damage suffered by the airline industry resulting from the total cessation of movement of goods as well as passengers was more than $200 million per day. By April 19, clouds from the volcanic ash had reached as far west as the eastern shores of the United States.

The Eyjafjallajökull eruption

VOLCANIC ERUPTION IN ICELAND

Iceland is a country of islands containing more than 200 volcanoes, some of them active. A large portion of the island is covered by massive fields of lava, while 15% of the area is covered by huge glaciers, among them Europe's largest glacier — the Vatnajökull — which has an area of over 3,475 mi^2 (9,000 km^2).

The volcanic activity produces immense heat which melts the snow, resulting in hundreds of miles of flowing rivers and spectacular waterfalls. A river's current, together with the steam from the columns of smoke which bursts forth from deep in the earth, powers turbines which create electricity providing 93% of Iceland's energy. Approximately 90% of homes in Iceland are heated by geothermal energy (power extracted from heat stored in the earth). Hot water is used for washing laundry and even to melt the snow on the streets and sidewalks. In fact, the name of the capital, Reykjavík, means Bay of Smokes, and the city was so named due to the ge thermal steam which rises from the ground.

However, the volcanic activity does not only bring blessing. O June 8, 1784, the volcano Laki, located in the southeast of Icelan erupted. The eruption lasted 8 months. Lava poured out at a rat of 303,700 ft^3 (8,600 m^3) per second. Volcanic ash spewed to a height of 9.3 mi (15 km), and within 6 weeks a significant portio of the northern hemisphere was covered. The ash clouds broug acid rain which resulted in serious breathing-related illness and the death of livestock which in turn caused massive hunger. Approximately 9,000 Icelanders died — 1/4 of the country's popula tion at the time. It is thought that the failure and destruction of Japan's rice harvest that summer and the subsequent deaths fro starvation of tens of thousands of people was due to volcanic dust which blotted out the sun's rays.

"If Hashem Will Not Protect"

VIRUSES AND BACTERIA

Not all dangerous natural phenomena are on the mega level. The microscopic world, tiny as it may be, is no less dangerous. For example, new and unusual strands of bacteria and viruses appear on the scene each year. Though not all bacteria are harmful, many develop resistance to antibiotics and medications and show no signs of disappearing.

"Whoever does not have trust in Hashem, cannot survive on this earth. He will either go out of his mind or commit suicide, for faith in Hashem is essential for all mankind, ranging from the simple person to the greatest sage." (Will of the Rebbe of Kosov)

DID YOU KNOW?
DOOMSDAY CLOCK

The American dropping of the atom bomb on Hiroshima and Nagasaki in 1945 demonstrated that mankind is so "developed" that it could wipe itself out along with all other living beings and vegetation. Therefore, in 1947, the board of directors of the *Bulletin for Atomic Scientists* at the University of Chicago came up with the "Doomsday Clock." The clock does not measure minutes and hours, but rather how close the world is to being destroyed. The closer the clock is to midnight, the closer the world is to global disaster.

Initially, the clock was set at 7 minutes to midnight. Since then it has been adjusted 19 times, depending on how close or how far we are to or from "Doomsday." The closest it came to 12 was in 1953 when the United States and the Soviet Union tested their thermonuclear devices, at which time the clock was set to 11:58 P.M. The most hopeful time was in 1991 when the United States and the Soviet Union signed the Strategic Arms Reduction Treaty, and the clock was set to 11:43 P.M. As of January 14, 2010, the clock was advanced to 11:54 P.M. One reason for the change is the renewal of the arms race after years of relative quiet. Other reasons include the increase in ecological hazards and new developments in nanotechnology and other scientific disciplines.

"The concept of *bitachon* applies only when used for the higher purpose of serving our Creator. Hashem will certainly assist such a person." (*Tiferes Shlomo, Chayei Sarah*)

Molten lava streams down a mountain slope.

A fountain of lava in Hawaii (USA)

When Hashem created Adam HaRishon, he took him aside and showed him all the trees of Gan Eden and said to him, "Look how eautiful and praiseworthy are all of My creations. All that I have created ave created for you. Try not to destroy My world, for if you do, there on't be anyone to fix it." (*Koheles Rabbah* 7:19)

LTHOUGH MANY OF the more frightening scenarios which could lead to the destruc-ion of the world are natural phenomena beyond man's control, the main dangers o mankind are brought about by man himself. Thus, the vast majority of threats to vorld survival are the results of scientific and technological development. Scientists egin research experiments without always knowing where they are headed or the otential results. The bitter truth is sometimes discovered only after many years. 3ut we mustn't panic: the world is not leaderless. Hashem sends the cure to all afflictions, and therefore dire predictions often prove to be misleading.

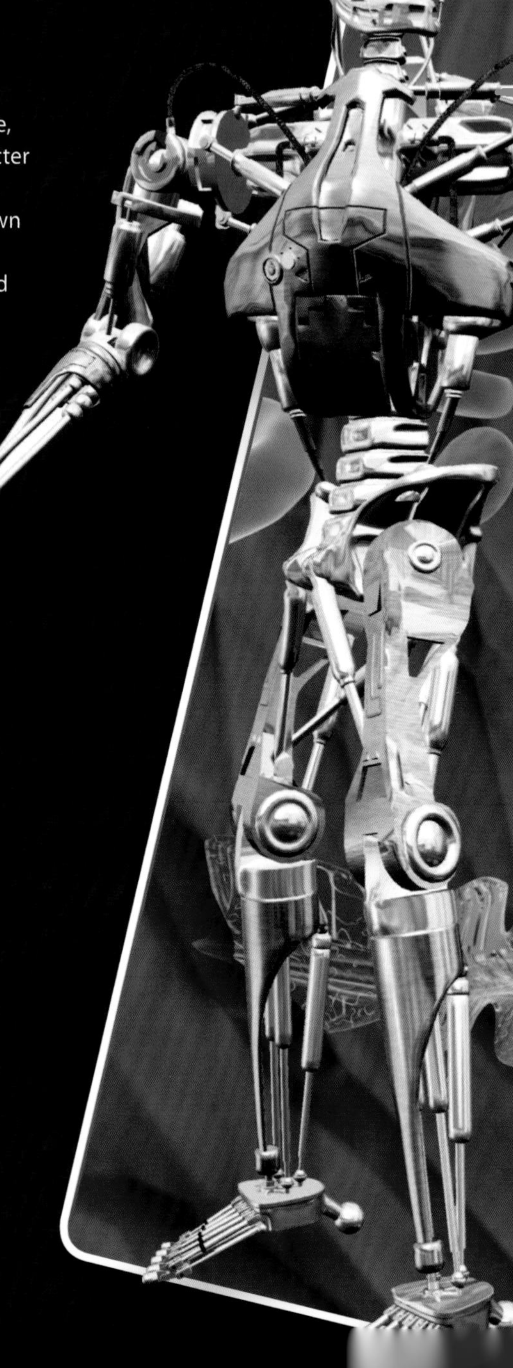

OMPUTER ADDICTION

n China there are already rehabilitation clinics for people, especially young people, vho have become addicted to computer games and surfing the Internet. As a matter of fact, there are even social psychologists who predict that one day mankind will nvent forms of entertainment that are so addictive that all of mankind we be drawn nto it and will lose total contact with the outside world.

Our *Gedolim* are right when they warn against the dangers of the computer and other electronic media.

REVENGE OF THE ROBOTS

Professor Hans Moravec from the Carnegie Mellon Robotics Institute in Pitts-ourgh, PA (USA), claims that by the year 2050 robots will have a mental capacity similar to that of human beings. The question is only whether it will be possible to program a robot sophisticated enough to commu-nicate like a regular human being but which does not mind being subservient to man.

BIOTECHNICAL ERROR

Biotechnology refers to using organisms and living creatures in the development and production of materials. The problem is that scientists experimenting with biotechnology not only cannot predict the results, but they have no control over the experiments. In fact, they rely more on miracles than on science.

Sounds strange? This is exactly how "Mad Cow" disease began. For years, farmers fed their cows straw which was enriched with the bones and flesh of animals, until it became apparent that this rich and nutritious menu causes cows and the people eating them to contract illnesses for which there is no cure.

A genetically engineered tobacco plant which expresses the gene of a firefly

"If Hashem Will Not Protect"

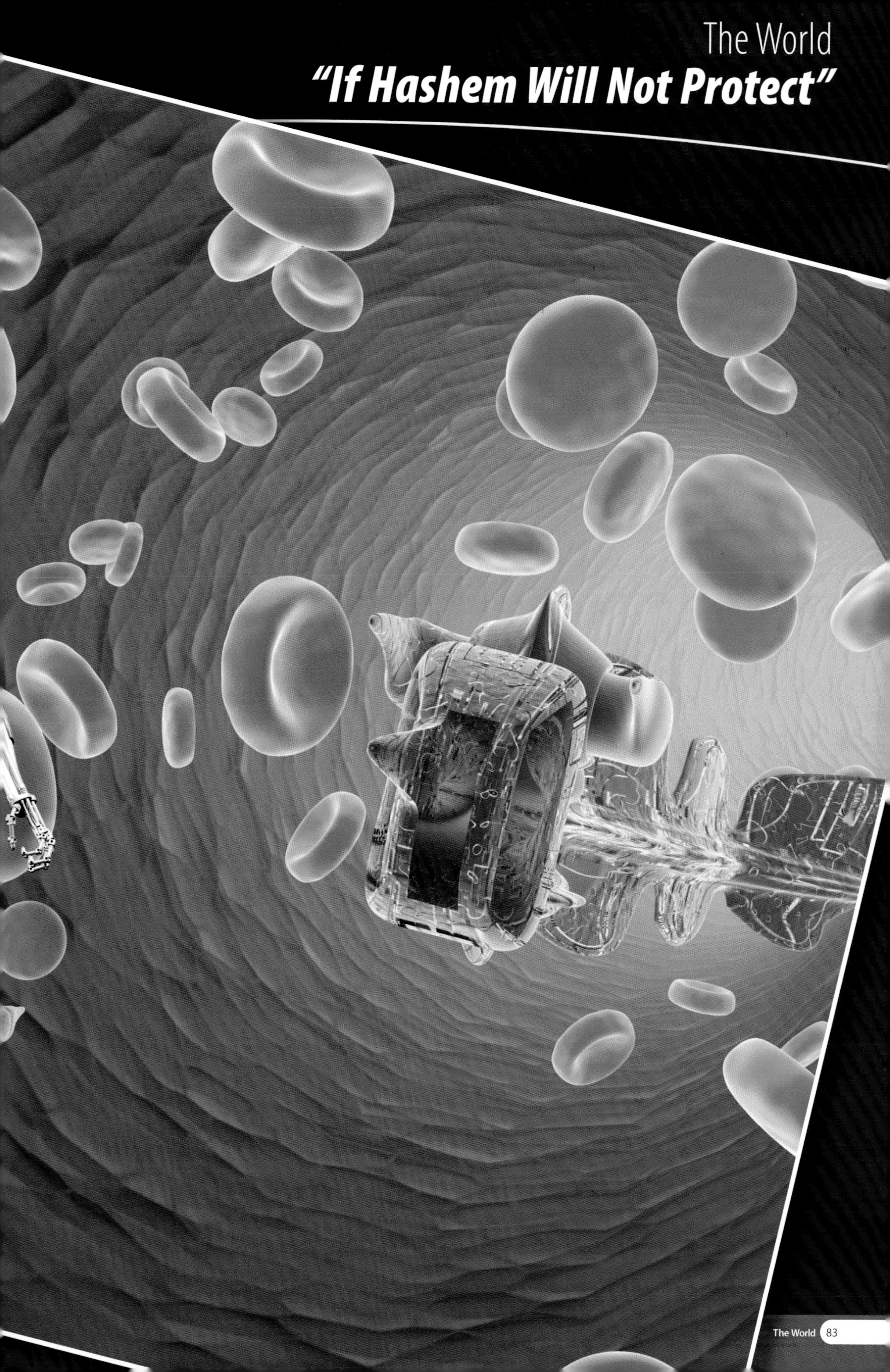

Unusual Talents 86

Large and Small 90

A Time to Play 94

Strange, Yet Interesting

How insightful was the person who said that had it not been for man's madness, the world would remain desolate, for there is no madness like human madness. Man, who was created with a weak soul and composition, is willing to travel to the ends of the earth, endure suffering at the hands of the elements, and place himself at the mercy of animals and other creatures — all in order to earn a few *dinarim* (pennies).

After he exhausts all of his faculties in his quest to amass money, he will use it to hire artisans to build for him some sort of solid dwelling place on this earth which he hopes will last for many years, though he knows full well that he has limited time remaining in his life to enjoy it.

Is there any greater insanity? The same may be said regarding pursuit of all worldly pleasures — it is mere foolishness. Nevertheless, it is what keeps the world afloat.

Rambam, Introduction to *Perush HaMishnayos*

WEIGHTLIFTING COMPETITION

On August 25, 2004, in Athens, Greece, Iranian-born Hossein Rezazadeg set a new weightlifting record by lifting 580 lb (263 kg) from the ground above his head. At the time, Hossein was 25 years old and weighed 231 lb (105 kg). The record for the heaviest weight lifted by a woman was set in 2006, also in Athens, when a Chinese woman named Chen Yanqing lifted 401 lb (182 kg).

A professional weightlifter

JUMP ROPE MARATHON

In December 2003, Australian Jed Goodfellow jumped rope for 27 consecutive hours in the Oasis Shopping Centre in Queensland, Australia, setting a new record. The rules permit only a 5-minute rest per hour.

JUMPING FROM A STANDING POSITION

In 1968 Erna Tvervaag set the standing long jump record — 12.2 ft (3.72 m). The standing long jump competition requires jumping from a stationary, hunched position.

In 1980 Rune Almen achieved the high jump — from a stationary position — record, passing a bar 6.23 ft (1.9 m) above the ground.

FASTEST JUMPER

In Podicherry, India, in 2004, the Indian jumper Namsibiam set the record for most jumps in a minute — 234, an average of 3.9 jumps per second.

LONGEST CONTINUOUS INSTRUMENT PLAYING

Kuzhalmannam Ramakrishnan surpassed his own world record of 36 hours by performing a 5-day Tabla (a pair of Indian Drums) marathon for 101 hours at Kannur, India.

The record for the longest continuous guitar-playing belongs to Brian Engelhart, who played 44 consecutive hours from June 14 until June 16, 2005, in Michigan (USA).

HEAVIEST WEIGHT LIFTED BY THE LITTLE FINGER (PINKY)

Barry Anderson of England showed extreme prowess in 2005 in Massachusetts (USA) when he managed to lift 137.8 lb (62.5 kg) using only his 2 pinkies.

IRON EAR

During an exhibition in Vienna, Austria, in October 2007, a Pakistani named Zafar Gill hung 137 lb (62.1 kg) of weights from his ear. He succeeded in raising them for a period of 10 seconds.

CHIN-UPS

Englishman Stephen Hyland's 2,220 chin-ups set a new world record. It took him 12.3 hours, which averages out to 180.4 chin-ups per hour or approximately 3 per minute.

The record for the one-minute chin-up is 40 and was set by Robert Natoli in Oswego, New York, on February 4, 2006.

FASTEST CRAWLER

A crawling contest requires contestants to advance with at least one knee touching the ground. In 2004, Christopher Hull of England managed to crawl on his belly a distance of just under a mile (1.5 km) in 36 minutes, an average of 1.6 mph (2.5 km/h).

LONGEST CONTINUOUS CRAWL

Arulanantham Suresh Joachim of Sri Lanka crawled continuously for 35.2 miles (56.6 km) next to the Queen Victoria building in Sydney, Australia. Joachim is the holder of 35, no less unconventional, records, granting him second place in the number of unusual records held. He keeps searching for new records that he can break, hoping to become the king of unconventional records.

Among his record-breaking feats are standing on one foot for 76 hours and 40 minutes. During the entire time he did not rest on any object nor did he even lean one leg against the other. He also rode up and down an escalator for seven consecutive days, walked 82.8 mi (133.3 km) with a bottle of milk on his head, and sat on a rocking chair for 75 hours.

Joachim commented that the time spent on the rocking chair was very productive in that it allowed him to contemplate his future plans, mainly searching for new unusual world records.

Unusual Talents

JUMPING OUT OF A PLANE WITHOUT A PARACHUTE

A Japanese by the name of Yasuhiro Kobo jumped out of a plane 1.9 mi (3 km) above the ground, without a parachute. After 1 minute of free fall, by manipulating his body, Yoshiru guided himself toward a parachute which had been thrown from the plane a few moments earlier. He attached himself to the parachute, pulled it open, and landed safely on the ground. He performed this feat in September 2000 in California before a large group of spectators.

HIGHEST NUMBER OF SIMULTANEOUS CHESS MATCHES

In February 2004, in England's Wellington College, British chess champion Andrew Martin competed in 321 chess matches simultaneously. Andrew won 294 games and lost only 1, while the remaining 26 ended in a stalemate.

LONGEST LECTURE

While some might find the subject of "Fundamentals of Hindi Grammar" quite fascinating, it is most likely that few people have even the slightest interest in it. Nevertheless, in December 2004, lecturer Narayanam Siva Sankar of India delivered a record 72-hour lecture on this topic. It is not clear who the audience was and what crime they were guilty of that they had to sit and listen to such a lengthy discourse.

MOST REVOLUTIONS AROUND THE EARTH

Russian cosmonaut Sergei Avdeyev orbited the earth a record 11,967 times over 3 tours of duty aboard the Mir Space Station.

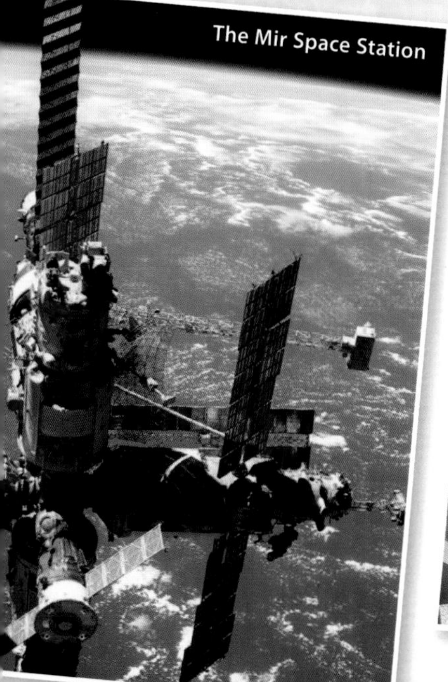

The Mir Space Station

LONGEST CONTINUOUS SWIM

In October 1989, Anders Forvass of Sweden swam a distance of 62.7 mi (101 km) in an 82 ft (25 m) long swimming pool. The small size of the pool made the swimming more difficult, requiring 4,040 laps, which he completed in a period of 24 hours — an average of 2.8 laps per minute.

LONGEST STAY UNDER WATER

For 69 days, from May 6, 1992, until July 4, 1992, Richard Presley remained in a structure which was lowered to the depths of the Key Largo Lagoon in Florida. This was part of a project researching how living in the depths of the ocean would affect people.

CROSSING THE PACIFIC OCEAN IN A ROWBOAT

Jim Shekhdar, a 54–year-old English businessman, spent 273 days and 13 hours crossing 9,041 mi (14,550 km) of the Pacific Ocean in a rowboat specially built for this purpose. He began in Peru in June 2000 and ended in Australia in March 2001.

FASTEST TALKER

Canadian Sean Shannon read the 260 words of "To be or not to be" from Shakespeare's play *Hamlet* in 23.7 seconds — a speed of 658 words per minute. The average person speaks at a rate of 200 words per minute.

LONGEST PAPER CHAIN

Sixty people from a Virginia (USA) college spent 48 consecutive hours constructing a paper chain, similar to what children make for sukkah decorations. The total length of the paper chain was 54.4 mi (87.5 km).

LONGEST LANYARD

Peter Edward of England spent 17.5 hours weaving a 12.3 mi (19.8 km) long lanyard (scoubidou) chain, the popular craft made from four nylon strings.

LONGEST BALLOON CHAIN

Those not interested in paper chains may pass their time making balloon chains, as students in Singapore did in July 2003. Not only did they blow up 5,239 balloons, they connected them, forming a .3 mi (.5 km) chain.

FARTHEST DISTANCE TRAVELED ON A LIFEBOAT

The farthest distance traveled on a rescue boat in which everyone survived was 802 mi (1,290 km), a journey which began in 1914. The expedition, named the Imperial Trans-Antarctic Expedition, led by Sir Ernest Shackleton, was to attempt a land crossing of the Antarctic continent via the South Pole, from the Weddell Sea in the northwest to the Ross Sea in the south. Two ships would be used. *Endurance* would carry the main party into the Weddell Sea, aiming for Vahsel Bay from where a team of 6, led by Shackleton, would begin the crossing of the continent. Meanwhile, a second ship, the *Aurora*, would take a supporting party under Captain Aeneas Mackintosh from Australia directly to Ross Island (at the Ross Sea) in order to lay supply depots containing food and fuel across the Great Ice Barrier, to enable Shackleton's party to complete their journey of 1,800 mi (2,900 km) across the continent.

Sir Ernest Shackleton

Endurance left South Georgia (to the northwest of Antarctica, in the South Atlantic Ocean) for the Weddell Sea on December 5, 1914, heading for Vahsel Bay. As the ship moved south, it ran into early ice, which slowed progress. Deep in the Weddell Sea, conditions got worse and worse until, on January 19, 1915, *Endurance* became frozen fast in an ice floe. The ship drifted slowly north with the ice through the following months. When spring arrived in September, the breaking of the ice and its later movements put extreme pressure on the ship's hull.

Trying to free *Endurance* from the ice

Shackleton was hoping that the ship, when released from the ice, could work its way back toward Vahsel Bay. On October 24, however, water began pouring into the ship. After a few days, Shackleton gave the order to abandon ship, and men, provisions, and equipment were transferred to camps on the ice. On November 21, 1915, *Endurance* finally slipped beneath the surface.

For almost 2 months Shackleton and his party camped on a large, flat ice floe, hoping that it would drift toward Paulet Island, approximately 250 mi (402 km) away, where he knew he would find supplies. By March 17, 1916, their ice camp was within 60 mi (97 km) of Paulet Island but, separated by impassable ice, they couldn't reach it. On April 9 their ice floe broke into two, and Shackleton ordered the crew into the lifeboats, to head for the nearest land. After 5 harrowing days at sea the exhausted men landed their 3 lifeboats at Elephant Island, near the northwest tip of Antarctica.

Because Elephant Island was far from any shipping routes, Shackleton realized that the chances of rescue were quite slim. He left his assistant Frank Wild and 21 people on Elephant Island and set out with 5 of his people on one of the lifeboats, the *James Caird*, in very severe weather conditions toward the island of South Georgia, 802 mi (1,290 km) north. They were equipped with nothing but a chronometer and sextant for navigational purposes. A navigational error of as little as 0.2 degrees would have drawn them into depths of the Atlantic Ocean without any chance of rescue.

The *James Caird* left Elephant Island on April 24, 1916; during the next 15 days it sailed through the waters of the South Atlantic Ocean, at the mercy of the stormy seas, in constant danger of capsizing. On May 8, the cliffs of South Georgia came into view, but the men couldn't land until the next day because of hurricane-force winds. They rode out the storm offshore, in constant danger of being dashed against the rocks. They finally landed on May 9 on the unoccupied southern shore, completing the longest recorded journey in a lifeboat.

After resting and recuperating, rather than risk another sea journey, Shackleton decided to try a land crossing of the island. No one had ever attempted this particular route before; even the most experienced mountain-climbers would find it challenging. Leaving 3 of his men at the landing point on South Georgia, Shackleton led the other 2 men over mountainous terrain for 36 hours to reach the whaling station at Stromness.

Shackleton immediately sent a boat to pick up the 3 men, while he set to work to organize the rescue of the Elephant Island men. He appealed to the Chilean government, which offered the use of *Yelcho*, a small seagoing tug, from its navy. *Yelcho* reached Elephant Island on August 30, 1916 — nearly 2 years after they had initially set sail on *Endurance* — and all 22 men were quickly evacuated.

There remained the men of the Ross Sea party, who were stranded at Cape Evans in McMurdo Sound, after *Aurora* had been blown from its anchorage and driven out to sea, unable to return. The ship, after drifting for many months, finally landed in New Zealand. Shackleton traveled there to join *Aurora*, and sailed with it to rescue the Ross Sea party.

Shackleton's men are rescued

LONGEST TRACTOR RIDE

The Russian Vasilii Hazkevich spent 72 days covering a distance of 13,172 mi (21,000 km) across Vladimir, Russia, on an ordinary unmodified tractor. The journey began on April 25, 2006.

SQUEEZING INTO ONE CAR

In August 2004, in Athens, Greece, 21 people squeezed into the tiny Mini Cooper car made by the BMW company.

Mini Cooper

Strange, Yet Interesting
Unusual Talents

FROM THE LAMB TO THE SWEATER

The 2004 International "Back-to-Back Challenge" held in New South Wales, Australia, required knitting a sweater in the shortest amount of time, from the time the wool was still on the sheep's back until the sweater was worn on a person's back. The winner was a team of knitters led by Australia's Pembroke Merriwa Jumbucks, with a record performance of 4 hours and 50 minutes. This included shearing the wool off the sheep, combing and spinning the wool, and then hand-knitting it into a finished product. Incidentally, the word Jumbucks is Australian slang for sheep.

LOUDEST SNORE

The loudest snores generally reach between 50 and 60 dB — similar to the noise of a passing bus 13 ft (4 m) away. However, those suffering from chronic snoring have been known to snore as loud as 80 dB. Most work environments forbid any noise above 90 dB.

DID YOU KNOW?

While in the midst of a sneeze it is impossible for a person to open his eyes; in fact, all bodily functions cease, including the heartbeat. A sneeze releases material at a speed of more than 230 ft or 70 m per second (157 mph or 252 km/h). A A A Choo! …. Bless You!

SNEEZING

Twelve-year-old Donna Griffiths of Britain sneezed for 978 consecutive days, beginning on January 13, 1981. Her estimated 3 million sneezes broke the previous record of "only" 194 days.

MOST CLAPS

Kent French of Wyoming set a world record by clapping 721 times in one minute. He also holds the record for most claps in one second — 16.

714,816,000 HICCUPS

In 1922 at the age of 28, American Charles Osborne suffered a hiccup attack. He could find no cure for this attack and therefore continued hiccupping for 68 years, until 1990. His first wife left him, but he married a second time, had 8 children and managed to lead a normal life. When the attack began he was hiccupping at a rate of 40 per minute. With time, however, he was hiccupping only 20 times a minute. Multiplying these hiccups over a 68 year period means that he must have hiccupped more than 714,816,000 times. The average person hiccups only 2,000 times in his entire life, and a hiccup attack does not usually last more than 5 minutes.

CONTINUOUS SINGING

In November 2005, German singer Hatmutt Timm sang for a consecutive 59 hours and 12 minutes before an audience which changed every 4 hours.

WHICH COMES FIRST: THE CHICKEN OR THE EGG?

On January 20, 2007, in the Ocean Gate Shopping Center in New Jersey, Rob Beaton set a world's record for holding the most number of eggs in one hand. Beaton held 17 medium-sized chicken eggs for 10 seconds.

HIGHEST NUMBER OF BLOOD DONATIONS IN ISRAEL

Eliezer Krauss has donated 229 pints of blood, giving him the record for the highest amount of blood donated in Israel.

Eleven members of the Sapir family have together donated 454 pints of blood to Magen David Adom (the Israeli equivalent of the Red Cross), making them the most generous donor family.

Only 4.6% of the Israeli population donates blood annually, but this low percentage is still higher than that of the United States and Europe.

MOST GENEROUS BLOOD DONOR

Maurice Creswick, 79, from Johannesburg, South Africa, donated his 350th pint of blood in 2005. The blood bank in South Africa reports that Creswick has donated 1 pint of blood every 2 months since the age of 18.

DID YOU KNOW?

Every year, Israelis donate 270,000 pints of blood, with 50% of the donors being between the ages 17 and 40 — 25% of whom are women. A person's body contains 1.6 gal (6 liters) of blood and he may donate 1 pint (450 ml) of blood at a time. After 2 days his body replenishes the lost fluid, and a month later all of his red blood cells are restored. A healthy person between the ages of 18 and 65 weighing at least 110 lb (50 kg) can donate blood every 56 days. However, in Israel, one may donate only every 3 months. Anyone over the age of 65 wishing to donate must receive permission from a doctor.

Every year 2,300 pints of blood (0.85% of donations) are rejected due to suspected illnesses which could be transmitted in a transfusion.

SOAP BUBBLES "SCIENTIST"

Fan Yang has bestowed upon himself the unusual title of "bubble scientist," and is the holder of all possible records related to soap bubbles. In 1992 in Germany, he displayed the largest spherical soap bubble in the world, with a diameter of 9.84 ft (3 m). In August 1997, in Seattle, WA (USA), he constructed a bubble wall 156 ft (47 m) long and 6.5 ft (2 m) high. In March 2000, in Paris, France, he managed to build 11 concentric circles of bubbles and in May 2006, in Madrid, Spain, he made a bubble so large that it encapsulated 22 people.

FOR A REALLY BIG TEA PARTY

The record for the world's biggest tea bag was broken on January 19, 2011, by the staff of Guinness Book of World Records' *Attack of the Show.* The bag weighed 151 lb (68.6 kg) – 150 lb (68.2 kg) of which was loose English Breakfast tea — the equivalent of 34,000 bags.

NANOTECHNOLOGY

Nanotechnology refers to building objects on a nanometer scale (a millionth of a millimeter or a billionth of a meter) using building blocks of molecules or even single atoms. Researchers are trying to develop a micro-robot the size of only a few atoms that will be able to take 1 atom and place it at a particular location and repeat this act over and over. Such a robot would enable the construction of any material at a very low cost. For example, it would be possible to take a piece of coal, composed of carbon atoms, break it down and construct a diamond — which is also composed of carbon atoms but organized in a different manner. Or reassembling the atoms of sand and adding a few ingredients would produce computer chips.

All forms of protein in a person's body are comprised of only 4 different types of atoms — the only difference between them is the ordering and the number of each one. When this nanotechnology becomes more developed, rather than prescribing medicine for symptoms, it will be possible to actually treat the illness by rearranging protein atoms.

Other uses of nanotechnology: Israeli Professor Aharon Gedanken developed a new material for making fabric. Clothes made from these fabrics will never give off a bad smell even if they are never washed.

Professor Gedanken, together with other scientists, developed a material to put on windows that prevents a build-up of dirt. The dirt simply rolls off the material without leaving any trace.

Other examples of nanotechnology that scientists are trying to develop include a special fabric with microscopic holes for desalination of seawater, a small biological sensor that can use a drop of blood to detect whether a person, G-d forbid, has cancerous growths, as well as an enzyme which would be able to locate the growth and kill it without affecting anything else. Scientists are also working on an injection of nanoparticles which will travel in our arteries and sweep them clear of any cholesterol.

LARGEST CANDLE

In February 2005, the Hussaini Drawing Society for Islamic Arts created a candle measuring 240 ft (73 m) and weighing 3,000 lb (1,360.7 kg). It held 12,000 wicks, which were lit by spectators as part of an exhibition.

SMALLEST BOOK

The smallest book in the world is 0.35 in. (9 mm) x 0.35 in. (9 mm). Every page contains 11 lines and 3 pictures. The book, published in 1994, was sold for $500 a copy. Only 100 copies were printed, half in English and half in Russian.

LARGEST BOOK

Michael Hawley, a scientist at the Massachusetts Institute of Technology (MIT) in Cambridge, MA (USA), published the largest book in the world — 5 ft (1.52 m) long and 7 ft (2.13 m) wide. It contains 122 pages and weighs 133 lb (63 kg). The book's title is *Bhutan: A Pictorial View of the Last Himalayan Dynasty.* It relates the story of the small Bhutan dynasty on the tops of the Himalayan Mountains and is accompanied by breathtaking pictures.

Only 500 copies of the book were printed, each costing $10,000. All proceeds from the sale of the book will go toward development of schools in Cambodia and Bhutan.

LONGEST CIGAR

How long is the world's longest cigar?

In May 2005 Patricio Pena spent several days rolling a cigar, but this was no ordinary cigar. The world's longest cigar, 61 ft (18.6 m) long, was made of 20 lb (9 kg) of tobacco and 100 leaves and was valued at $2,500.

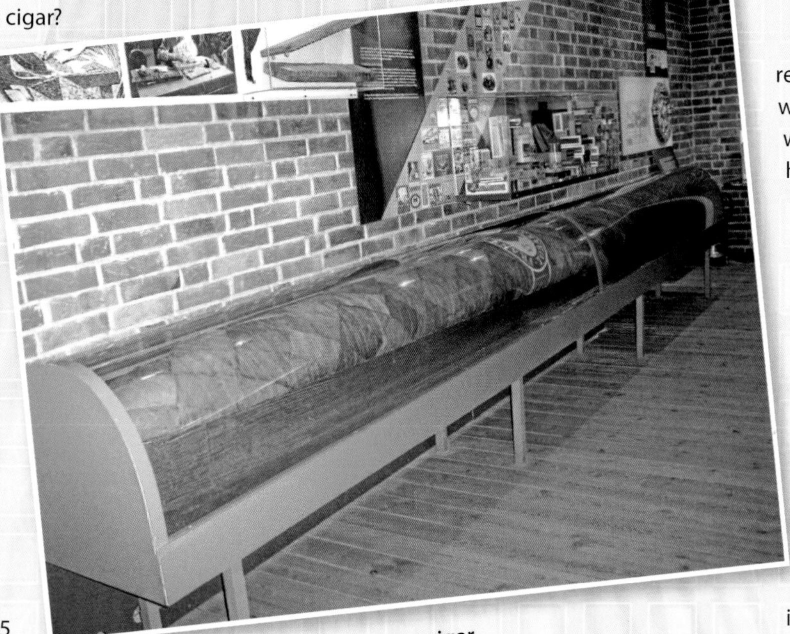

The world's longest cigar

SMOKING STATISTICS

As of 2010, 6 trillion cigarettes are sold worldwide per year. China is the largest consumer and producer of cigarettes in the world, with over 350 million Chinese smoking 2 trillion cigarettes per year — 1/3 of world cigarette consumption. About 15 billion cigarettes are sold daily worldwide — 10 million every minute.

Smoking rates in the United States have dropped by half from 1965 to 2008 — from 42% to 21% of adults. In Israel, adult smoking rates have dropped from 42% in the 1980s to 23% in 2008. In the developing world, however, tobacco consumption is rising by well over 3% per year.

Smoking is the #1 cause of preventable death in the world. It kills 5 million people per year worldwide, or 1 person every 8 seconds.

Smoking-related diseases kill 1 out of 10 adults globally. These include heart disease (the #1 cause of death in the United States, and the leading type of death caused by smoking), stroke, cancer, and lung disease. Almost 90% of lung cancers in men and 80% of lung cancers in women are caused by smoking.

Fifty percent of those who start smoking in adolescence will go on to smoke for 15 to 20 years, and 1/2 of long-term smokers will die from tobacco use. Every cigarette smoked shortens your life by 5 minutes — about the time it takes to smoke it.

There are over 4,000 toxic or carcinogenic (cancer-causing) chemicals in cigarette smoke, and tobacco is extremely addictive. In fact, most drug addicts claim that tobacco is even more addictive than drugs.

The bottom line: *Venishmartem* ***me'od*** *lenafshoseichem*!!! JUST SAY NO!!!

WORLD'S LARGEST PENCIL

In August 2007, New Yorker Ashrita Furman set the new record for the world's largest pencil, at 76 ft (23.16 m) and 22,000 lb (10,000 kg). The pencil has a 200 lb (90.9 kg) eraser, and it is filled with 4,500 lb (2,045 kg) of graphite that is 10 in. (25.4 cm) thick. It is painted with 50 gal (189 liters) of yellow paint. It is estimated that 2 million pencils could be made from this one.

Furman has set 329 world records so far, and is the world record holder for most world records currently held by one person (127). Among some of his feats are: most pancakes caught in 1 min (27), fastest mile (1/3 km) hopping on 1 foot (27 min, 51 sec), most hopscotch games completed in 24 hours (434), and eating the most Jello with chopsticks in 1 min (16.04 oz/ 454 gm).

Furman breaks records "in order to show people what is possible if they truly believe in their own potential. We should always push ourselves to do something greater."

If someone can use this philosophy to catch pancakes and play hopscotch, imagine what we can do with it when learning Torah or doing *mitzvos*!

LARGEST STONE STATUE UNDER CONSTRUCTION

For over 60 years, the Ziolkowski family has been working in the Black Hills of South Dakota in the United States on an immense monument to memorialize Native American leader Crazy Horse, whose victory over the United States Army's 7th Cavalry made him a legend. The gigantic statue depicts the famous Indian chief riding a horse and pointing into the distance.

The monument is being carved out of Thunderhead Mountain on land considered sacred by some Native Americans, about 8 mi (13 km) away from Mt. Rushmore. Thus far, more than 8 million tons of boulders have been removed in hundreds of blasts.

The sculpture's final dimensions are planned to be 641 ft (195 m) wide and 563 ft (172 m) high. The head of Crazy Horse will be 87 ft (27 m) high; by comparison, the heads of the four U.S. Presidents at Mt. Rushmore are each 59 ft (18 m) high. The length of the Indian leader's arm will be 656 ft (200 m) and 6,000 people will be able to comfortably stand on it. When finished, it will be the world's largest sculpture, making the pyramids in Egypt and the Presidents on Mt. Rushmore appear miniature in comparison.

The mountain carving was begun in 1948 by the patriarch of the family, sculptor Korczak Ziolkowski. Ziolkowski died in 1982. The project has no fixed completion date.

The memorial is to be the icon of a huge educational/cultural center that will include the University and Medical Training Center for the North American Indian and the Indian Museum of North America, and will honor the heritage of the 20 million Native Americans, the original settlers of the continent, who were evicted by the early American pioneers.

LARGEST STONE STRUCTURE

The statue of 4 American presidents: George Washington, Thomas Jefferson, Theodore Roosevelt, and Abraham Lincoln, which is carved into the rocks of Mt. Rushmore in South Dakota, is the largest stone statue in the world. The image of each president is a towering 59 ft (18 m) high. This impressive memorial was carved by Gutzon Borglum along with 400 other people over a period of 14 years between 1927 and 1941. In the course of the work, more than .5 million tons of stone and rocks were blasted.

LARGEST GIFT

The Statue of Liberty: 9/11/2001

The largest gift ever given was the Statue of Liberty on the edge of New York City, which towers to a height of 305 ft (93 m) from its base until the tip of its torch. The statue was designed by the French sculptor Frédéric-Auguste Bartholdi and was initially intended to be a gift from the French people to the people of the United States in honor of America's centennial celebration in 1876. However, the sculpture arrived in the United States only 10 years later, dismantled into 350 pieces. After 4 months of assembling, the statue was finally placed on what has been its home ever since. The statue itself is made of a skeleton of iron and steel covered with bronze plates. During the first years, the bronze shimmered with a golden hue, but as the years went by the bronze plates took on a greener appearance.

The torch before it was attached

In 1986, 100 years after its assembly, widespread renovations were done at a total cost of $70 million. The old bronze torch was replaced by a torch plated with solid gold. Interestingly, France originally intended for the Statue of Liberty to stand at the Suez Canal as a symbol of peace among nations. However, Ismail Pasha, the khedive (ruler) of Egypt, refused to accept the gift.

Strange, Yet Interesting
Large and Small

San Alfonso del Mar

LONGEST ROLLER COASTER

Nagashima Spa Land is a major amusement park in Mie Prefecture, Japan. It is best known for its roller coaster, Steel Dragon 2000, which is the longest roller coaster in the world — 8,133 ft (2,479 m) — as well as the 5th tallest, and was built at a cost of $50 million. Although great efforts were made at insuring the roller coaster's safety, which included protection against earthquakes, Steel Dragon 2000 was shut down for 3 years after one of the trains was thrown off the track while in operation and 2 passengers were seriously injured.

LONGEST FENCE

Australia's Dingo Fence or Dog Fence is a pest-exclusion fence built to keep dingoes out of the southeastern part of the continent (where they had largely been exterminated) and protect the sheep flocks. It is the world's longest fence, stretching 3,488 mi (5,614 km) — large enough to circle the entire State of Israel 3 times. The fence is dug 1.1 ft (33 cm) into the ground and rises to a height of 6.2 ft (1.9 m). It was finished in 1885.

LARGEST SALTWATER SWIMMING POOL

The world's largest saltwater swimming pool is found in San Alfonso del Mar, a resort in Algarrobo, Chile. The pool is 0.6 miles (1 km) long, with an area of 20 acres, and holds over 66 million gal (250 million liters) of water. It is the length of 64 Olympic-size swimming pools.

The large pool uses water pumped from the Pacific Ocean that is then filtered and treated to supply the pool. The pool is 115 ft (35 m) deep, making it the world's deepest pool as well. It is heated to a temperature of 79°F (26°C) — warmer than ocean water. In spite of its vast size, the water still has a crystal-clear blue color using far less chemicals than an ordinary pool. The sand which surrounds the pool is also heated.

In the next few years, a new record will be set for the world's largest pool, in Sharm el Sheikh, which is being built by the same company that built San Alfonso del Mar.

LARGEST ADVERTISEMENT

From 1925 to 1934, the car company Citroën's name was emblazoned in lights on the Eiffel Tower. The advertisement used a total 250,000 light bulbs in six colors, with the bottom letter being 69 ft (21 m) high. The lights were visible from as far as 24 mi (38 km) away.

LARGEST SNOWMAN EVER BUILT WAS A SNOW-WOMAN

The world's largest snowperson was built in Bethel, ME (USA), in 2008, and was named Olympia Snowe, in honor of the U.S. senator from Maine. The snow-woman was 122 ft, 1 in. (37.21 m) tall and weighed 13 million lb (5.9 million kg). Her eyelashes were made from skis and her scarf was 100 ft (30.48 m) long. Two 27 ft (8.2 m) tall trees were used as arms, and her nose was 8 ft (2.4 m) long.

TALLEST FOUNTAIN

The world's tallest fountain is King Fahd's Fountain (Jeddah Fountain), in Jeddah, Saudi Arabia. At full pressure, the fountain sends a stream gushing forth at a speed of 233 mph (375 km/h) to a height of 853 ft (260 m). Every minute, 7,000 gal (26,500 liters) of water, weighing more than 18 tons, are thrown upwards.

King Fahd's Fountain

HIGHEST MEMORIAL STATUE

The Gateway Arch, also known as the Gateway to the West, is situated on the banks of the Mississippi River in St. Louis, MO. The arch, built in memory of the early American pioneers who settled the West, stands 630 ft (192 m) tall and is 630 ft (192 m) wide at its base, making it the tallest monument in the United States. Construction of the arch started in 1963 and was completed in 1965. The monument opened to the public in 1967. Within each leg are 2 elevators. Each can carry 40 passengers to the observation deck on top.

The Gateway Arch cost $15 million to build and is made from 4,644 tons of stainless steel and 34,570 tons of reinforced concrete. St. Louis law forbids building any structure above the height of the arch.

DOMINO THEORY

On November 18, 2005, 4.1 million dominoes were toppled, breaking the previous world record of "only" 3.9 million set in 2004. For 2 consecutive months, dozens of people worked on setting up the dominoes in a large exhibition hall in Holland. The first domino was pushed and for the next hour and a half all the dominoes fell one after the other.

The record was marred by controversy, as 4 days before this, a sparrow flew into the hall and knocked over 23,000 dominoes. After several futile attempts to catch the bird, it was shot.

MICROSCOPIC CHESS SET

A microscopic chess set no bigger than a match head could possibly be the smallest board game in the world. The board is 0.14 in. x .01 in. (3.5 mm x 2.5 mm) and the gold and silver playing pieces range between 0.006 in. (0.15 mm) and 0.01 in. (0.3 mm) high. The set took 6 months to complete.

The set is the work of Russian micro-miniaturist Vladimir Aniskin. He uses powerful microscopes and equipment that he designed himself and says that he must work between his heartbeats to create his tiny pieces.

LARGEST AND SMALLEST CHESSBOARDS

The world's largest wooden chess set, 78.7 x 78.7 ft (24 x 24 m), was built by the Faculty of Physics in Vilnius (Vilna) University in Lithuania in honor of FiDi 40 Physics Day. Each square of the board measures 9.84 x 9.84 ft (3 x 3 m). The king is over 9.84 ft (3 m) high.

The smallest handmade, conventional chess set, 0.5 in^2 (33 mm^2) in area, was designed by Jaspal Singh Kalsi from India. The "largest" piece, the king, is 0.5 in. (13 mm) tall and the smallest piece, the pawn, is 0.28 in. (7.2 mm) tall. The diameter of the base of each piece is 0.12 in. (3.1 mm).

CHESS GAME WITH THE MOST MOVES

Goran Arsovic and Ivan Nikolic from Serbia finished their chess game in a draw after 269 moves, making it the chess game with the most known number of moves. The game, which took place on February 17, 1989, lasted over 20 hours.

A Time to Play

MOST SIMULTANEOUS CHESS GAMES

Kiril Georgiev achieved a chess record by playing against 360 players simultaneously. The event took place in the Expo Center in the Bulgarian capital of Sofia before a large crowd of spectators. Georgiev won 284 of the games, lost 6, and ended 70 in a draw.

For every move, Georgiev had to walk a total of 0.3 miles (0.5 km) to reach all of the chessboards and players. It therefore took 10 hours of play to reach move 19. At move 24 there were only 50 opponents left. The last game was completed after 14 hours and 14 minutes.

CHESS PRODIGIES

One measure of a chess prodigy is the age at which he or she gains the International Grandmaster title. As of August 2009, there are 1,328 International Grandmasters listed in the World Chess Federation (Fédération Internationale des Échecs — FIDE).

In 1958, Bobby Fischer earned the title at age 15 years, 6 months, making him at the time the youngest holder of the title — which he held for 33 years. The youngest is now Ukrainian Sergey Karjakinn, who was 12 years and 7 months old when awarded the title.

CHECKERS CHAMPION

The world checkers champion is a computer program which is able to calculate 500 billion possible checkers moves, guaranteeing a win — it even defeated the human world champion. It has been proven that when two people play a checkers match without committing any errors, the game will always end in a draw.

THE INVENTION OF SUDOKU

Sudoku is a logic-based combinatorial number-placement puzzle. The goal is to fill a 9 × 9 grid with numbers so that each column, each row, and each of the nine 3 × 3 sub-grids (also called "boxes," "blocks," "regions," or "sub-squares") contain all of the numbers from 1 to 9. The puzzle constructor provides a partially completed grid, which usually has only one solution.

The predecessor to Sudoku began in China many years ago and was known as the "Magic Square." The modern Sudoku was designed by Howard Garns, a 74-year-old retired architect and freelance puzzle constructor from Indiana, and first published in 1979 by Dell Magazines as "Number Place." Garns died in 1989 before getting a chance to see his creation turn into a worldwide craze.

The puzzle was introduced in Japan by the Nikoli puzzle company under the name Suuji, which means "the digits must be single" or "the digits must occur once." Later, by using the first letter of each word, the name was abbreviated to Sudoku.

A retired judge named Wayne Gould came across the game in 1997 and spent the next few years developing a computer program to generate Sudoku squares. In 2004 he convinced the British newspaper *The Times* to publicize the puzzle game, resulting in the craze as we know it today.

INVENTION OF THE CROSSWORD PUZZLE

Crossword puzzles today are an integral part of any respectable newspaper. Although it may seem that they have been around forever, they are in fact a relatively recent invention. They were first created in the 19th century in England. On December 21, 1913, Arthur Wynne of Liverpool published the first crossword puzzle (called a "word-cross puzzle") in a newspaper called *New York World*. It looked much different from the crosswords used today and had no black squares.

At first, only the *World* carried the new puzzle as a weekly feature. But in 1924, a small publishing firm, Simon and Schuster, published the first collection of *World* crossword puzzles in book form. The craze began, and Simon and Schuster's success was launched. Soon after, crossword puzzles began appearing in British newspapers, and from there the craze spread to newspapers all over the world.

Interestingly enough, *The New York Times* was one of the last newspapers to begin publishing a regular crossword puzzle.

TELEPHONE

The record for the greatest number of people participating in a game of "Telephone" was set on April 15, 2005, at the Somerville School in New Jersey (USA), where 814 people participated in the event.

SIMON SAYS

In 2006, 1,169 children gathered in Victoria Park in Glasgow, Scotland, to play the children's game "Simon Says." It is not known who won or how long the game lasted.

MOST EXPENSIVE YO-YO

The world's most expensive yo-yo was designed by jeweler Sidney Mobell. It was valued at $10,000 at the time. It contains 119 gemstones: 44 diamonds, 25 rubies, 25 sapphires, and 25 emeralds.

DID YOU KNOW?

The Yo-Yo was invented in the Philippine Islands when 16th century hunters hiding in trees would throw a rock tied to a cord up to 20 ft (6.1 m) long at wild animals beneath them. The cord enabled retrieval of the rock after missed attempts.

MOST POPULAR BOARD GAME

Monopoly is considered the world's most popular board game. In 1903 Elizabeth Magie (pronounced "McGee") came up with an idea for an educational board game which she called The Landlords Game. Properties were not purchased but only rented. One of her goals was to teach people about the dangers of giving so much power to landlords who were able to demand high rents. The game was played on a board made up of 40 spaces arranged 10 per side. The four corner squares were Mother Earth (collect $100), Jail, Public Park, and Go To Jail. In the center space on each side of the board was a railroad. The rest of the spaces consisted of properties and fines that had to be paid.

The game became very popular, but it was not mass-produced and therefore people made their own boards with slight changes to the rules. The Landlords Game was granted a U.S. patent in 1906, and again in 1924 when Magie made changes to the game.

The game became more and more popular, and underwent changes. Eventually Charles Darrow improved on the game, patented it, and in 1935 sold the rights to Parker Brothers, who made more changes and named the game Monopoly. Parker Brothers began mass-producing the game which immediately became a big hit. It is estimated that since that time, 200 million games have been sold throughout the world, not to mention the many new versions which have developed.

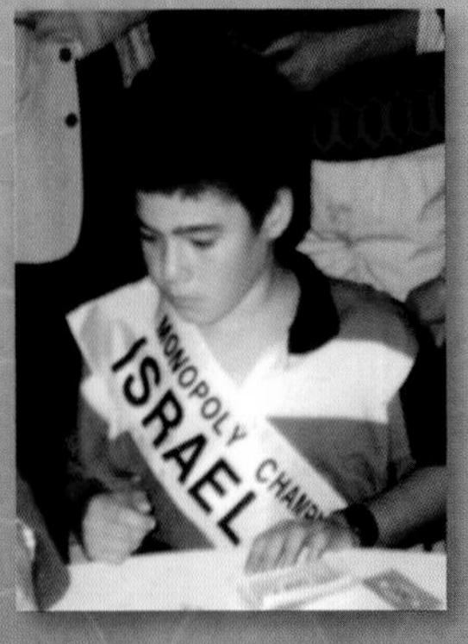

13-year-old Chen Shabtai, Israel national Monopoly champion, 2nd place winner at the 1988 Monopoly World Championship

Sidney Mobell with his Monopoly set

MOST EXPENSIVE MONOPOLY GAME

The most expensive Monopoly set is a special board designed by jeweler Sidney Mobell of San Francisco, CA (USA). It is made of gold. It weighs 32 lb (14.5 kg) and is embedded with 165 gemstones, including 60 diamonds, 47 sapphires, and 24 rubies. The dice are embedded with 42 diamonds. The 28 title cards are gold-plated, and the tokens are made of 18 karat solid gold. The game is valued at $2 million.

LARGEST TOY STORE

The world's largest toy store is Hamley's in London, which was established in 1760 by William Hamley. The 54,000 ft^2 (5,000 m^2) store has 7 floors, containing more than 40,000 types of toys.

Every floor in the store is dedicated to a different type of toy:

Basement: Lego, construction, and inter active toys.

Ground floor: Soft toys.

1st floor: Board games, thinking games, and puzzles.

2nd floor: Baby and preschool toys.

3rd floor: Girls' toys (dolls, strollers), arts and crafts, etc.

4th floor: Trains, models, and remote-control games, and games requiring assembly.

5th floor: Boys' games — cars, guns, etc

Hamley's is also one of the most popular tourist sites in London, with 6 million visitors from all over the world walking through its doors every year. Visitors testify that it is impossible to leave the store empty-handed.

BABUSHKA

On April 25, 2003, Yulia Brodskaya of Russia finished painting her 51 nesting ("Babushka") dolls, which fit one inside the other. The largest of these nesting dolls is 21.7 in. (55 cm) and the smallest is .12 in. (0.3 cm), making this the largest Babushka series in the world.

LARGEST TOY STORE CHAIN

The largest chain of toy stores in the world is Toys R Us, based in New Jersey (USA). The chain has 1,677 branches in 30 countries all over the world. The flagship location, Toys R Us Times Square, located in Times Square, New York City, is by far the most impressive. The entrance hall contains a huge, 102 ft (31 m) Ferris wheel, as well as a towering, 52.5 ft (16 m) tall dragon weighing 5 tons. There is a 2-story-tall Barbie Doll house whose parts are life-size. If you have an allergy to the color pink, we would not recommend entering the doll house. Toys R Us bills itself as "The best toy store in the world."

The ferris wheel at Toys R Us Times Square (N

A Time to Play

WORLD'S LARGEST TETRUS GAME

Dutch students transformed a 16 floor university building into a giant tetrus game 322 ft (98 m) high. The lights which were lit and extinguished in the rooms were used as the game's bricks.

LARGEST PUZZLE

The world's largest puzzle was completed in Singapore in June 2002. The puzzle, 37.8 ft (11.5 m) long and 35.1 ft (10.7 m) wide, consists of 212,320 pieces.

LARGEST COMMERCIALLY SOLD PUZZLE

In 1985, using the theme "Put It Together," the British Monadnock United Way assembled the world's largest commercially sold jigsaw puzzle, breaking the Guinness record previously held by Hallmark and Macy's. It had 15,520 pieces and was 82 ft (25 m) long and 56 ft (17 m) wide.

COMMERCIALLY SOLD PUZZLE WITH THE MOST PIECES

The Spanish company Educa Borras produces the commercially sold puzzle with the highest number of pieces. The puzzle, made up of 24,000 pieces, is 14 ft (4.28 m) long and 5.2 ft (1.57 m) wide. The picture on the puzzle, called "Life — The Great Challenge," was painted by New Zealand artist Royce B. McClure. The puzzle retails for $279.95.

The first people to complete the puzzle were Scott Slater and his wife P.J. from Sacramento, CA (USA). They began putting the puzzle together in May 2007, and managed to complete it 34 days and 200 combined working hours later.

RUBIK'S CUBE

In 2006, Toby Mao of California (USA) set a new world record by solving the Rubik's Cube puzzle from a completely mixed-up state in only 10.48 seconds.

MOST POPULAR BUILDING TOY

In 1932 a carpenter named Ole Kirk Christiansen from the Danish village of Billund began creating wooden games for his 12–year-old son. He made several games before he came up with the idea of a toy which could be changed from day to day based on the child's desire. This would add interest and variety, and the child would therefore never get bored. So began the Lego company.

The Lego company has manufactured over 3.41 billion Lego pieces. Every second of the day, 7 Lego games are sold somewhere in the world. The word Lego is a contraction of the Danish words *leg* and *godt*. *Leg godt* means "play well" in Danish. Coincidentally, the word lego means both "I study" and "I put together" in Latin. The second Latin name is certainly justified, as it is possible to build 9.15 million different structures from 6 small (.79 x 1.58 in./2 x 4 cm) pieces of Lego.

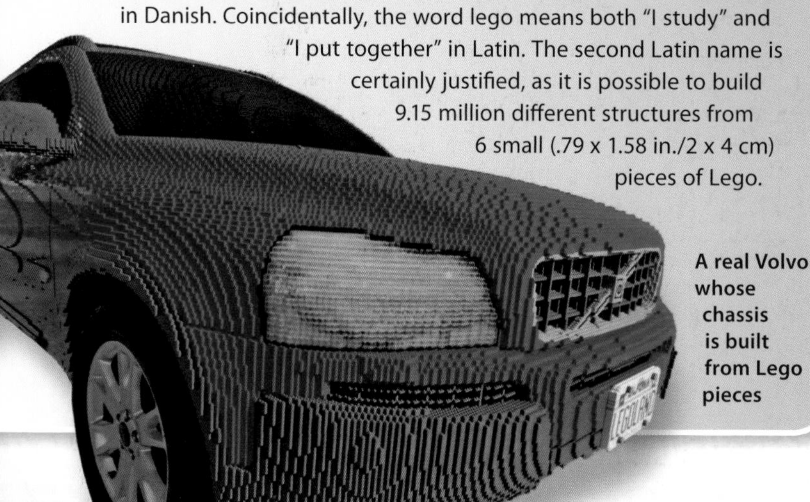

A real Volvo whose chassis is built from Lego pieces

WORLD'S MOST ANNOYING ALARM CLOCKS

The following is a selection of alarm clocks which are guaranteed to wake you up no matter how deeply you are sleeping.

WAKE-UP PUZZLE: This alarm clock will definitely get you out of bed! It wakes you up by firing four puzzle pieces into the air. Your task is to pick up the pieces and put them back in the alarm clock — which won't turn off until then.

FIND THE PEG: Mission impossible — this ball-shaped clock consists of many "nodules," and only one of them can turn off the alarm. Furthermore, from the moment the alarm begins to ring, the clock does not stop rolling all over the room. What can you do if you want to sleep a little longer? Throw the ball against the wall and hope that the right button will be pressed.

THE HOVERING CLOCK: At wake-up time this clock rises and beings to hover all over the room — all the while emitting earsplitting shrieks and sounds.

ACOUSTIC GRENADE — This clock emits such a loud explosive sound that it will wake up all the residents in a 12–story building (think of the savings). The only way to be saved from the explosion is to wake up from your slumber and immediately return the "grenade" pin to its place.

HIDE AND SEEK: This is the most annoying of all the clocks. The moment it begins to ring it falls to the floor and its wheels take it anywhere, perhaps into a closet or under a set of drawers. Every few minutes it finds a new hiding place, making it very difficult to find.

"Not by Bread Alone …" 100

"Drink Sweet Beverages" 104

Fruit of the Land 108

"His Palate Is Sweet" 112

From the Fat of the Land 116

Who Nourishes All

Food is man's sustenance; it is what keeps the soul connected to the body. One who does not eat will quickly die and his soul will leave his body, G-d forbid.

Because eating connects the body to the soul, we must eat properly and in a holy way.

If a person eats and eats purely for his own pleasure, then his body has overpowered his soul. However, if a person eats in an appropriate and holy way, wanting only to nourish his soul, then his soul has overpowered his body—"A *tzaddik* eats to satisfy his soul" (*Mishlei* 13:25). Whether the body or the soul will dominate a person depends on how he eats, for eating is the connection between the body and the soul.

Hilchos Chadash 3

"THIS IS THE WAY OF TORAH: EAT BREAD WITH SALT" (*Pirkei Avos* 6:4)

Bread with salt is considered the most basic form of eating, for all flavors are contained in bread and salt. In fact, the words לחם (bread) and מלח (salt) have the same letters. There is a strong connection between bread and salt. Bread absorbs all flavors and tastes, while the strength of a food's flavor is directly proportional to its salt content. Salt plays a major role in the taste of our food because it is very lofty indeed: "The covenant (*bris*) between Hashem and the world has been made with salt since the six days of Creation" (see Rashi on *Vayikra* 2:13). Bread and salt are therefore deeply intertwined.

The blessing recited on bread is of such significance that not only does it come before the *berachos* on all other foods, it absolves a person from having to recite more *berachos* on any food which is part of the meal. Although all other foods may have a sweeter taste than bread, it satisfies and sustains us as no other food can.

Taste is a type of knowledge, as the verse states, "Teach me good *ta'am* (literally, flavor and taste) and wisdom" (*Tehillim* 119:67). The sweetness of knowledge is of the utmost importance, as the verse states, "(Torah is) sweeter than honey and drippings from the honeycombs" (*Tehillim* 19:11). Bread, however, does not have a sweet taste. This is because it absorbs all flavors, and therefore each individual flavor is not detected.

(excerpted from *Hilchos Netilas Yadayim liSeudah uVetzias HaPas*)

Chazal taught that eating bread with salt and drinking a pitcher of water in the morning is extremely healthy. Besides the benefits to the body, a morning meal of bread, salt and water helps a person teach and study Torah. His words are heard and his learning remains with him.

A person who places too much emphasis on delighting in food and drink cannot learn Torah. The Maharsha says that this is why eating morning bread with water gives wisdom to the simple, as well as helps a person study and teach Torah. Bread is the food that gives man wisdom. It is said that the moment a child begins to eat bread he gains wisdom. Water, as well, is the most basic drink. Other foods and wine only serve to confuse the mind.

MOST COMMON AND IMPORTANT FOOD

Since the days of Adam HaRishon, the most common, basic food in the world is bread in all its varieties and forms.

BREAD CONSUMPTION

The biggest bread consumers in the world are the Germans, followed by the French. Israel is 7th in the world in bread consumption per person. The average Israeli eats 295 lb (134 kg) of bread per year. It is estimated that NIS 1.5 billion per year is spent on bread, half of which is supplied by Israel's three major bakeries: Angel, Davidowitz, and Berman. The rest of the bread is supplied by 550 smaller bakeries as well as stores selling bread. Each month, 2,000 tons of bread are returned to the bakeries. The main customers of the stale bread are farmers who feed it to their calves.

HUNGRY FOR BREAD AND THIRSTY FOR WATER

The area of land available for growing crops has dropped by 40% in the past 30 years. Despite this, since the 1960s agricultural produce has grown by 78% and the general production of food has risen by 170%. During this same period of time, food production in Africa has dropped by 12%.

Approximately 1/3 of the earth's inhabitants still suffer from some level of hunger and malnutrition. The water situation is not good either, as 1.2 billion people in the world have no access to drinking water while 2.4 billion people drink contaminated water.

FAVORITE FLAVOR

The most preferred flavor in foo is chocolate, which surpass banana and vanilla by a 3-to-1 margin. This mea that for every vanilla- or banana-flavored product, there are chocolate-flavo food products

LARGEST FOOD COMPANY

The Nestlé food corporation, established by a Swiss man named Henry Nestlé in 1866, is the largest food company in the world. There are Nestlé factories in 86 countries throughout the world, including 2 in Israel. Nestlé employs 309,000 workers and was ranked 51st in the Fortune 500 companies in 2009, with revenues of $107.6 billion and profits of $10.43 billion.

"Not by Bread Alone . . ." (Devarim 8:3)

DETERMINING HOW FOOD TASTES

In addition to a person's senses of taste and smell, his nose and mouth are packed with sensory nerve endings that are sensitive to heat, cold, and touch. These play a big role in how food tastes to us. Other sensations which affect how we taste are actually connected to the sense of touch: the tickling feeling of bubbles of carbonated drinks, the "crunchy" feeling of chips and other crisp snacks, and even the burning sensation of hot pepper.

HOT PEPPERS

A "hot" food has nothing to do with taste, smell, or temperature.

Chili peppers produce a compound called capsaicin, which causes the mucous membranes to let sodium and potassium enter the membranes in larger amounts. This signals the nerve cells the same way heat signals them — and that's why you feel a burning sensation when you eat the peppers. Drinking cold water may help, but drinking fatty liquids such as milk is more effective in stopping the burning sensation because capsaicin breaks down more easily in fat than in water.

Because this burning feeling is not related to taste, capsaicin has the same effect on all sensory nerve cells. That is why your eyes will burn if you touch them after you touch a hot pepper.

SPICINESS FELT IN THE NOSE

The pungency of horseradish is felt especially in the nostrils. The active ingredient in horseradish, isothiocyanate, works in a similar way to capsaicin in that it produces a burning sensation. However, unlike capsaicin, it produces vapors which cause a burning sensation in the sensory nerve endings of the nose.

The isothiocyanate evaporates quicker than capsaicin and therefore the burning sensation in the nostrils disappears faster than the pungency of pepper in the mouth.

MINT

Menthol, found in mint candies and toothpaste, affects cells sensitive to temperature in the opposite fashion—it produces a feeling of cold rather than burning. It enters through the olfactory epithelium of the pharynx and the nose, reaches the nerves which are responsible for the sense of cold and heat, and increases their sensitivity to cold. Eating mint candies with a closed mouth does not provide a totally refreshing taste, but if you inhale after the menthol has affected the nerve endings, it produces a strong sensation of cold.

TANNIN

Saliva in the mouth contains a protein called mucin which gives the saliva viscosity (thickness) and oiliness. Unripe fruits, nut peels, and red wine contain compounds known as tannins. They mix with the mucin proteins, causing the saliva to lose its viscosity. This creates that dry and puckery feeling in the mouth after a person eats unripe fruit or drinks red wine. The "dryness" caused from this sensation, known as astringency, is not real but just a feeling, and therefore drinking water will not solve the problem. A wine taster who rolls wine in his mouth determines among other things the level of astringency in the wine.

"ALWAYS ROOM FOR SWEET THINGS" (*Megillah* 7b)

Even though they will usually eat only when hungry, animals will eat sweet food even when completely full. The cat family is an exception. They will not eat any food if they are not hungry, no matter how sweet it is.

LARGEST FOOD CONSUMPTION PER FAMILY

In every country, the "food basket" per family differs in its quantity, makeup, and cost. The biggest food consumers are the Germans. An average German family, consisting of parents and 2 children, eats a large quantity of meat, many soft drinks, beer, wine, mineral water, milk products, bread, fruit, vegetables, pizza, and salads, spending on the average $500 per week on food.

In Japan, the same size family eats a lot of fish, vegetables, fruits, dressings, and rice. They spend an average of $317 per week on food.

In Israel, a family of parents and 2 children eats many fruits and vegetables, bread, eggs, milk and milk products, meat, snacks, and soft drinks. Their average food outlay is $150 per week.

LOWEST FOOD OUTLAY PER FAMILY

In refugee camps such as Bredjing in Chad, a family consisting of parents and 4 children spends an average of $1.3 per week on their food basket, which consists of wheat, rice, dry peas, and a small amount of vegetables and water.

In poorer East Asian countries such as Bangladesh and Bhutan, and in Black African countries, the average extended family, consisting of 12 people (parents, children and their spouses), spend $5 a week on food, which includes rice, many vegetables, a bit of fruit, meat, and a small amount of drinks.

WORLD'S BEST-KEPT SECRET

The Coca-Cola soft drink, introduced in 1886, is the most well-known brand name soft drink in the world as well as the best kept secret in the food industry — only 10 people have ever learned the secret formula. The formula, referred to as "Merchandise 7X," is held in SunTrust Bank's main vault in Atlanta, GA (USA). Today, the company's 2 directors and the chief chemist are the only ones who know the formula, and it is rumored that for security reasons they will never travel or fly together. However, in order to receive a *kashrus* certification in Israel, the managers agreed to make an exception and reveal the ingredients—without revealing the quantities of each ingredient and the exact method of preparation.

EATING AND SPIRITUALITY

The more spiritual a person, the lighter his food intake. The generation that traveled through the desert, known as the Generation of Wisdom, ate manna which was very thin. On Shabbos, a more spiritual day, they ate bread of unusual taste. Jewish people eat milk and dairy products during the week, while on [the more spiritual days of] Shabbos and Yom Tov they eat more delicate foods. On Yom Kippur, the most spiritual of days, they are like angels for whom there is nothing in the world which is sufficiently spiritual for them to eat — they therefore fast on that day. (HaRav Pinchas miKoritz)

The word "sugar" is shared by most languages. Some examples: *sukar* (Hebrew), *zucker* (German), *sucre* (French), *azúcar* (Spanish), *zucchero* (Italian), *shuga* (Japanese).

HONEY — THE NATURAL HEALER

The Rambam writes about the healing powers of honey — it purifies the blood and is good for a person's digestive system. However, he recommends limiting its intake in keeping with the verse, "When you find honey, eat what is sufficient for you" (*Mishlei* 25:16). He suggests mixing it in warm water and drinking it first thing in the morning when it is most effective. A dosage of 1.8 oz (50 gm) is enough, and it should not be drunk too many times in one day.

Honey also invigorates and strengthens the body during periods of tiredness, as we find regarding Yehonasan the son of King Shaul: "He dipped it into the honeycomb and then brought his hand to his mouth and his eyes lit up" (*I Shmuel* 14:27).

During both World Wars, the Russians would use honey to dress wounds in order to protect them from infection and to help them heal. They would also use this "royal jelly" as natural penicillin.

MOST EXPENSIVE JAM

The most expensive jam in the world was displayed by the British food company F. Duerr and Sons in September 2006. It was manufactured in honor of the company's 125th anniversary. The Fine Cut Seville Orange Marmalade is sold in crystal jars and among its ingredients are 62-year-old whiskey, vintage champagne, and of course edible gold crumbs. One 2.2 lb (1 kg) jar sells for $9,996, and the proceeds are donated to an organization for needy children in Manchester, England.

MOST EXPENSIVE CAVIAR

The word caviar comes from the Persian word *khag-avar*, which means "the roe-generator" — roe is fish eggs. The most expensive caviar in the world is the almas (meaning diamond), which is produced from the eggs of the beluga fish. The beluga is a non-kosher fish from the sturgeon family found mainly in the Caspian Sea. Most types of caviar are from the sturgeon family, and the most expensive are generally the black ones. The almas, however, is white as a pearl and the brighter it is, the higher the price.

Only one restaurant in the world sells almas—Caviar House and Prunier in London. A kilo (2.2 lb) of caviar served in a 24-karat dish sells for $25,000. Kosher caviar is made from salmon roe.

Caviar House and Prunier, London

LONGEST-LASTING FOOD

Honey lasts longer than all other foods — it never spoils. In ancient times, honey was used to preserve food, as well as, *lehavdil*, bodies Embalming cream used by early Egyptians was honey-based, and jars of honey were placed next to the bodies of Egyptian kings. In the grave of the Egyptian pharaoh Tutankhamen there was found a jar of honey which had remained in good and edible condition for more than 3,000 years.

THAT'S SOME PIZZA!

The 12-in. (30 cm) Pizza Royale 007, the world's most expensive pizza, was made by chef Domenico Crolla and bought by Maurizic Morelli at public auction for $4,200. The money was donated to th Fred Hollows Foundation in England.

The pizza is topped with an assortment of some of the world's most expensive (and *treif*) foods, such as lobster marinated in cognac, caviar soaked in champagne, sunblush tomato sauce, Scottish smoked salmon, venison medallions, prosciutto and vintage balsam vinegar. In addition to all these fine ingredients, it is topped with a significant amount of edib 24-karat gold flakes.

World's most expensive jam

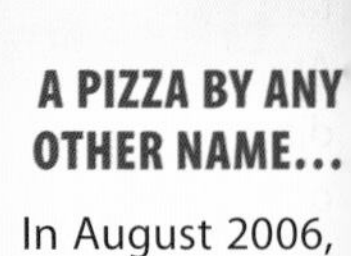

A PIZZA BY ANY OTHER NAME...

In August 2006, Iranian President Ahmadinejad publicized a presi dential order forbidding the use of Western words and expressions which had crept into the Persian language. The Persian Academy of Language has introduced more than 2,000 alternative words and expressions. The ne word for pizza is loosely translated as "flexible loaves of bread."

MOST EXPENSIVE CATTLE MEAT

John McLeod owns an Australian meat exporting company which produces the world's most expensive cow meat. For 60 days before being brought to the slaughterhouse, the cows are fed hay which has been soaked in Cabernet Merlot wine ($12 per bottle). While they eat their gourmet hay, the cows listen to classical music. Steaks from these cows sell for $90 a portion, or $164 per lb ($360 per kg). Demand for this meat is so high that McLeod can't keep up with it.

"Not by Bread Alone ..."

LARGEST CHEESE

At the 1964 World's Fair in New York, the Wisconsin Pavilion displayed the world's largest cheese. Using 16,000 cows to produce 170,000 quarts of milk, Wisconsin certainly had the ingredients required to produce a cheddar cheese which measured 14.5 x 6.5 x 5.5 ft (1.6 x 2 x 4.42 m) and weighed 34,591 lb (15,960 kg).

GREATEST CHEESE CONSUMERS

Greece is the greatest cheese consumer in the world. The average Greek consumes 62.8 lb (28.5 kg) of cheese every year, while the average Israeli eats 35.3 lb (16 kg) of cheese per year.

LARGEST SANDWICH

The world's largest sandwich was displayed in April 2004 in Zocalo Square in Mexico City, Mexico. The sandwich, prepared with mayonnaise, meat, and fresh lettuce, weighed 7,006 lb (3,178 kg). A sandwich this size can feed 31,780 children.

MOST POPULAR AND MOST DANGEROUS SWEETENER

The synthetic sweetener aspartame is the most common artificial sweetener in the world, as well as the unhealthiest. The most dangerous ingredient in aspartame is methanol alcohol. Eating too much aspartame can cause 75 different side effects. Among them are memory loss, headaches, dizziness, vomiting, sleeping and sight disorders, irregular heartbeats and problems with the nervous system, allergies, and asthma.

MOST DANGEROUS FOOD COLORS

In the purification process of coal there remains a black tar derivative which is used to produce benzene, carbolic acid, and naphthalene. These raw materials are used to make the most harmful food colors in the world—black, purple, blue, and bright colors such as yellow and red. What remains of the coal is used to tar roofs and pave roads.

The "azo" group color compounds are slightly less harmful. These are cheaper to produce and make up approximately half of all dyes used in food. They are comprised of nitrogen and nitrous acid.

MOST HARMFUL FOOD COLORING

The synthetic blue dye known as Brilliant E133 is derived from coal tar and can be combined with the synthetic orange-yellow dye tartrazine (E102) to produce various shades of green. The E133 dye is considered extremely unhealthy and has been known to be the cause of concentration problems and hyperactivity. It has been banned in many countries, among them Argentina, Bulgaria, Czechoslovakia, France, Italy, and Turkey.

Tartrazine is from the "azo" family of dyes and appears to cause the most allergic and intolerance reactions of all the "azo" dyes, particularly among asthmatics and those who can't use aspirin. It has been outlawed in Norway and Austria.

CHOPSTICKS

The fork and knife are virtually unknown in many Far Eastern countries. The Japanese, the Chinese, and the residents of other countries in the region eat everything, including rice, with chopsticks. These are simple sticks approximately 12 in. (30 cm) long. More than 25 million trees are chopped down each year in order to manufacture the 45 billion wooden chopsticks used by the Chinese people.

FIRST FORK

The fork was invented approximately 1,000 years ago. Forks were originally straight and two-tined and called "split spoons."

FIRST TIN CANS

In 1810, Peter Durand from Britain registered a patent on preserving food in tin cans. Two years later, in 1812, Thomas Kensett set up a small canning plant on the New York waterfront and began producing America's first hermetically sealed salmon, lobsters, oysters, meats, fruits and vegetables. The first cans were expensive, and the food inside them could be frighteningly poisonous. Moreover, they were so thick and heavy that they required ingenuity to open, using hammers, knives, chisels or rocks. The practice among American soldiers was to shoot them open.

Ermal Fraze from Kettering, OH (USA), came up with the idea of a ring on the top portion of the can for easy opening. In 1959, he invented what is known today as the flip-top can, originally called the pop-top can (or easy-open can).

Canning factory, 1904

FIRST CAN OPENER

In 1858, 48 years after cans were invented, Ezra Warner of Waterbury, CT (USA), patented the first can opener. In 1866, J. Osterhoudt patented the tin can with a rotating key opener that you can still find on sardine cans. In 1930, the first electric can opener was unveiled.

EAT YOUR FOOD IN HAPPINESS (*Koheles* 9:7)

- Hashem fulfills the wishes of those who recite a blessing on their food and drink. (*Tikkunei Zohar* 18)
- When a person goes in the ways of Hashem, Hashem brings him closer. And because Hashem is pleased with him, he is able to derive great joy from eating his bread and drinking his wine. (Zohar, *Shemos* 29a)
- Food and drink bring joy and drive away sadness and worry. The happier a person is, the better he is able to think, as we find Yitzchak Avinu needing to eat before bestowing the blessing upon his son Yaakov. (Rabbeinu Bachya, *Bereishis* 1:21)

MOST COMMONLY USED OIL

The most popular oil contained in food the world over is sunflower seed oil. In Israel, however, the most commonly used oil is soybean oil, which on its own has almost no flavor and is therefore mainly used for cooking.

BIGGEST OLIVE OIL PRODUCER

The Mediterranean basin countries produce 99% of the world's olive oil. The largest manufacturers are Spain, Greece, and Italy. Israel has 81 mi^2 (52,000 acres or 210,000 dunams) of olive trees used for making oil, with an estimated annual yield of 7,000 tons — supplying only 66% of the country's annual consumption.

MOST EXPENSIVE COCKTAIL

Jay Malik from Manchester, England, has produced the world's most expensive cocktail, which costs $51,000 per glass. The ingredients of the cocktail are vintage champagne, aged cognac, and other valuable liquors. The astronomical price, however, is not due to the ingredients but rather to the way it is served. The cocktail stick is made of a 6.5 karat pink tourmaline gemstone, and instead of the usual green olive on the end of the stick is an 18 karat white gold ring set with a 2 karat diamond. The cocktail is served by a waiter accompanied by 2 armed security guards.

COFFEE CONSUMPTION

Finland leads the world in per capita coffee consumption — 26.4 lb (12 kg) of coffee drunk per year per person. Canada is ranked 11th, with 14.3 lb (6.5 kg) of coffee drunk per person per year. The United States is in 26th place (9.24 lb/4.2 kg) and Israel ranks 34th (8.36 lb/3.8 kg). Surprisingly, Italy and France, the countries most associated with coffee consumption and the "café society," rank only 15th (19.8 lb/5.9 kg) and 19th (11.88 lb/5.4 kg), respectively.

DID YOU KNOW?

During the hot summer days, ice consumption in Israel reaches 250 tons daily.

WATER AND ICE

Water is the only material in the universe which expands when frozen. The converse is also the case: ice is the only material whose volume is less when it is transformed into liquid.

MOST POPULAR DRINK

After water, the world's most popular drink is tea. Every year, 79 billion gal (300 trillion liters) of tea of all types and flavors are drunk throughout the world. Mineral water is next, at 42 billion gal (160 trillion liters) per year, followed by coffee at 26 billion gal (100 trillion liters).

MOST COMMON TEA

Black tea, popular in the United States, Europe, and North Africa, comprises 90% of all teas sold in the world. Green tea, which has a gold or bright green color, comprises slightly less than 10% of teas sold throughout the world. Both types of tea are made from leaves of a bush called Camellia sinensis. Black tea, however, undergoes an oxidizing process which changes the chemical balance and taste of the tea leaves. Green tea does not undergo any processing and therefore has a more delicate taste.

CAFFEINE

A cup of tea contains much less caffeine than a cup of coffee (see chart, below). Herbal tea is not made from tea leaves but rather from plants that are caffeine-free.

Caffeine is most commonly found in 60 types of plants, and it repels insects and parasites. It is found in high quantities in coffee beans, tea leaves, cocoa, cola nuts, and chocolate. For an adult, drinking approximately 3 mg of caffeine per day for every kg (2.2 lb) of body weight is considered reasonable and harmless.

Caffeine is absorbed quickly in the body, temporarily raising blood pressure and increasing heart rate. It also interferes with the body's absorption of iron. The effects of a cup of coffee can last 3 hours. However, the most significant effects begin 30 minutes after drinking.

Consumption of 600 mg of caffeine per day is considered poisonous, and can cause anxiety, headaches, quicker heart rate, restlessness, nervousness, overreactions and sleeplessness. The caffeine content of 72 cups of coffee is deadly.

CAFFEINE CONTENT IN 1 CUP (240 ML) OF DRINK
(Doesn't include special, "gourmet" coffees)

Drink	Caffeine content (mg)
Turkish Coffee	65+
Espresso	77
Filter Coffee	108–145
Instant Coffee	57
Decaffeinated Coffee	3–6
Tea	15–60
Decaffeinated Tea	1–4
Herbal Tea	0
Coca-Cola	35
Chocolate Milk	5

A 3.5 oz (100 gm) chocolate bar contains between 60 and 120 mg of caffeine.

FIRST TEA BAG

The first tea bag as we know it was invented in 1908 by Thomas Sullivan of New York.

BIGGEST TEA DRINKERS

The people of Ireland drink more tea than anyone else in the world. The average Irish citizen drinks an average 1,177 cups of tea per year, which is equivalent to 3.2 cups per day.

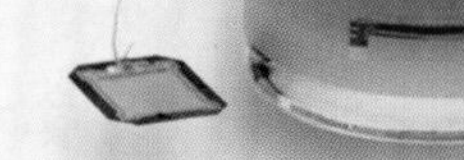

"Drink Sweet Beverages" (Nechemiah 8:10)

BEVERAGE OF KINGS

The Aztecs of Mexico believed that cocoa beans are a gift from Heaven which gives a person energy and wisdom. Thus, the scientific name for the cocoa tree—Theobroma—means "gift of G-d" in Latin.

The Spanish conqueror Hernando Cortez had visited the court of Emperor Montezuma in Mexico and was presented with a golden goblet of "*chocolatl*." Realizing he had stumbled across something amazing, Cortez sent a ship filled with cocoa beans and cocoa-making equipment back to Spain.

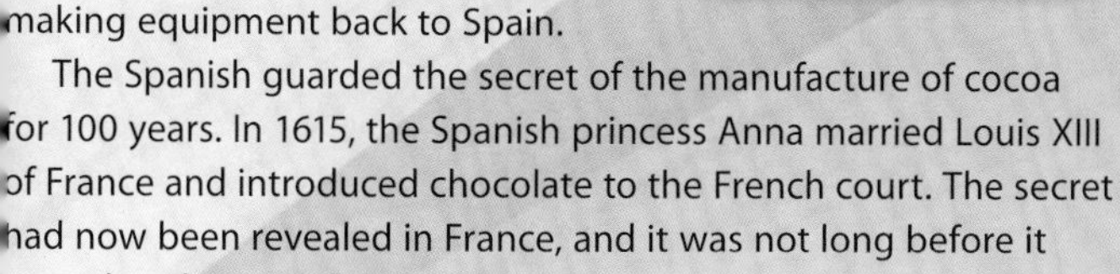

The Spanish guarded the secret of the manufacture of cocoa for 100 years. In 1615, the Spanish princess Anna married Louis XIII of France and introduced chocolate to the French court. The secret had now been revealed in France, and it was not long before it spread to the rest of the world.

Cocoa beans

In contrast to tea and coffee, the price of cocoa was quite high, mostly because of the miniscule amount that had been imported. Therefore, it was found mainly in the king's court and among the nobility.

BIGGEST MILKSHAKE

A number of milk-beverage manufacturers in the United States banded together in New York in August 2000 to prepare the world's largest milkshake — a 6,000 gal (22,700 liter) classic Black & White shake—the equivalent of 50,000 shakes! Ingredients included 4,270 gal (16,164 liters) of milk, 1,526 gal (5,776 liters) of ice cream, 67 gal (254 liters) of chocolate syrup, 67 gal (254 liters) of pure vanilla, and 70 gal (265 liters) of all-natural flavor (i.e., sugar, cocoa, stabilizers). The Black & White (vanilla with chocolate syrup) is the world's most popular milkshake flavor.

REWARD FOR PROVIDING DRINK FOR ANOTHER

R' Yochanan said: "So great is providing drinks to travelers [and so terrible is not offering drinks to them] that it distances those who are near, draws near those who are far; causes the sins of the wicked to be ignored, and causes the *Shechinah* to rest on the prophets of the Ba'al. Even unintentionally not providing for another is viewed as intentional."

"Distances those who are near" — This refers to Amon and Moav. They were living near the Jewish people, and yet it was decreed not to accept any of their converts because they did not offer food and drink to the Jewish people who entered their borders, as it is written, "Because they did not offer you bread and water on the way when you went out of Egypt" (*Devarim* 23:5).

"Draws near those who are far" — This refers to Yisro, who came from Midian. As a reward for having instructed his daughters, "Call him and let him eat some food" (*Shemos* 2:20), he merited that his descendants would convert and be members of the Sanhedrin which sat in the Beis HaMikdash.

"Causes the sins of the wicked to be ignored"—This refers to Michah. The smoke from his idol's altar would mix with the smoke from the altar at Shilo, which was only 3 *mil* (2.1 mi or 3.24 km) away. The angels wanted to move him, but Hashem instructed them not to harm him, for he offered his food to travelers.

"Causes the *Shechinah* to rest on the prophets of the Ba'al" — This refers to the prophet Ido's friend who lied and claimed to be a true prophet, but in fact he was a prophet of the Ba'al. In spite of this, as reward for giving Ido food and drink, he was able to receive the word of Hashem.

"Even unintentionally not providing for another is viewed as intentional" — When David fled from Shaul, Yehonasan forgot to give him food for his journey. Rav Yehudah says in the name of Rav, "If only Yehonasan had given David two loaves of bread for his journey when he fled from Shaul, the Kohanim of Nov would not have been killed, Doeg HaEdomi would not have been denied entry into the Next World, and Shaul and his three sons would not have been killed." (*Yalkut Shimoni, I Shmuel, remez* 130)

LAND FLOWING WITH MILK AND HONEY

Israel has the highest average yearly milk output per cow in the world — 3,078 gal (11,653 liters). In 2nd place is the United States, with an average of 2,634 gal (9,970 liters) per cow. The dairy beverage market in Israel is estimated at close to NIS 900 million. The milk for these drinks comes from the milking of 120,000 cows, which produce a total of 333 million gal (1.26 billion liters) of milk per year.

MOST PRODUCTIVE COW

Kibbutz Tze'elim are the proud owners of Gina, the cow holding the world record for milk production. Between the years 1989 and 2003, Gina produced a total of 44,006 gal (166,572 liters) of milk, an average annual output of 3,143 gal (11,898 liters) of milk.

HIGHEST MILK PRODUCTION

The 91.1 million tons of milk produced yearly make India the highest milk-producing nation in the world.

Chateau d'Yquem wine

MOST EXPENSIVE WINE

The most expensive commercially sold wine is the French white wine Chateau d'Yquem from the Sauternes-Gironde region made in 1787. The price of a bottle fluctuates between $56,000 and $64,000. This wine is the sweetest in the world and is made of a mixture of 80% Semillon grapes and 20% sauvignon blanc.

WHITE WINE FROM RED GRAPES

White wine can be manufactured from red grapes. In order to make white wine, it is necessary to separate the skins from the grapes before the fermentation process. The skin is what gives the wine color, taste, and fragrance. White wine from very dark grapes whose skin has been removed may have a pink tint. This type of wine is called "blush."

BIGGEST WINE CONSUMERS

More wine is drunk per capita in Luxembourg than in any other country in the world — with the average person drinking 20 gal (75.5 liters) per year. This is followed by Italy with 14 gal (53 liters), then France with 13.4 gal (50.6 liters). The United States trails far behind, at 2.2 gal (8.3 liters).

Apart from the Moslem states that forbid the drinking of wine, the annual wine consumption of the average Israeli is among the lowest in the world, at 1.85 gal (7 liters).

LOWEST WINE CONSUMPTION PER CAPITA

The lowest annual wine consumption per capita is found in Egypt, where the average person drinks only two spoonfuls of wine per year.

DOES WINE REALLY BRING JOY?

A blood-alcohol concentration of 0.1% will lift a person's spirits and give him self-confidence. However, his ability to concentrate will drop, his reaction time will increase, his reflexes will weaken, and even under this slight influence of alcohol his tongue will "loosen" and he will become very talkative.

When the blood-alcohol concentration reaches 0.2%, coordination decreases, vision becomes blurred, self-control continues to weaken which can lead to violent outbursts, and there is a feeling of heaviness and tiredness.

When the concentration reaches 0.3%, it becomes difficult to walk or even to stand up straight, the ability to express oneself becomes difficult, the person can feel dizzy or nauseous, and he might throw up.

At a 0.4% blood-alcohol concentration, the drunkard becomes apathetic, ceases to react and becomes oblivious to his surroundings. It is at this point that the situation can be life-threatening. A high concentration of alcohol can directly affect the brainstem, which controls the respiratory system and the heart rate.

A concentration of 0.5% can cause a person to lose consciousness. Body temperature will drop, and a person will lose control over basic bodily functions.

Alcohol depresses the activity of the hormone ADH and causes dehydration.

UNTIL THE EFFECTS OF WINE HAVE WORN OFF

The liver breaks down approximately 90% of the body's alcohol intake. About 5% is broken down by the kidneys and the other 5% is exhaled. The "breathalyzer test used by the police measures the concentration of alcohol in a person's exhaled breath. This can determine the percentage of alcohol in the bloodstream.

The rate at which alcohol leaves the bo is approximately 0.5 oz (15 ml) per hour. Th means that an entire hour is required for t body to rid itself of the amount of alcohol found in 1 cup of beer (4%), and 2 hours ir order to rid itself of the alcohol content of glass of wine (12%).

Alcohol has a stronger effect on wome than on men because women naturally ha less of the special enzyme that breaks dow alcohol and eliminates drunkenness.

FIRST DIET DRINK

The first diet carbonated soft drink was invented in 1952. The drink, ginger ale, wa manufactured by the Kirsch company of Brooklyn, NY. The drink, originally named "No-cal beverage," was produced for the benefit of those suffering from diabetes.

FIRST CANS

The first cans were invented in 1957 and slowly began replacing glass bottles in th sale of carbonated drinks. Five years later, in 1962, flip-top cans for easy opening we invented. The use of plastic bottles for drinks began in 1970.

FIRST DRINKING STRAW

The first straws were made by the Sumerians living in Aram Naharayim and were used for drinking beer and oth fermented drinks (in order to avoid the solid byproducts of fermentatic These earliest drinking straws were hollow stems of rye-grass—literally made of straw.

The modern straw as we know it was invented in 1888 by Marvin Sto It was simply a spool of paper for which he registered a patent. After numerous experiments, Stone came to the conclusi that the ideal straw is 8.5 in. (21.5 cm) lon and must be narrow enough to prevent lemon seeds from passing through it.

"Drink Sweet Beverages"

THE INVENTION OF COCA-COLA

John Pemberton, a pharmacist from Atlanta, GA (USA), registered a patent in 1885 for a drink called French Wine Coca. It was advertised as the perfect stimulant for nerves and energy. The drink contained a small amount of cocaine and a bit of wine. A year later, Pemberton removed the wine and added caffeine as well as the abstract of the cola nut, which has a bitter taste.

Pemberton's partner renamed the drink Coca-Cola, thinking that two words beginning with the same letter would be attractive advertising. At first the drink was marketed by traveling salesmen as medication against headaches, nausea, and stomachaches. The original color of Coca-Cola was green.

The 1st Coca-Cola bottle

COCA-COLA AND THE UNITED STATES

Coca-Cola is such an American icon that countries that break their diplomatic ties with the United States will immediately evict the American ambassador as well as close down all Coca-Cola plants. During the period of the Arab boycott against Israel in 1951, many Coca-Cola plants in Arab countries were shut down. In Iraq, the local producer of Coca-Cola was publicly hanged in the market square.

MOST SOLD SOFT DRINK

Coca-Cola is the most well-known brand name product in the world. More than 6 billion people, 94% of the world population including those who live in remote villages, have heard of the drink.

Every second, millions of people throughout the world are drinking more than 9,600 bottles of different forms of Coca-Cola which are produced in 1,500 factories in 200 countries. The daily consumption of Coca-Cola exceeds 773 million cups and bottles, amounting to approximately 51 million gal (193 million liters). If all the bottles of Coca-Cola ever sold were placed side by side, they would encircle the earth 20,051 times.

SOFT DRINKS IN SPACE

NASA has decided to include Coca-Cola as part of the astronauts' menu on the space shuttles. The Coca-Cola company invested $250,000 in developing a special canteen which is connected to the astronauts' space suits.

GREATEST BEER DRINKERS

In Czechoslovakia, the average person drinks 41 gal (154 liters) of beer per year — the largest per capita beer consumption in the world. Ireland comes in second place at 32 gal (120 liters) per person, followed by England at 26 gal (100 liters) per person, and the United States at 22.5 gal (85 liters). Far behind is Israel, where the average person drinks only 3.6 gal (13.5 liters) of beer per year.

It is estimated that at any moment, 0.7% of the world population is drunk.

MOST WIDELY SOLD BEER IN ISRAEL

Goldstar is Israel's most popular beer, with approximately 30 million bottles sold annually. Goldstar was also the first beer produced in Israel for commercial use. Sales began in 1950, and the traditional recipe has not changed in the past 50 years.

PRAISE FOR THE FRUITS OF ERETZ YISRAEL

In a place called Shichin, a mustard root produced three branches. The workers who guarded the field cut one of these branches to serve as a roof for their hut. Within this branch they found 3 *kavin* (a very significant amount) of mustard.

"I had mustard growing in my yard," said R' Shimon ben Chalafta, "and I could climb as high on it as one climbs a fig tree."

Once they brought 2 radishes to Rabbi Yehudah HaNasi which had grown in the 10 days between Rosh Hashanah and Yom Kippur. They were the size of a camel-load.

Another person planted turnips. They grew so quickly that as he finished planting, he was able to pick the freshly grown turnips and take them to the market to be sold.

(*Talmud Yerushalmi, Pe'ah* 7)

Rami bar Yechezkel traveled to Bnei Brak. He saw goats eating under the fig trees. Fig honey dripped from the figs while milk dripped from the goats, and the 2 mixed together. He said, "This is literally 'a land flowing with milk and honey.'"

Rav Yaakov ben Dostai said, "From Lod until Ono is a distance of 3 *mil* (2.1 mi or 3.24 km). Once I left before dawn and I walked in fig honey up to my ankles." (*Kesubos* 111b)

Why is Eretz Yisrael compared to a deer? To tell you that just as the deer are fastest of all animals, Eretz Yisrael is the fastest of all lands in causing its fruits to ripen. Does this mean that just as the deer's… meat is not fatty, so too Eretz Yisrael's… fruit is not rich? Therefore, the verse states, "Flowing with milk and honey": richer than milk and sweeter than honey. (*Kesubos* 112a)

Breadfruit tree

Heaviest jackfruit

LARGEST FRUIT

The largest edible fruit is the jackfruit, from the breadfruit family. The average jackfruit grows on the trunk of the tree or on one of its branches and weighs between 22 and 55 lb (10–25 kg). The larger ones can weigh as much as 132 lb (60 kg) each.

Jackfruit is very prevalent in India, where the main consumers are poor people. It is found in Southeast Asia, the tropical South American countries, and has even made its way to Hawaii.

MOST POPULAR PRODUCE

Tomatoes are sold more than any other produce—60 million tons from almost 10,000 different varieties every year. Next highest is banana (44 million tons sold per year), followed by apples (36 million tons), oranges (34 million tons), and watermelon (22 million tons).

LONGEST AND HEAVIEST CARROTS

John Evans from Palmer, AK (USA), located 40 mi (64 km) north of Anchorage, grew the world's heaviest carrot in 1998 — 18.985 lb (8.6 kg). In 2007, Joe Atherton from Nottinghamshire, England, grew the world's longest carrot — 19 ft, 1.96 in. (5.841 m).

LARGEST MARROW

The world's largest marrow (also known as summer squash), grown by Ken Dade from Norfolk, England, weighed 113 lb (65 kg) and required 2 men to carry it to a stand at the National Amateur Gardening Show in Somerset.

GIGANTIC PUMPKIN

Grown in Rhode Island (USA) by Joe Jutras from North Scituate, the world's biggest pumpkin was shown at the Topsfield Fair of Massachusetts in 2007, weighing 1,689 lb (766 kg). This surpassed the previous world record by 187 lb (85 kg).

CHAMPION OF THE CRUCIFERAE

John Evans is the proud holder of 7 world records for giant vegetables. Besides the carrot mentioned above, he has held the record for the heaviest of the following cruciferous vegetables:

Green cabbage — 76 lb (34.4 kg); 1998
Cauliflower — 31.25 lb (14.1 kg); 1997
Broccoli — 35 lb (15.8 kg); 1993

LARGEST/HEAVIEST VEGETABLES

Here are some other world-record vegetables:

VEGETABLE	WEIGHT/ LENGTH	GROWER AND COUNTRY
Cucumber	36.1 in. (91.7 cm)	Alf Cobb England
Lemon	11 lb, 9.7 oz (5.265 kg)	Aharon Shmuel Kfar Zeitim, Israel
Potato	24.9 lb (11.3 kg)	Khalil Semhat Tyre, Lebanon
Tomato	7 lb, 12 oz (3.51 kg)	Gordon Graham United States
Watermelon	268.8 lb (121.9 kg)	Lloyd Bright United States

Fruit of the Land

MOST EXPENSIVE WATERMELON

One of the main problems people have with watermelons is how to store the large, round-shaped fruit in the refrigerator. In the late 1980s, farmers from Zentsuji in Kagawa, Japan, invented a cube-shaped watermelon which could be easily packed and stored. They began growing watermelons in glass boxes and the fruits assumed the square shape of the box. These watermelons are available all over Japan, proudly displayed with a party ribbon tied to the stalk. The main drawback of these watermelons is their price, which ranges from $137 to $202 per watermelon.

LARGEST APPLE CONSUMERS

Israel holds 1st place in apple consumption per capita. At the height of the apple season, Israelis eat 2 million apples daily. During the month of Tishrei, mainly on Rosh Hashanah, Israelis consume a total of 14,000 tons of apples. Apple orchards are spread over 45,000 dunams (11,120 acres, or about 17 mi^2) of land, with 90% of Israel's apples being grown in the Galil and Golan regions. In addition, approximately 85,000 tons of apples are stored in temperature-controlled environments, which allows them to be sold the entire year.

LARGEST STUFFED CABBAGE

The largest stuffed cabbage was made by Chef Lazar Kovacs of Hajduboesoerrmen, Hungary, and measured 944.9 ft (288 m).

BAL TASHCHIS

The village of Bunyol is located half an hour's drive from Valencia, Spain. Its claim to fame is the tomato fight which marks the end of the annual La Tomatina festival, and which takes place in the streets of the city.

On the last Wednesday of August, many dignified and respectable adults gather together with mischievous youth and tens of thousands of tourists from all over the world. They all become infected by the city's frivolous mood and they spend the day from 11:00 in the morning until 1:00 the next morning (14 hours!) throwing tomatoes at each other. The tomato fest's security force insists that tomatoes be squashed before being flung at someone, in order to avoid injury. Police are on hand to keep order and make sure safety instructions are followed in the juicy red streets. Since 1975, the festival has been run by a commercial company which, among other things, supplies participants with 330,690 lb (150,000 kg) of fresh tomatoes.

The annual tomato fight began on a hot August day in 1945. On the day of the annual parade, a group of irritated youngsters began to "boo" the performers and a skirmish broke out. Groups of young people began throwing things at each other. They grabbed vegetables from the agricultural stands lining the street. Soft and ripe tomatoes were the most popular throwing item, and from then on the village decided to make the tomato fight into an annual event.

DID YOU KNOW?

There are 7,500 different types of apples in the world, among them the Rome Beauty, Granny Smith, Pink Lady, Early Strawberry, and Fall Wine. The foliage of an apple tree gathers sunlight and converts the energy of sunlight into nutrients for the tree, which nourishes the growing fruit. This is just one more wondrous example of Hashem's kindness.

DID YOU KNOW?

A French botanist named Tournefort provided the tomato with the Latin botanical name, *Lycopersicon esculentum,* which translates to "wolf peach" — peach because it was round and luscious, and wolf because it was erroneously thought to be poisonous.

MOST EXPENSIVE SEEDS

The Hazera Genetics company in Israel has developed a strand of yellow cherry tomatoes known as Summer Sun. This hybrid became a hit in Europe, where the seeds sell for about $160,000 a pound ($350,000/kg). With that sum of money, one could purchase 35 lb (16 kg) of gold—and there would still be money left over.

Ten grams (0.35 oz) of seeds are required to sow 1 dunam (¼ acre) of Summer Sun tomatoes, which in turn produces 6 tons of the vegetable. An experienced farmer can grow 44 lb (20 kg) of produce, on average, from a single seed. The Summer Sun, which contains about 3 times the sugar level of ordinary tomatoes—making it literally as sweet as honey—is sold in Europe for about $12 per lb (about $25 per kilo). The company sells only 4.4 lb (2 kg) of Summer Sun tomato seeds per year, mainly to French farmers.

FRUIT SPREAD

The Black Sapote fruit, known as the chocolate pudding fruit, is from Colombia, South America. This black fruit, which is extremely sweet, can be spread on a slice of bread in the same manner as peanut butter or eaten with a spoon the way you'd eat chocolate pudding or ice cream.

MOST WATER-LADEN FRUIT

Cucumbers contain 98% water—more than any other fruit or vegetable. Watermelons, lettuce, and tomatoes are comprised of 95% water.

DRIEST FRUITS

Legumes are the driest produce, containing only between 5 and 15% water.

MOST INTOXICATING FRUIT

The African Marula tree, which can grow up to 49 ft (15 m) high, produces 2 tons of fruit each season. The marula fruit is approximately the size of an apricot. It has a fibrous texture, a sour flavor, and a very large pit. At the height of the African summer in February, the fruit ripens and gives off a very strong scent, which can be smelled great distances away. Elephants, giraffes, antelopes, monkeys, and other grass eaters and rodents are attracted to the smell.

The elephant herd captures the marula grove for itself and forcefully drives away all other animals. The elephants then butt the tree with their foreheads, which knocks down the ripe fruits. As the fruits hit the ground, the yellow peel splits open. This begins a natural process of fermentation which produces alcohol.

Elephants, who as we know have very good memories, remember that it is worth their while to wait. They therefore guard the fallen marula fruit during the three-week fermentation period. Following fermentation (which usually occurs in March — around Purim time!), the elephants begin eating the fruit, which contains 3% alcohol (equivalent to the average beer).

For those of you who are unaware, elephants are not in the habit of drinking beer on a regular basis. Eating the fruit therefore makes them confused. They cannot walk straight and they bump into each other and fall down. At times the elephants become violent and aggressive the way drunkards do. At a certain point they are unable to guard their precious marula trees, and this allows other animals to join the party.

DRUNK, BUT NOT FROM WINE

Sometimes when a bird eats a bit too many grapes, it becomes drunk. Grapes contain very small amounts of yeast which naturally ferments in the bird's stomach, producing alcohol. This causes the bird to become intoxicated, and it cannot fly straight.

WORLD RECORD FOR COTTON PRODUCTIO

Israelis Yagev Kilman of the Zabar-Kama Field Crop Cooperative and Gil Gershowitz of Kibbutz Dan set a world record by growing 540 lb (240 kg) of cotton fiber per dunam (a dunam is a quarter of an acre, or 10,764 ft^2/1,000 m^2) — 3.5 times greate than the world average, which is 154 lb (70 kg). This was achieved using unique hybrid cotton known as Acalpi, which was developed by the Israeli Hazera Genetics Company. This cotton combines record high yields with high-quality fiber, and is especially suitable for regions where long-fiber cotton is difficult to grow.

WORLD RECORD FOR TREE PLANTING

Forests throughout the world are rapidly being cut down in order to make room fo building cities, to sell trees for industry, an to create energy. Israel is the only country in the world that has entered the 21st century with an increase in its number of tree A large percentage of the forests were planted by the Jewish National Fund (KKL) with more than 200 million trees having been planted since 1950. The forests serve a variety of purposes — improving the environment, "green lungs," creating rest, recreation and vacation spots, providing trees for industry, and improving areas of animal-grazing.

Fruit of the Land

URIAN FRUIT

he durian is undoubtedly the fruit about vhich you will find the most differing and xtreme opinions. The Asians, who love it, efer to it as the King of Fruit, while Westrners cannot tolerate its terrible smell. ts chemical makeup changes depending n how ripe it is, and its odor can be deected miles away. Travel and food writer ichard Sterling wrote, "Its odor is best lescribed as bird droppings, turpentine nd onions, garnished with gym sock." On the other and, the 19th-century British aturalist Alfred Russel Vallace famously described ts flesh as "A rich, butterke custard highly flavored with almonds, but intermingled with wafts of flavor that call to mind cream cheese, onion sauce, brown sherry and other incongruities. The more you eat of it, the less you feel inclined to stop."

Durian is also one of the world's most expensive fruits. The price depends on where it is grown, its shape, its size (it can weigh as much as 11 lb/5 kg), its ripeness, and its taste. The price can fluctuate between $1.15 and $22.75 per lb ($2.50 and $50 per kg).

Despite its popularity in many East Asian countries, in Singapore, it is forbidden to bring durian fruit into trains, buses, and other public areas. There are signs explicitly stating this.

No smoking
Fine $1000
No eating and drinking
Fine $500
No flammable goods
Fine $5000
No durians

Durian fruit

LARGEST COLLECTION OF USEFUL PLANTS

Moshe Wallach's orchard contains the largest variety of fruit trees in the world. Located in Israel, at Kibbutz Ein Shemer between Hadera and Afula, he grows more than 300 different types of fruits. Exotic fruit trees are seen alongside Israeli fruit trees. He also has citrus trees, subtropical fruit trees, and spice and medicinal plants from all over the world.

None of the trees are a result of *kilayim*; rather, every tree and plant is precisely the way Hashem created it. Among the unusual trees in the orchard is the "miracle berry," which after it is eaten causes everything else that is eaten during the next four hours to taste sweet.

Wallach also has an unusual type of *esrog* known as the "finger citron (*esrog*)," which is shaped like the palm of a hand with many fingers. It can be used to make jam, but cannot be used as one of the *arba'as haminim* on the holiday of Sukkos. There is also a fruit which tastes like peanut butter, the Peruvian ground cherry (Cape gooseberry), a huge pitanga fruit, guavas without seeds, red annona fruits, and much more.

DID YOU KNOW?

Every year about 150 people are killed by a coconut falling on their head.

Inga

Finger citron

Red annona

FIRST ICE CREAM

It is told that 2,200 years ago, Alexander the Great ate ice mixed with honey and nectar for desert. Some 1,900 years ago, the cruel Emperor Nero of Rome is said to have sent teams of runners (slaves) to the mountains to bring snow and ice to cool the fruit drinks he was fond of.

The first ice cream store opened in New York City in 1776.

FIRST ICE CREAM MACHINE

In 1843, housewife Nancy Johnson invented a hand-cranked freezer that established the basic method of making ice cream still used today. In 1851, Jacob Fussell turned his milk dairy into a very successful ice cream factory. Fussell is considered the father of ice cream, one of America's national foods.

FIRST ICE CREAM IN ISRAEL

Fridle (Pedya) and Bracha Feldman, owners of the Feldman Ice Cream Company, began producing ice cream in 1945 during the period of the British Mandate. The ice cream was originally made to be served on top of cakes in the famous Kapulsky café in Rehovot. However, soon everyone wanted Feldman's ice cream. In 1963, their factory was established in Rehovot's industrial area.

FIRST ICE CREAM FACTORY IN ISRAEL

Israel's first ice cream factory was established by the Strauss dairy company. In 1936, the Strauss family, German-Jewish immigrants who moved to Nahariya at the time of the British Mandate, set up a small dairy farm. When she saw that the milking business was not successful, Hilda Strauss began making cheese, which did prove successful. In 1950, she introduced her first line of ice cream.

LARGEST ICE CREAM FACTORY IN ISRAEL

Strauss is Israel's largest ice cream company, with 50% of the country's ice cream sales — an NIS 800 million industry. The huge international company Nestlé enjoys 40% of the Israeli ice cream sales, while the remaining 10% is divided among smaller companies.

A MONTH OF ICE CREAM

In 1984, American president Ronald Reagan announced that the month of July would hereby be "National Ice Cream Month." He suggested that loyal and patriotic Americans should observe the month with "appropriate ceremonies and activities."

FIRST ICE CREAM CONE

It is not clear who invented the ice cream cone. Some say it was invented in New York in 1896 by Italian immigrant Italo Marchiony. Others consider the first waffle used as an ice cream cone as the first cone. In 1904, Syrian immigrant Ernest Hamwi sold hot waffles at the World's Fair in St. Louis, MO (USA), next to ice cream vendor Charles Manches. When Manches ran out of serving cups, Hamwi rolled his waffle into a cone shape, and produced an ice cream cone. It was only 18 years later, in 1922, that the ice cream stick was invented.

MOST POPULAR ICE CREAM FLAVOR

Vanilla is the world's most popular flavor of ice cream, with 26% of the ice cream sold throughout the world being vanilla-flavored. Next comes chocolate at 13%, followed by strawberry at 4.8%. Among Israelis the most popular ice cream flavor is chocolate.

UNUSUAL ICE CREAM FLAVORS

There's really no accounting for taste. The following unusual flavors are eaten by ice cream lovers around the world: avocado, garlic, smoked salmon, tomato, cucumber, bean, pumpkin, corn, mushroom, Rockford cheese, pickle, and even chili pepper.

ICE CREAM CONSUMPTION

As with many food records, the United States ranks first among ice cream consumers. The average American eats 5.8 gal (22 liters) of ice cream per year. The average European eats 4 gal (15 liters), while in Israel the average is only 2.64 gal (10 liters).

HOW TO MAKE REAL POPSICLES

When a cup of juice is frozen, the bottom portion becomes a mass of sweet, solid ice, which is not at all like a Popsicle. The secret to making a real Popsicle is to add Jell-O (gelatin) powder to the liquid, half the amount required for making Jell-O. The powder uniformly spreads the ingredients and keeps the Popsicle frozen. Enjoy!

By the way, researchers have found that the Popsicles we buy take 142 licks to finish.

Fridle (Pedya) Feldman

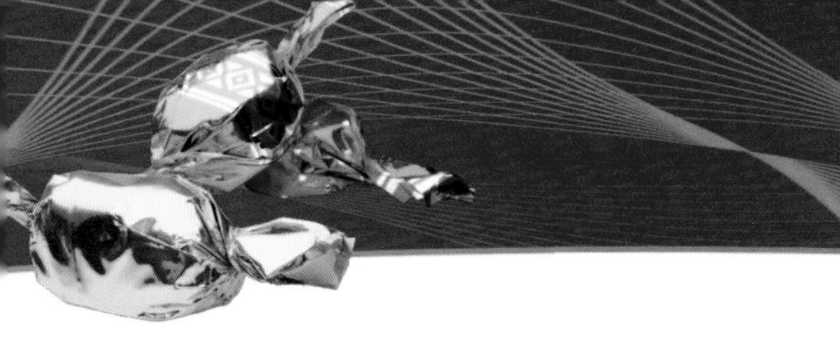

"His Palate Is Sweet" (Shir HaShirim 5:16)

LARGEST PUMPKIN PIE

The world's largest pumpkin pie, assembled in Windsor, CA (USA), in 2005, took 6 hours to bake and 5 hours to cool off. It measured 12 ft (3.65 m) in diameter and weighed 2,020 lb (916.3 kg).

LARGEST GUMMY BEAR

A record-breaking Gummy Bear was created in 1999 in Hagenow, Germany. It weighed in at 1,395 lb (632.7 kg) and was 5.5 ft (17 m) tall.

MOST POPULAR SNACK FOOD IN ISRAEL

Bamba, manufactured by Osem, is Israel's most popular snack. Every minute there are 450 bags of Bamba produced, which amounts to 27,000 per hour. Every 4th snack sold in Israel is a bag of Bamba.

The original Bamba was a cheese-flavored snack brought from the United States in 1964, but it didn't sell well. Before closing down the business, the company experimented with coating the Bamba with peanut butter, which resulted in immediate success.

To manufacture Bamba, large quantities of crushed corn are compressed, heated, and pushed through a cylindrical mold. They are then cut into pieces and coated with peanut butter.

OLDEST SNACK

The oldest known snack is popcorn which, of course, is made from popped corn. It was invented a few thousand years ago by the native peoples of the Americas.

MOST POPULAR SNACK

Popcorn is the world's most popular snack, largely due to its low price. In order to prepare popcorn, all that is needed is a handful of low-priced seeds, a bit of heat, oil and salt.

Popcorn became popular as a snack among poor people during the Great Depression (1929–1939). During World War II when the entire world was suffering from a sugar shortage, which caused snack prices to skyrocket, popcorn consumption tripled.

WHY DOES CORN POP AND TURN INTO POPCORN?

When vegetable seeds are heated up, their water molecules begin to "dance" with full energy in all directions, until they quietly and easily evaporate. A popcorn kernel, however, is covered with a strong and impermeable peel which traps the vapor, and therefore the molecules continue to dance. The pressure from the built-up steam finally causes the kernel to pop with a loud noise. This allows the steam to escape, dragging with it that white fluffy starch. The hard yellow material inside the popcorn is what remains of the peel.

There is also a special popper that can pop walnuts and grains of rice.

LARGEST LOLLIPOP

On August 27, 2009, Ashrita Furman of New York unveiled the world's largest lollipop. It weighed 6,706 lb (3,041 kg) and was 10 ft (3 m) in diameter and 10 in. (25 cm) thick. The huge red candy was made of sugar and corn syrup, which was melted in 100-gal (380 liter) pots. With the stick it is 25 ft (7.50 m) high.

SWEETER THAN HONEY

England is the largest consumer of sweet snacks in the world, with the average citizen consuming 34 lb (15.5 kg) of snacks per year.

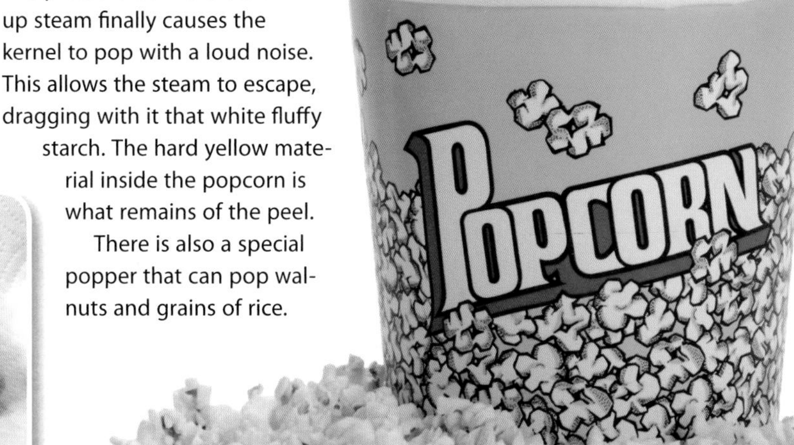

FIRST CHOCOLATE

In 1828, a Dutch chemist named Conrad Van Houten discovered the process of transforming cocoa into something resembling chocolate as we know it. The first modern chocolate bar was invented in 1847 by Englishman Joseph Fry, who patented the process. Daniel Peter of Vevey, Switzerland, invented the first milk chocolate in 1875. Using milk powder invented by fellow-countryman Henry Nestlé, the two of them went into partnership and created the Nestlé company, which grew to become the largest food manufacturing company in the world. In 1879, another Swiss man named Rudolph Lindt revolutionized chocolate-making by developing a process called "conching."

CHOCOLATE IN OUTER SPACE

Chocolate, mainly the dark and bitter variety, is considered an energy-rich food and is an essential component of the diet of soldiers on the battlefield, as well as an item on the spaceship menu of the NASA astronauts. Chocolate contains fats, carbohydrates, proteins, minerals (mainly iron, calcium, and magnesium), vitamins (mainly B_2 and riboflavin). Dark chocolate is also rich in antioxidants, which positively affects the immune system, the heart, and blood pressure. Antioxidants also help prevent clotting and ease tension.

MOST EXPENSIVE CHOCOLATE

Danish born Fritz Knipschildt, who in 1999 founded Knipschildt Chocolatier in South Norwalk, CT (USA), makes the most expensive chocolate in the world. The "Madeleine" is a handmade, 1.5 oz (40 gm) chocolate ball that sells for $250 and must be ordered in advance.

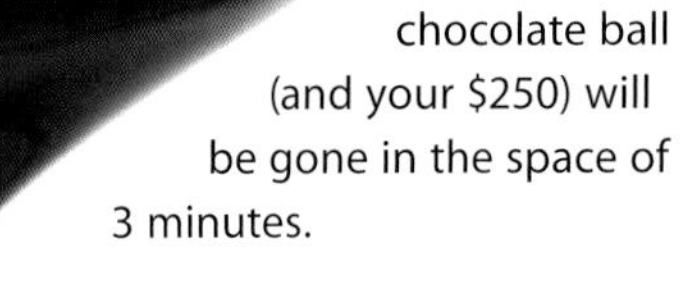

The Madeleine contains a creamy truffle ganache made from French Valrhona chocolate blended with fresh cream infused with vanilla pods and pure Italian truffle oil. Each chocolate is delivered with a personally signed card explaining how it was made and bearing a unique serial number.

If you can hold out and eat slowly, your chocolate ball (and your $250) will be gone in the space of 3 minutes.

FIRST CHOCOLATE IN ISRAEL

Elite's first product, known as "Shamnonit" chocolate, was introduced to Israel in 1934. It eventually became known as "Cow Chocolate" or "Red Cow" due to the cow shape stamped into the bar, even though these names never appeared on the wrapping and the cow in the picture is not even red — it is set in a red background. During the period of "austerity" in Israel (1949–1959), Shamnonit chocolate remained one of the food vouchers distributed to citizens. Nowadays, Elite's "Cow Chocolate" makes up 63.2% of the Israeli chocolate market. In other words, out of every 10 chocolate bars sold in Israel, more than 6 of them are the Elite cow.

Cocoa beans

LARGEST CHOCOLATE CONSUMERS

The Swiss eat more chocolate than anyone else in the world. The average Swiss citizen eats close to 22 lb (10 kg) of chocolate per year. The average western European eats 15.4 lb (7 kg), the average American eats 11 lb (5 kg), while the average Israeli eats only 6.6 lb (3 kg) of chocolate per year. Chocolate is an $80 billion per year industry which is controlled mainly by a few large international companies.

DID YOU KNOW?

In one of Mozart's operas, *Così Fan Tutte*, there is an aria that mentions chocolate. Perhaps it is for this reason that chocolate companies call their higher quality pralines by his name and have his picture on the wrapper. However, there really is a special Mozart chocolate. The original "Mozartkugeln" (Mozart ball) was invented by candy maker Paul Fürst in Salzburg, Austria, in 1890. The Fürst Company still sells these handmade chocolates using the original recipe.

"His Palate Is Sweet"

ARGEST HERSHEY'S KISS

he largest Hershey's Kiss was con-
ructed in Hershey, PA (USA) in 2007
nd required over 3 mi (5 km) of foil to
over. The Hershey's Kiss weighed
0,450 lb (13,812 kg), had a 7 ft (2.13 m)
ng plume, was 12 ft (3.65 m) high and
2 ft (3.65 m) wide.

OW COTTON CANDY IS MADE

e machine used to make cotton candy nsists of a small bowl within a larger owl. Sugar is poured into the small bowl d food coloring is added. The sugar owl is spun at high speed, while heat-s near the edge melt the sugar, which squeezed out through tiny holes by ntrifugal force. The sugar then solidi-s in the air and is caught in the large owl surrounding the sugar bowl. A stick, ne, or even hands may be twirled to ther the sugar strands.

During the Middle Ages, sugar was nsidered a luxury and therefore sold r 9 times the price of milk.

EARLIEST SOURCES FOR GUM

"One may not chew *matztichi* (similar to the modern Hebrew word for gum — *mastic*) or rub one's teeth with it for healing purposes on Shabbos, but it is permitted to do so if one wants to get rid of a bad odor in his mouth" (*Shulchan Aruch, Orach Chaim* 328:36). The *Magen Avraham* explains that *matztichi* is a resin which is used in the manufacture of tar, while the *Mishnah Berurah* adds that it is a type of resin with a pleasant scent.

FIRST COMMERCIAL GUM

Chicle-resin, derived from Sapodilla trees grown in the forests of Mexico, is the predecessor to the chewing gum as we know it today. When Christopher Columbus landed on the shores of America he commented about the "strange" Indian custom of chewing chicle-resin. However, the story of modern chewing gum began in 1869 when Mexican dictator Antonio Lopez hired American Thomas Adams to find an inexpensive substitute for rubber used for the tires of wagons. After many failed experiments with chicle-resin, a moment before throwing out the useless, sticky rubber, Adams decided to try to market chewable rubber without even adding any scent or flavor. His success was immediate. Nowadays, there are more than 1,000 gum manufacturing companies.

TREAT MOST HARMFUL TO THE ENVIRONMENT

Gum is considered very harmful to the environment, as it sticks to sidewalks and streets and takes at least 5 years until it naturally decomposes. In England, the Environmental Protection Agency spent £150 million on cleaning the streets and public buildings from gum. Singapore law forbids importing gum, and those caught chewing it are punished with heavy fines.

COUNTRY THAT CHEWS THE MOST GUM

The average American citizen chews an average of 2.2. lb (1 kg) of gum per year, making the United States the leader in gum-chewing. Like many other treats, chewing gum was distributed all over the world during World War II, thanks to American soldiers. More than 150 billion sticks of gum were sent to American soldiers on the front lines in order to lessen their feeling of thirst. The soldiers found other uses for gum such as emergency sealants for leaks in the hydraulic system of tanks and other motor vehicles.

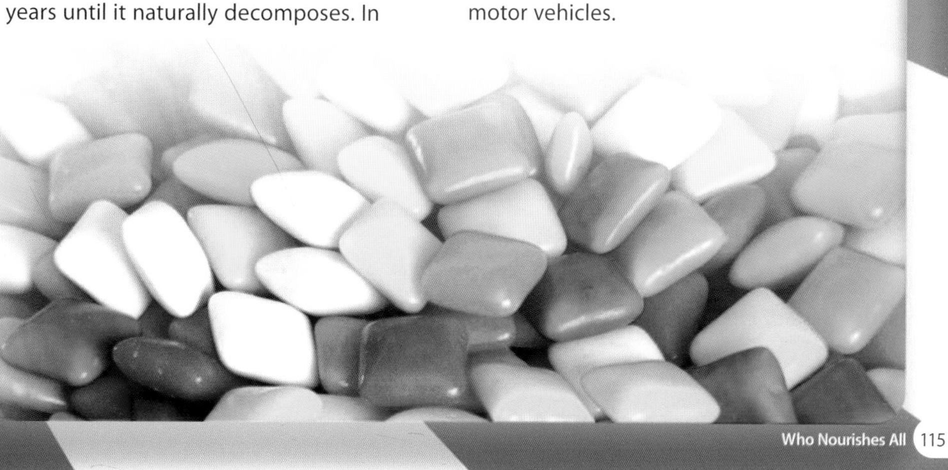

EATING MEAT SHORTENS LIFE

The Rambam tells us that the two most important things for being healthy are 1) not to overeat and 2) to exercise (*Hilchos De'os* 4:14–15). He also writes that the reason people in early generations lived for close to 1,000 years was because they did not eat meat — it was only after the Mabul (the Flood) that people were given permission to eat meat (see *Me'am Lo'ez, Bereishis*, vol. I, p. 199).

The Rambam prefers fowl to red meat, and suggests people choose non-fatty birds — not too young but not more than 2 years old. He also says that chicken soup has many healing properties. Chicken, pheasant, pigeon and turtledove are the healthiest, and waterfowl such as duck and geese are the least healthy.

In terms of red meat, Rambam says that the healthiest meat is from a kid or a 1-year-old lamb. Cow and adult goat and sheep are the least healthy. He says to stay away from fatty meat as well as meat that is aged and salted. In his opinion, the best cuts are the front part of the meat that is attached to the bone such as the shoulder, chest and ribs.

SEGULAH FOR A LONG LIFE

The saintly Reb Pinchas of Koritz said that overeating is the work of the *yetzer hara*. The more a person eats, the further he distances himself from Hashem. A person who overeats must learn to eat less, for while he is eating he is being judged Above. Rav Pinchas said that there are many animals which spend their entire lives eating and live for a very short time—some for not even half a year. However, a camel eats the least of all animals, and they can live as long as 80 years.

THE CALORIE

A calorie is the energy needed to increase the temperature of a gram of water by 1°C. The calorie unit listed on food products is actually a kilocalorie, or large calorie, and it is the energy required to raise 1 kg of water by 1 degree. In practice, the calorie is the amount of energy which a certain weight of food adds to a person's body.

HOW MANY CALORIES DO YOU BURN IN A DAY?

Basal metabolism is the amount of calories a person burns in a single day — without doing any activity whatsoever. To figure out basal metabolism, a man should multiply his body weight in kg by 1 and a woman by 0.9. This will be the average calories burned in 1 hour. For example, a man who weighs 70 kg will burn 70 calories per hour, while a woman will burn only 63. Now multiply this number by 24 (the hours in a day) to get your basal metabolism. In the above example, the man's basal metabolism is 1,680 calories per day, while the woman's is 1,512 calories.

A person who is awake burns 15% more calories above his basal metabolism (252 additional calories for a man: 1,680 + 252 = 1,932). A person studying in yeshiva who takes a half hour walk burns 50% more calories per day (1,680 + 840 = 2,520). A teacher who stands most of the day and also spends half an hour exercising burns 70% more calories (1,680 + 1,176 = 2,856). A man weighing 70 kg who is involved in hard physical activities can burn 3,220 calories per day.

COUNTRY RICHEST IN CALORIES

The average person consumes 3,000 calories daily. The country with the highest per capita caloric intake is the United States, where the average person consumes 3,754 calories per day. Israel is in 11th place, at 3,554 calories per day.

MOST NUTRITIOUS FOOD

Hashem in His kindness made many delicious and nutritious foods for us to eat and enjoy. There are countless opinions on what are the world's most healthy foods. Here is one list:

- Sea vegetables (seaweed): contain all 90 minerals known to exist (20–200% more than land vegetables), have high levels of vitamins C, D, K and B. Have more vitamin A than carrots.
- Cacao (chocolate bean): one of the highest antioxidant foods in the world. Has 10 times more magnesium and chromium than any other food.
- Quinoa: a grain (but not *chametz*). Has the highest nutritional profile of all grains. Has high levels of fiber and B vitamins, and all 8 essential amino acids. High in zinc, potassium, calcium, and vitamin E.
- Kale: a green leafy vegetable. Has high levels of chlorophyll, vitamins A, C and K, folate, potassium, magnesium, iron, lutein and phytochemicals. Great source of calcium, folic acid, vitamin B6, and manganese. High in fiber.
- Berries: very good for cleaning the body of waste and toxins. High in vitamins C and E, calcium, folic acid, phytochemicals, and fiber.

The New York Times listed the following foods as "must-eats":

- Beets
- Cabbage
- Swiss chard
- Cinnamon
- Pomegranate juice
- Prunes
- Pumpkin seeds
- Sardines
- Turmeric
- Blueberries
- Canned pumpkin

From the Fat of the Land

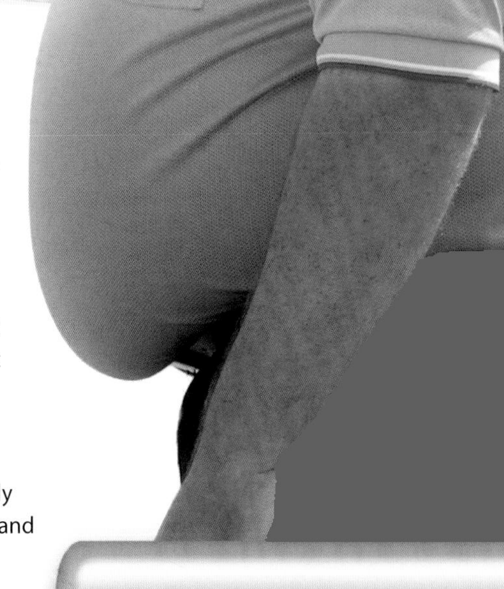

OST WASTEFUL FOOD

robably the least efficiently utilized food in the orld is beef. It takes great time and expense to raise ie animals, and even then only 50% of the animal is ctually eaten. Other parts of the animal are thrown vay. Cows around the world consume food con- ining enough calories to feed 8.7 billion people. y way of contrast, 300 million Americans consume od which could feed a billion people in poorer ountries.) If the American people would reduce their eat and poultry consumption by a mere 10%, the me resources could be used to produce more than 2 million tons of wheat. This could feed more than 5 million starving people for an entire year.

To raise a calf from birth to one year old, it must e fed approximately 5 million calories. However, ie meat produced from his slaughter supplies only 55,000 calories — which is just 5% of the amount iat he eats. This amounts to a loss of 95%. This without taking into account the costs of raising ie animal, shipping, and preparation of the final roduct.

The same area needed for raising animals, if used produce grains and vegetables, would yield 10 mes the amount of food.

ALORIES PRODUCED FROM A ONE DUNAM 0,764 FT²/1,000 M²) FIELD

ONE DUNAM	MILLIONS OF CALORIES
Cows for milk	250
Cattle for meat	86
Sheep for meat	77
Chickens laying eggs	158
Wheat	1,400
Peas	300
Potatoes	2,400

USCLE, FAT, AND AGE

uring its growing years, the body requires 50 alories per kg (2.2 lb) of body weight per day. The ecommended caloric intake for a 130 lb (59 kg), 15- ear-old boy is therefore approximately 2,950 per ay. When a person stops growing his needs drop, a 145 lb (66 kg), 20-year-old man who does light hysical activity requires only 30 calories per kg of ody weight — approximately 1,980 calories per day.

The biggest calorie consumers are the muscles. ne kg of muscle requires 100 calories per day, as pposed to 1 kg of fat which needs only 7 calories er day. Therefore, the lower a person's muscle eight, the fewer calories he requires.

From the age of 25, a person begins to lose iuscle weight at an average of 0.25 kg per muscle er year. Therefore, a person interested in watching is weight must lower his daily caloric intake by 250 alories every 10 years.

LEAST SATISFYING FOODS

A cucumber is the least nourishing of all fruits and vegetables. A cucumber weighing 3.5 oz (100 gm) contains only 12 calories. However, cucumbers are much easier to digest than celery, which contains only 19 calories per cup. The fact that the celery is more difficult to chew and digest means that it burns more calories than the amount it contributes to the body.

COST OF DIETING

The amount of money invested annually throughout the world in development and production of diet foods is $50 billion.

THE "PRICE" OF PIZZA

A slice of pizza contains approximately 400 calories and takes about 4 minutes to eat. Burning these 400 calories requires 1 hour of strenuous activity at the gym.

EATING AND DRINKING

The average person eats 66,138 lb (33,000 kg) and drinks more than 19,814 gal (75,000 liters) of liquids during his lifetime.

BEYOND NATURAL MEANS

During World War II, the Nazis forced Jewish prisoners to do backbreaking work for 10 hours a day, yet they received a food ration of only 180 calories per day.

SOUL-SEARCHING

Approximately 83% of Israelis do not watch their weight. The people most concerned about their weight are those between the ages of 35 and 44 — 21% of them watch what they eat. In the 45–54 age range, only 14.7% watch their weight. The Chareidi population in Israel is more likely to be conscious of the food they eat — 28% compared to only 17% of the secular population. In the general population, women (21%) are more calorie conscious than men. Awareness of calorie intake is higher among those with higher education and higher income.

POPULATION GROWTH

The United States' 300 millionth resident was born in 2007. At the same time, it was publicized that 30 million people, 10% of the population, weigh more than 330 lb (150 kg).

LONGING FOR THE PAST

According to the Israel Central Bureau of Statistics, in 1950 the average caloric intake per person stood at 2,600 calories per day. This was during the time of "austerity," when people stood in line for an egg or a bottle of oil. By 1960, Israelis were consuming 3,000 calories per day. In 1995, there was a large jump in the amount of advertising for food products, and from then on more calories were added to the Israeli daily menu every year. The daily consumption is now holding at about 3,554 calories per day. These additional calories generally come from treats, soft drinks, and snacks — which are rich in calories. The rise in quality of life has resulted in less physical activity such as walking and even light housework, and this is also responsible for weight gain. The real problem is that this is only the beginning; unhealthy eating and lack of exercise are expected to reach their peak in 20 years, when today's children will be adults. *Heh-chacham einav b'rosho* (*Koheles* 2:14): The best time to start eating healthy and exercising is NOW!

Men of War	120
Fighter Aircraft	124
Battleships	130
Submarines	132
Tanks	134
Cannons and Guns	136
Bombs and Missiles	138
Unconventional Weapons	140
Nuclear Warfare	142

Armies and Wars

Someone was once speaking about wars. He remarked that leaders fight with each other over some issue, resulting in much senseless bloodshed. He added that much of the foolishness of previous generations, such as *avodah zarah* in which they would kill their own children and bring them as an offering to some idol, is long gone. However, the wars remain.

He mocked their wise men — how they invest time and research into building such wonderful weapons that can destroy thousands of lives in one shot. Is there anything more nonsensical than killing and destroying for no reason?

Chayei Moharan

YOUNGEST GUERILLA LEADERS

Johnny and Luther Htoo, 12-year-old Burmese twins (born 1987), were the leaders of a band of guerilla fighers called God's Army. Their soldiers viewed them as gods and obeyed their every command. In January 2000 they stormed a hospital in the Thai town of Ratchaburi, taking 700 people hostage for 24 hours. In the end, they surrendered to the Thai army, and the number of their supporters dropped from 300 to a mere 20.

DRAFTING CHILDREN

In 1976, President Francisco Macías Nguema of Equatorial Guinea in Central Africa sent notices requiring army service for all boys between the ages of 7 and 14. The letter stated that parents who refused to send their sons would either be imprisoned or face death by firing squad.

WAR OF THE CHILDREN

The Children's Crusade was the unusual attempt to free the Holy Land from Muslim rule. It was organized in the year 1212 by a 12-year-old French shepherd boy named Stephen of Cloyes. Stephen began his quest with impassioned speeches, where he managed to convince the crowd that he could work miracles. Over 20,000 children joined him and his adult followers. He led his "army" through the French port city of Marseilles on the Mediterranean coast, believing that the sea would split when they got there and he and his followers would march to Jerusalem on dry land. This of course did not happen. Two merchants came to the port and directed the children onto 7 boats, which set sail for Tunisia. There, the children were sold into slavery.

Children in the military

SOLDIERS WITH BABY TEETH

In Israel's War of Independence in 1948, hundreds of young boys 12 years of age and up were drafted into the Israeli army. Their job was to build fortifications, pass messages, and provide any necessary help to hospitals. In addition, the 15-year-olds were given guard duty in military outposts.

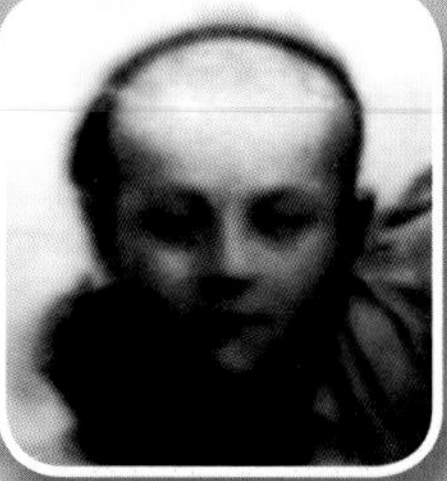

Nissim Ginny *Hy"d*

The youngest person ever to fall in battle defending the State of Israel was 9-year-old Nissim Ginny. Nissim was born in Jerusalem's Old City in 1938. His father, Yitzchak Ginny, had immigrated to Israel on his own from Turkey following in the footsteps of his father, who fell in battle in Jerusalem during World War I. Nissim's mother, Miriam, was an immigrant from Morocco. The couple had 4 children. The youngest, Aryeh, died during the Yom Kippur War.

During the War of Independence, the children of the Old City, who were very familiar with the alleyways of the Jewish Quarter, served as relays between stations. There was no radio communication, and they were constantly exposed to enemy fire. They spent their time dodging bullets and shell fragments. They delivered information, arms, and food between the stations. Nissim served as a relay and a lookout. He would spend sleepless night after sleepless night at his post.

On May 27, 1948, Nissim completed his watch and was making his way home to eat. The boy scheduled to relieve Nissim never came and Nissim was called back until a replacement could be found. When he returned to his post, he noted suspicious movement. When he put his head out to check what was happening, a Jordanian sniper shot in his direction. The bullet struck a gun which was at the post, the barrel exploded, and the fragments flew toward Nissim, injuring him critically. After a day of pain and suffering, he died of his wounds at the tender age of 9.

When the family returned after the Jewish Quarter had been liberated in the Six Day War (1967), nothing remained of what had been their home, and there was no remembrance of Nissim either. It was only several years later that a picture was found of Nissim standing next to other children in his *cheder* — a young boy sporting a large yarmulke.

THE CANTONISTS

The Cantonist decree of 1827 was one of the most heartbreaking tragedies endured by the Jewish nation during their long exile. During the reign of Czar Nicholas I, there was a special law which al lowed the drafting of eight-year-old Jewish children into the Russian army. The main goal of this terrible decree was to integrate Jews and other non-Russian minorities into Russian society (in order to erase their religious and national identities), and to baptize them into Christianity. Unfortunately, the plot was somewhat successful, and approximately 1/3 of those drafted became Christians against their will. In spite of all the indescribable difficulties, most of the Jewish children stayed faithful to Judaism.

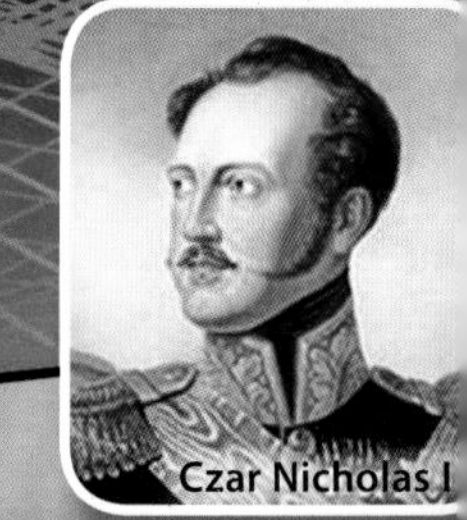

Czar Nicholas I

Until 1827, a person could pay to get out of the draft. However, in that year, Nicholas I did away with this possibility and required the entire Jewish community to send a certain amount of children for service. These unlucky ones were imprisoned in a small room until army representatives would arrive to take them to the camps. The weeping mothers stood at the window of the room and begged their sons not to leave the faith under any circumstances. Even if they were threatened with death, they were admonished to withstand all the physical and emotional pain and stay Jewish.

Obligatory military service was for 25 years. Until age 20 the boys worked on Russian farms, and after that they were put on the front lines until the end of their service. Many died sanctifying the Name of Hashem while holding on to their faith.

THE UNITED NATIONS

When World War II ended (1945), the heads of states decided to create an international organization that would return peace and tranquility to the world. They named it the United Nations (UN). The first meeting took place on January 10, 1946, in London, where representatives of 51 countries met. Israel was accepted into the organization on May 11, 1949, as the 59th member. Today the UN is located in New York City and every nation in the world is a member, except Taiwan, Kosovo, and Vatican City. The UN General Assembly meets 3 months a year.

Men of War

LARGEST ARMY

The Chinese army has an estimated 2.8 million soldiers (regular as well as reserve), making it the largest in the world. The Russian army is a distant 2nd with 1.52 million soldiers, followed by the United States army with 1.37 million and India with 1.3 million.

WORLD ARMY

The total cost of maintaining armies and weapons all over the world is estimated at $790 billion, which amounts to 10% of all production in the world. There are 28 million full-time enlisted soldiers, as well as 45 million on reserve duty. There are also 30 million people serving in auxiliary army-related positions. This adds up to 103 million people serving in the armed forces throughout the world.

ARMY WITH THE LARGEST EXPENSES

The Israeli army has the largest expenditures per capita of any nation in the world — $1,470 per person per year. Kuwait is in 2nd place, at $1,110 per person, and then Norway at $880. Saudi Arabia is in 4th place ($690 per person per year).

LARGEST ARMS PROVIDER

The United States, the so-called guardian of world peace and freedom, is the largest arms provider in the world. Their annual export of arms to all parts of the globe reaches astronomical proportions. There have been many wars in which both sides were using weapons provided by the United States. According to the Pentagon, arms sales by the United States to other nations reached $38.1 billion in 2009.

Biggest Purchasers of American Arms

COUNTRY	AMOUNT SPENT
United Arab Emirates	$7.9 billion
Afghanistan	$5.4 billion
Saudia Arabia	$3.3 billion
Taiwan	$3.2 billion
Egypt	$2.1 billion
Iraq	$1.6 billion
NATO	$900 million
Australia	$818 million
South Korea	$716 million

The United States has also been involved in every war which has taken place anywhere in the world in the past 100 years.

Incidentally, there are 370,000 American soldiers stationed in 48 countries outside the United States.

THE ISRAELI MILITARY

Israel has 187,000 soldiers in compulsory service and an additional 445,000 reservists. This adds up to 1 out of every 6 able-bodied citizens serving in some capacity (1 out of 11 total residents). By comparison, in other countries, the accepted ratio of people serving in the armed forces is 1 solider for every 500 residents.

ARMY IN LONGEST CONTINUOUS EXISTENCE

The oldest army unit in the world which is still functioning is the Vatican's Swiss Guard, which consists of between 80 and 90 soldiers. The Guard was formally established in 1506, but is known to have been in existence even before 1400.

Recruits to the Guard must be single Catholic men with Swiss citizenship who have completed basic training with the Swiss military, and who received certificates of good conduct. They must be between the ages of 19 and 30, and at least 5 ft., 9 in. (174 cm) tall. They also have to have either a high school diploma or a professional degree.

Candidates must apply for the job. New guards are sworn in every year on May 6 in the Vatican's San Damaso Courtyard.

LONGEST WAR

The longest war in history was the Hundred Years War, between England and France. It lasted 115 years, from 1338 until 1453. From the creation of the world, there have been only 290 years in which there were no wars. (Chances are that there were wars during these years, but they were not recorded by historians.)

BLOODIEST WARS

The Second World War (1939-1945) is the bloodiest war of all time. An estimated total of 55 million people were killed: 16 million soldiers and 39 million citizens (including 25 million Russians and 8 million Chinese).

During World War II, 3 million Polish Jews were murdered, as well as 3 million Polish solders and citizens — 22% of the Polish population of 28 million.

The total number of people killed in World War I was 16.5 million: 9.7 million soldiers and 6.8 million civilians.

In the war involving Paraguay against Brazil, Argentina, and Uruguay (1864-1870), Paraguay's population dropped from 1.4 million to only 220,000. Out of this low number, only 30,000 of them were men — the only Paraguayan men left alive after the war.

HIGHEST NUMBER OF LOSSES IN A WAR

The number of losses suffered by the Russian army during World War II was 85 times greater than the combined losses of the English and American armies. During the war, 135,000 Russian soldiers were judged and executed by their own army for desertion and cowardice. Thousands more died after being sent to labor camps for even less severe infractions. The number of Russian soldiers killed by the Red Army itself was higher than the total number of American soldiers killed in the entire war.

GREATEST BOMB CASUALTIES

World War II saw the greatest bomb casualties. The bombs dropped on the city of Dresden in Nazi Germany resulted in the deaths of more than 600,000 Germans. The March 10, 1945, firebomb raids over Tokyo killed approximately 140,000 people, while 600,000 Japanese died from conventional bombing. The atomic bomb dropped on Hiroshima (see page 142) caused 170,000 deaths, and the one dropped on Nagasaki caused 80,000.

MOST COSTLY WAR

The total cost of World War II has been estimated at $1.5 trillion — 10 times greater than the cost of all other wars in history combined. It is estimated that the United States spent $550 billion fighting this war.

GREATEST NAVAL BATTLE

The largest number of ships and jets that ever took part in a naval battle was in the Battle of Leyte Gulf in the Philippines in October 1944 (World War II). The battle involved 231 ships — 166 belonging to the Allies and 65 belonging to Japan. There were also 1,996 planes used — 1,280 American and 716 Japanese. Six American and 26 Japanese ships sank in this battle.

MOST MASSIVE BATTLE

The final attack of the Russian army into Berlin in April 1945 (World War II) involved a total of 3.5 million soldiers, 52,000 cannons and mortars, 7,750 tanks, and 11,000 planes from both sides.

BLOODIEST BATTLES

The highest number of casualties ever suffered in a battle was in the First Battle of the Somme in France, which took place over a 4.5 month period from July 1 until November 19, 1916 (World War I). The number of soldiers killed in that battle was 1.284 million — 624,000 English and French, and 660,000 German.

The Battle of Stalingrad (Russia) lasted from July 17, 1942, until February 2, 1943 (World War II). There were approximately 1.2 million soldiers and civilians killed and 650,000 injured. After the battle, only 1,500 citizens remained alive in the city from a pre-war population of more than 500,000 people. Ironically, Russia is considered to have "won" this battle.

GREATEST NUMBER OF LOSSES IN A SINGLE DAY

On the first day of the First Battle of the Somme during World War I, 60,000 British soldiers were killed. By comparison, the number killed in 7 wars of the State of Israel — from the 1948 War of Independence until the 2006 Second Lebanon War — is 10,081. The number of Jewish deaths in battle since the beginning of the Jewish settlement in 1870 is 21,182.

The First Battle of the Somme

LARGEST NAVAL INVASION

The largest naval invasion in military history was carried out by the Allied forces in Normandy, France, in World War II. The invasion, which started in June 1944, was carried out by land, sea, and air. During the first 3 days, 38 battalions — which included 745 ships — reached the Normandy shore. They were assisted by 4,060 landing craft, 185,000 soldiers, 20,000 motor vehicles and 347 mines. The air strike involved 18,000 paratroopers who jumped out from 1,090 planes. There were 13,200 planes which were airborne to assist and protect the 42 divisions from the air. Within a single month, 1.1 million soldiers, 200,000 motor vehicles, and 750,000 tons of equipment had landed in Normandy.

GREATEST SEA EVACUATION

At the beginning of World War II (September 1939), a large group of British soldiers known as the British Expeditionary Force arrived in France led by Lord John Gort. They did not fight until the German invasion of France and the Low Countries (Holland, Belgium and Luxembourg) on May 10, 1940.

Thanks to the Germans and their *blitzkrieg* ("lightning war") tactics, the British Expeditionary Force found themselves suddenly cut off from the French forces with no chance of winning the battle. Lord Gort ordered a quick evacuation from the shores of Dunkirk, Belgium, using all Allied ships available. Two French divisions remained behind to protect the evacuation, named Operation Dynamo. In 1 week, a total of 338,226 men — 218,000 British soldiers and 120,000 French soldiers and civilians — were evacuated over the English Channel to the shores of Dover in England.

The evacuation was partially carried out by private citizens who owned boats. More than 900 ships took part: commercial vessels, fishing boats, yachts, and rescue ships. Nineteen British destroyers were damaged, while an additional 9 British and 3 French destroyers and 200 small ships were sunk during the operation.

DID YOU KNOW?

John Henri Dunant (a. k. a. Henri Dunant) was a Swiss businessman and social activist. In 1859, at the age of 31, he passed by the battlefield right after the Battle of Solferino in modern-day Italy. France was fighting on the side of Piedmont-Sardinia against Austria, which had occupied much of today's Italy.

Thirty-eight thousand wounded, dying and dead soldiers were still on the battlefield, and there appeared to be little attempt to provide care. Shocked by these scenes of the dead and dying as well as by the lack of medical care, Dunant organized the civilian population to provide first aid and other help to the injured and sick soldiers.

When he returned home to Switzerland, Dunant immediately sat to record his experiences in his book, *A Memory of Solferino*. In the book, Dunant calls for medical staff to accompany armies during war as well as the founding of relief agencies which would also work during times of peace. The book inspired the creation of the International Red Cross, whose purpose is to provide help for people who are injured in war and natural disasters such as flooding, earthquakes, plagues, and famine. Refugees and prisoners of war are given medical care, food, and clothing. Prisoners of war are visited by organization representatives who check the conditions of imprisonment and deliver letters to and from their relatives. In 1901, Dunant received the world's first Nobel Peace Prize.

LONGEST MODERN-ERA SIEGE

The Siege of Leningrad, the longest recorded siege in the 20th century, lasted for 880 days, from August 1941 until January 1944 (World War II). The siege was a military operation carried out by the German army attempting to capture the city of Leningrad in the Soviet Union. More than 250,000 bombs were dropped over the city during the course of the siege.

THE FOOTBALL WAR

The Football War, also known as the Hundred Hours War, was a 4-day war between the Central American countries of El Salvador and Honduras. In 1969, the Hondurans evicted many El Salvadoran farmers who had been living in Honduras and working the land for the past few generations. Their land was divided among Honduran farmers.

Despite the great tension, in June 1969, the 2 countries competed in 3 qualifying matches for the 1970 World Cup. There was fighting between fans at the 1st game (which Honduras won), and after El Salvador won the second match, El Salvadoran fans attacked the Honduran fans with great violence. The 3rd match was a play-off, with El Salvador winning 3-2 in overtime. A few weeks later the El Salvadoran government attacked Honduras, and the fighting continued for 4 days. A ceasefire agreement was signed. Only 11 years later, on October 30, 1980, the two countries signed a peace treaty.

About 1,000 soldiers and 2,000 civilians were killed in the war. In addition, the war led to a suspension of each country from the Central American Common Market for 22 years.

MOST DAMAGING CIVIL WAR

The bloodiest civil war in world history was the Taiping (Great Peace) Rebellion in China from 1851 to 1864, during which the Southern Ming loyalists fought against the army of the ruling Qing (Manchu) dynasty. Leading the rebellion was Hong Xiuquan, who established the Taiping Heavenly Kingdom (Heavenly Kingdom of Great Peace) with Nanjing as its capital. An estimated 25 million people — civilians and soldiers — were killed during this rebellion. Afterwards, Hong Xiuquan was sentenced to death.

BIGGEST ANTI-WAR PROTEST

On February 14, 2003, many anti-war protests took place throughout the world. The largest of these protests took place in Rome, where 3 million people protested the American threat to invade Iraq. On the same day, 1.3 million people took part in a peace rally in Barcelona, Spain, and another million participated in a peace march in the streets of London. From police estimates in the various countries, it appears that protest rallies took place in 600 additional cities throughout the world.

MOST ACCEPTED WORLD TREATY

Every country in the world has signed on the Geneva Convention, which outlines the rules of behavior during times of war. This was the first time in world history that any sort of treaty gained full world recognition. The last two countries to sign this pact were Nauru and the Republic of Montenegro.

FIRST AIR FORCE

The Prussian army was the first to use a hot air balloon for military purposes. The balloons were used for scouting missions in their war against France near Strasbourg in September 1870.

The British Royal Air Force (RAF) is the world's first air force. It can trace its history back to 1878 when the No. 1 Balloon Company of the Royal Engineers was formed. In 1911, the Air Battalion of the Royal Engineers was created, which became the No. 1 Squadron of the Royal Flying Corps a year later. The RAF was made its own unit in 1918. By the end of World War I (1918), the RAF was already the largest air force in the world.

Military airship

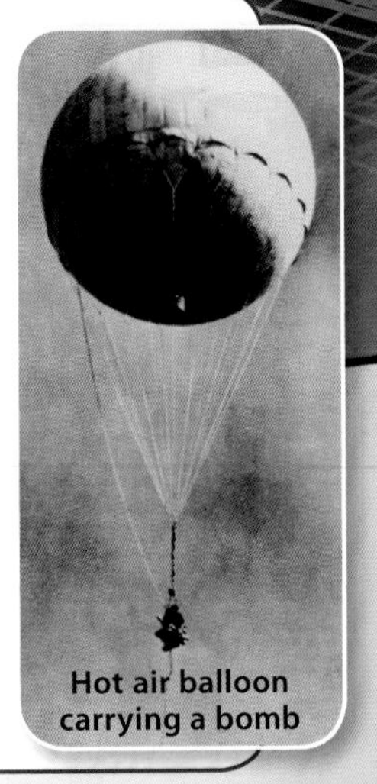

Hot air balloon carrying a bomb

LARGEST AIR FORCE

The largest air force in history was the American Air Force at the end of World War II. In July 1944, it had 79,900 aircraft and was serviced by 2,411,300 soldiers. The Air Force was established when the United Sates entered World War I in 1917. It became a separate, independent branch of the military in 1947. Today there are 650,000 soldiers flying more than 2,400 fighter planes (an additional 1,000 aircraft are in storage), 3,500 helicopter gunships, cargo transport helicopters and planes, spy planes, unmanned planes, and other types of aircraft.

The air section of the American Naval Fleet has 4,000 planes, plus additional aircraft from 9 large aircraft carriers and naval bases throughout the world.

The Russian air force has 175,000 soldiers, 1,550 fighter planes, and an additional 390 helicopter gunships.

MOST EXPENSIVE BOMBER

The most expensive bomber as well as the most expensive plane ever built was the B-2 Spirit, also known as the Stealth Bomber. Manufactured by the American company Northrop, it was first flown in 1989. The cost of a single plane is $2.2 billion, which amounts to $30 per gram of plane — 3 times the price of gold. This is why only 21 planes have been manufactured thus far.

The Stealth Bomber is designed in a way which allows it to "disappear" and avoid enemy radar detectors. It is also constructed from materials which are radar-absorbent and is equipped with the most sophisticated electronic stealth equipment. Despite its astronomical price — which is mainly due to the enormous development costs — serious defects have been discovered. For example, the layer of radar-absorbent material which lines the plane does not remain durable in water for too long. Therefore, following any mission flown in rain, the plane requires a special, long treatment in order to renew the layer. B-2 planes participated in the bombings of Iraq in 1991 and 2003, in Bosnia, and in the war against Afghanistan.

General Characteristics of the Stealth Bomber:

Length: 69 ft (21 m)
Height: 17 ft (5.18 m)
Wingspan: 172 ft (5.18 m)
Weight: empty — 46 tons; loaded — 170 tons
Maximum speed: 604 mph, 972 km/h, Mach 0.95
Cruise speed: 541 mph, 870 km/h, Mach 0.85
Range: 6,900 mi (11,100 km)
Ignition: 4 engines manufactured by General Electric. The engines are buried within the wing to conceal the induction fans and hide their exhaust.
Maximum flying altitude: 50,000 ft/9.47 mi (15,200 m)
Crew: 2 people sitting side by side

An F-117A Nighthawk Stealth Combat Aircraft

A B-52 bomber plane with its ammunition

Fighter Aircraft

FASTEST BOMBER

The American F-14 bomber manufactured by General Dynamics is the fastest bomber in the world. It can travel at a maximum speed of 1,544 mph (2,485 km/h, Mach 2.34).

The F-14 can carry missiles and bombs weighing up to 6 tons.

Other Characteristics of the F-14:

Length: 62 ft, 9 in. (19.1 m)
Height: 16 ft (4.88 m)
Maximum flying altitude: 50,000 ft/ 9.47 mi (15,200 m)

A fighter aircraft crosses the sound barrier

HEAVIEST BOMBER

The heaviest bomber in the world is the Boeing B-52, known as the Strato Fortress. Its maximum weight at takeoff can reach 227 tons.

The B-52 can transport 12 short-range, thermonuclear cruise missiles, 24 bombs weighing 750 lb (340 kg) under its wings, and 8 additional missiles or 84 bombs each weighing 500 lb (227 kg), in the plane's underbelly.

Other Characteristics of the B-52:

Length: 159 ft, 4 in. (48.5 m)
Wingspan: 185 ft (56.4 m)
Maximum speed: 650 mph (1,050 km/h) — with the aid of 8 jet-stream engines

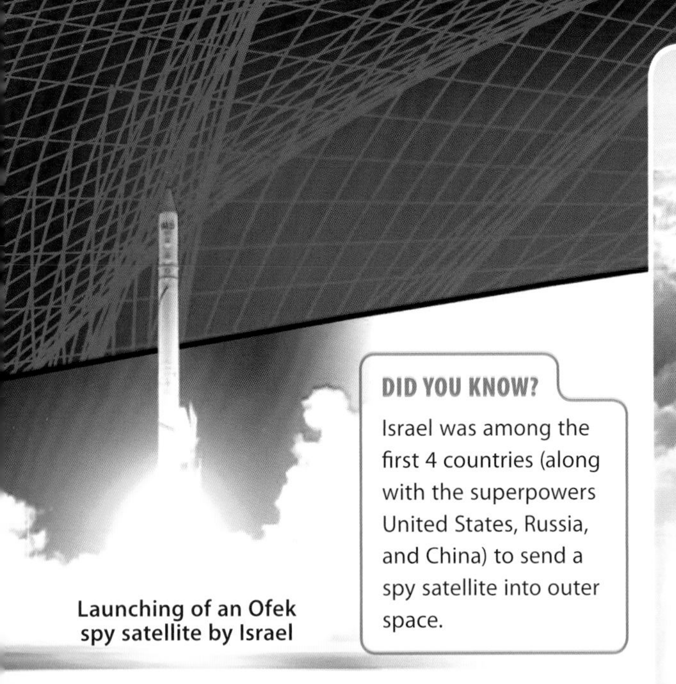

Launching of an Ofek spy satellite by Israel

DID YOU KNOW?

Israel was among the first 4 countries (along with the superpowers United States, Russia, and China) to send a spy satellite into outer space.

BEST RECONNAISSANCE AIRCRAFT

The Lockheed SR-71 jet, known as the Blackbird, made its flying debut in December 1964. Despite its great age it is still considered the fastest, highest-flying, and most advanced jet in the world. (See also page 161.)

The Blackbird can fly at a maximum speed of 1,988 mph (3,200 km/h, Mach 2.61), and can reach an operational altitude of 80,000 ft/15.15 mi (24,000 m). The SR-71 is a record-holder for its class of jet in a few categories:

Absolute speed: 2,193.2 mph (3,529.6 km/h, Mach 2.88).

Absolute altitude: 85,069 ft/16.11 mi (25,929 m).

Flight Distance: 3,682 mi (5,926 km).

The Blackbird was retired from active duty in 1990 because it was thought that the spy satellites as well as reconnaissance high-altitude aircrafts of the U-2 model could accomplish the same missions at much less cost. However, based on the lessons learned from the Gulf War (1991), it was returned to active duty in 1997.

FIRST RECONNAISSANCE AIRCRAFT

In 1950, America's Central Intelligence Agency (CIA) put out a tender for the building of a reconnaissance aircraft which would gather precise information from all parts of the world. The jet would have to fly at an altitude of higher than 12.5 mi (20 km), far higher than all Russian battle planes and surface-to-air, anti-aircraft missiles, and even above the detection capability of radars.

In 1955, the 1-seat U-2 reconnaissance aircraft successfully carried out its first flight, reaching an altitude of 80,000 ft/15.15 mi (24,000 m). It was equipped with cameras developed for it by the Kodak company. It reached a speed of 510 mph (821 km/h), and flew for a distance of 3,500 mi (5,633 km).

The U-2 mission was kept secret until 1960, when one was shot down over Soviet skies near the Ural Mountains. The pilot successfully parachuted to safety, but was taken into captivity. He was returned home to the United States only 21 months later.

After that incident, the U-2 planes no longer flew over the Soviet Union, but they continued to gather pictures of Soviet missiles from various other parts of the world. After the Soviets developed surface-to-air missiles capable of reaching an altitude of 82,000 ft/ 15.53 mi (25 km), the U-2 was replaced by the faster and more advanced SR-71.

SMALLEST UNMANNED AERIAL VEHICLE

The AeroVironment Company in Monrovia, CA (USA), developed a small Unmanned Aerial Vehicle (UAV), which looks like a robotic flying insect. They named it the Black Widow, after the poisonous spider. This micro-UAV, whose size without the wings is that of a dragonfly, carries a small surveillance camera. It can enter buildings, take pictures of what is happening there, and transmit sharp and clear color pictures to a command station as far as 1.1 mi (1.8 km) away. The wings of the micro-UAV, 6 in. (15 cm) long, are made from very thin polythene film similar to camera film and a simple, carbon-fiber skeleton. The UAV can reach an altitude of 769 ft (234 m) above ground, such that the ordinary eye would not be able to detect it and the sound of the miniature motor would not be heard.

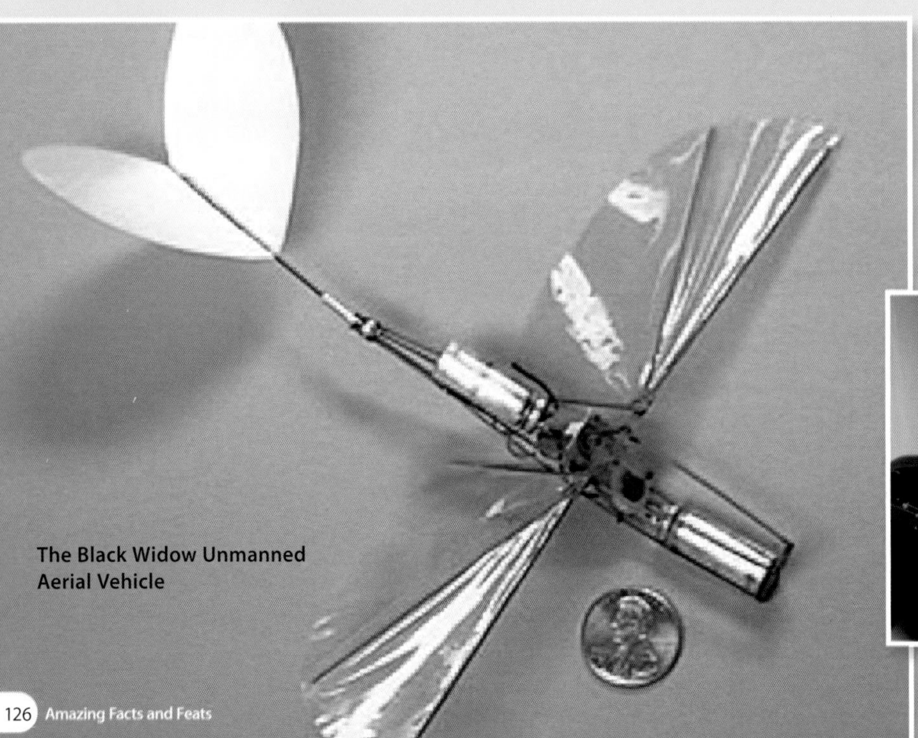

The Black Widow Unmanned Aerial Vehicle

The Black Widow's control room

Fighter Aircraft

VORLD'S BEST ATTACK HELICOPTER

he 2-seater American attack helicopter nown as the Apache is designed to attack round targets such as tanks. It is consid- red the best attack helicopter in the world.

The helicopter's 2 engines are manufac- ured by General Electric, and have 1,587 hp each — hich is equivalent to the power of 30 cars.

The Apache is equipped with a gunner which ngages close-range targets with one M-230, 30-mm automatic cannon ttached to a turret under the helicopter's nose. It is also equipped ith 1,200 bombs and 16 Hellfire missiles from the fire-and-forget odel which need no other guidance from the helicopter once they ave been fired. The missiles are so precise that they can strike some- ing the size of a Coke can from half a mile away. The Apache can be quipped with Hydra 70 rocket pods on four hard points mounted n stub-wing pylons. External fuel tanks can also be arried by the pylons to increase range and mission time.

The Apache's advanced maneuverability, its high survivability, and s ability to work day and night, in all weather, together with the ellfire missiles, have transformed it into the best attack elicopter in the world.

ther Characteristics of the Apache:

ength: 58.17 ft (17.75 m)
eight: 16.7 ft (5.1 m)
mpty weight: 10,758 lb (4,880 kg)
oaded weight (a full fuel tank and ammunition): ,000 lb (9,525 kg)
aximum speed: 226 mph (365 km/h)
aximum altitude: 21,000 ft/4 mi (6.4 km)
ying distance without refueling: 428 mi (689 km)

ARGEST AND MOST VALUABLE IRPLANE GRAVEYARD"

e AMARC base in Tucson, AZ (USA), is known as the rplane Desert Graveyard. The base stores the surplus the American Navy and Air Force. The dry desert mate allows storage under the open sky, with low aintenance costs. At the site one can find almost ery type of plane which served or is still serving the merican Air Force and Navy, as well as plane parts om the German Air Force.

The newer planes are coated with a special sub- ance, and are inspected once every 4 months so that there's a war they will be able to be quickly restored fighting capability. The older planes are stored in a orehouse until they are needed for spare parts or pur- ased by foreign armies.

In a separate, isolated site are stored C-123 Provider anes that were used in the Vietnam War (1961–1975) spray the jungles of Vietnam with chemicals in or- r to defoliate them. ("Defoliate" means to take off e leaves.) This was done to expose the hiding places the Viet Cong enemy and to eliminate their food urces. It is forbidden to enter this storage site due the dangerous chemicals that were flown on these anes. The estimated value of the equipment stored at MARC is over $10 billion.

HEAD-UP DISPLAY

F-16 fighter planes are equipped with an Israeli invention called a Head-Up Display. A Head-Up Display (HUD) is a transparent screen that gives data with- out requiring the user to look away from what he or she is looking at. The HUD gives data such as the enemy plane's altitude and speed, and what it is armed with. The system also lets the pilot send both air-to-air and air-to-surface missiles by tracking the location of the enemy plane or ground target without having to steer the nose of the plane toward the target. On the display a camera is in- stalled, which documents where the pilot looked during the time of the flight.

A Helmet-Mounted Display (HMD) is a device used in some modern aircraft, especially combat aircraft. HMDs display information similar to that of an HUD on an aircrew's visor, thereby allowing him to obtain information in the direc- tion his head is pointing. Sometimes the device is called a Helmet-Mounted Sight and Display (HMSD) or Helmet-Mounted Sights (HMS).

G-FORCE

G-force is an object's acceleration relative to free-fall. In a military aircraft, as acceleration or deceleration increases, the pilot experiences a higher g-force. A g-force which is too high may prevent blood from reaching the pilot's brain. His peripheral vision will become progressively worse, until he may experience tunnel vision. The pilot may possibly become color-blind, black out, or at times even lose consciousness completely.

Positive, or "upward" g-force drives blood downward to the feet of a seated or standing person.

In the F-16 fighter plane, the pilot's seat is angled 30° to lessen the verti- cal distance between the heart and the brain, such that during sudden ac- celeration and deceleration as well as sharp turns, the effect of g-force on the bloodstream to the pilot's brain will be far less and allow a higher capability of maneuvering. On shorter pilots the vertical distance from the heart to the brain is naturally less.

MOST POPULAR BATTLE PLANE

The F-16 Fighting Falcon is the most popular battle plane in the world. It was designed as a lightweight, daytime air battle fighter. However, it became a successful multi-purpose aircraft, mainly due to its relatively low price. The original models cost about $12 million, and the later ones sell for approximately $18.8 million — about half the price of the competing F-15.

More than 4,200 F-16s have been manufactured. It serves more than 24 armies throughout the world, and the United States continues to manufacture it for export purposes.

The F-16's empty weight is approximately 10 tons, and when the fuel tank is full and it is loaded with missiles and cannons, the weight can reach 12.8 tons. To allow for more distance, it is possible to store additional fuel tanks weighing 10.75 tons. Therefore, the takeoff weight can reach a maximum of 23.55 tons.

The F-35

MOST EXPENSIVE AIRPLANE DEVELOPMENT

The highest amount ever invested in the development of an airplane was $276 billion for the F-35 — slated to become the American Air Force's next fighter plane. The plane was manufactured by the Lockheed Martin Company. The F-35 is also referred to as Lightning II, as a tribute to the P-38 Lightning which served the United States during World War II. The F-35 is a multi-purpose, stealth fighter. It is quick and has great maneuvering ability. Its targ ing exactitude and the amount of weapon can carry make it superior to any competit plane. In addition to the United States, the countries of England, Italy, Holland, Turkey Australia, Norway, and Israel also participa in its development. The United States is pl ning to purchase 2,334 such planes to rep the F-16, F-15, and other planes. Despite th astronomical development costs, the large number of orders lower the price of the F- to "only" $50 million per plane.

Fighter Aircraft

An F-16 fighter aircraft

An F-16 aerial refueling

F-16 aircraft bombing Iraqi oil fields

F-22 fighter aircraft

The F-22 Raptor

COST OF AN HOUR OF FLYING

The cost of 1 hour of flying the F-14 fighter plane is estimated at $1,689, while an hour of flying an F-15 is estimated at "only" $1,073. However, when adding the price of the plane and the operating and storage costs, and then dividing it by the number of flying hours, the price per flight hour reaches $20,000 and perhaps even more.

'ST AND MOST EXPENSIVE MULTI-ROLE PLANE

e Lockheed Martin/Boeing F-22 Raptor is a single-seat, twin-engine, 5th genera-n fighter aircraft that uses stealth technology. It is considered the best multi-purpose plane the world. However, due to its $250 million price, it is used only by the American army. It was signed primarily as an air superiority fighter (a fighter aircraft used to enter and seize control enemy airspace), but has additional capabilities that include ground attack, electronic war-e, and signals intelligence.

The Raptor carries one M-61A2 Vulcan 20 mm rotary cannon, air-to-air missiles, 2 M-9 Sidewinder short-range missiles for self-protection, and air-to-surface weapons ch as bombs with the sophisticated Joint Direct Attack Munition (JDAM) guidance stem.

her Characteristics of the F-22 Raptor:

ngth: 62 ft, 1 in. (18.90 m)
ight: 16 ft, 8 in. (5.08 m)
ngspan: 44 ft, 6 in. (13.56 m)
pty weight: 43,430 lb (19,700 kg)
aded weight: 64,460 lb (29,300 kg); 80,500 lb (36,500 kg) with 2 external fuel tanks
ximum speed: 1,220 mph (1,963 km/h, Mach 1.60)

LARGEST NAVY

The United States Navy is the largest in the world, with 570,000 soldiers staffing more than 300 boats and 4,000 planes.

FIRST AIRCRAFT CARRIERS

American pilot Eugene Ely was the pilot credited with the first shipboard aircraft landing. On January 18, 1911, Ely landed his Curtiss pusher airplane on a platform on the armored cruiser USS *Pennsylvania* anchored in San Francisco Bay (CA), using the first-ever tail hook system.

The first ship upon which aircraft could take off and land was the British HMS *Argus*, part of the British naval fleet. The first landing on the ship was made on October 1, 1918, by Lt. Col. Richard Bell Davis. The flight deck was 566 ft (172 m) long, with space for 20 parked planes.

LARGEST AIRCRAFT CARRIER

Half of the world's aircraft carriers are operated by the United States. The Nimitz class supercarriers, named for Admiral Chester Nimitz, are a group of 10 nuclear-powered aircraft carriers in the service of the United States Navy. These are the largest aircraft carriers and most expensive ships ever built, with an overall length of 1,100 ft (335 m), a flight deck 235 ft (77 m) wide, and an area of 4.5 acres — equivalent to a neighborhood containing 36 spacious, standalone houses.

The Nimitz is a nuclear-powered, steam-driven ship with 4 nuclear reactors which boil water for steam. Instead of the gas turbines or diesel-electric systems used for propulsion on many modern warships, the carriers use 2 pressurized water-reactors which drive 4 propeller shafts. These can produce a maximum speed of over 36 mph (58 km/h) and a maximum 280,000 hp (the equivalent of 2,200 family cars). The reactors need only be refueled once every 932,000 mi (1.5 million km). This means that the ships are capable of operating for over 20 years without refueling and are predicted to have a service life of over 50 years.

All 10 carriers were constructed by Newport News Shipbuilding Company in Virginia (USA). The 1st ship was commissioned in May 1975, and the 10th and last, in January 200

An aircraft carrier, when laden with 90 planes on its deck, can weigh as much as 98,000 tons. A large elevator lowers the planes to the storage area in the belly of the ship. The air fleet includes F-18 and F-14 battle planes, EA-6B electronic warfare aircraft, early-warning aircrafts from the E-2 series, S-3 surveillance aircrafts, and Skyhawk helicopters.

TAKEOFF AND LANDING ON AN AIRCRAFT CARRIER

An aircraft carrier's deck is generally 1,100 ft (335 m) long — too short for battle planes, which require an area of between 1,640 ft (500 m) and 3,280 ft (1,000 m) for takeoff and secure landing.

In order to land, a device called a catapult is attached to the front wheel of the plane. The catapult is steam-powered with great pressure and can accelerate even the heaviest of battle planes from a standing position to a speed of 170 mph (273 km/h) in only 3 seconds.

Landing on a flight deck is one of the most difficult and dangerous things a navy pilot will ever do. The planes are required to land in this small area while their motors are operating at almost full capacity, so that if anything should go wrong they can immediately take off on their own without requiring the aid of the catapult. To land on the flight deck, each plane needs a tail hook — an extended hook attached to the plane's tail. The pilot's goal is to snag the tail hook on one of four arresting wires, which are sturdy cables woven from high-tensile steel wire. The arresting wires are stretched across the deck and are attached on both ends to hydraulic cylinders below deck. The ropes halt the plane almost instantaneously.

LARGEST STAFF OF SAILORS

An aircraft carrier is staffed by 3,200 sailors and 2,500 air personnel — a total of 5,700 workers. These include aircrew, technicians, mechanics, and flight supervisors; more than 3 times the crew of any other ship in the world. The ship's kitchen prepares more than 20,000 meals per day.

For the sake of comparison, there are 6,000 soldiers in the entire Israeli Navy.

LARGEST BATTLESHIPS

The Japanese battleships *Yamato* and *Musashi*, constructed in 1941 (during World War II), were the largest battleships ever built. Each one had a displacement capacity of 73,000 tons, overall length of 863 ft (263 m), and width of 128 ft (39 m). Each ship had 9 cannons of 18 in. (460 mm) diameter which were installed in 3 turrets — the largest caliber of naval artillery ever fitted to a warship. Each cannon was 75.5 ft (23 m) long and weighed 162 tons.

The cannons were capable of firing high-explosive or armor-piercing shells weighing 3,219 lb (1,460 kg) for a distance of 25 mi (40 km). The *Musashi* was sunk on October 24, 1944, in the Philippine Sea by 10 bombs and 17 torpedoes. The *Yamato* was sunk by American battleships in April 1945.

Battleships

SAS-100

FASTEST COMBAT BOAT

The fastest battleship in the world is the experimental hovercraft of the American fleet named SAS-100. It is 75 ft (23 m) long, and despite its great weight — 100 tons — in tests conducted in Chesapeake Bay, MD, it reached a speed of 104 mph (168 km/h, 92 knots).

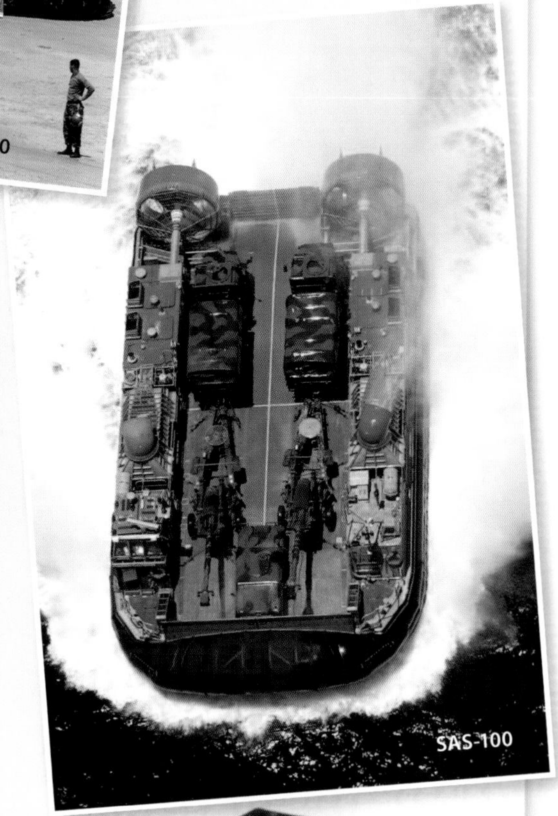

LARGEST MILITARY HOVERCRAFT

The Russian hovercraft *Zubr* is the largest military hovercraft in the world. It is 187 ft (57 m) long and weighs 400 tons. When adding the weight of the 3 tanks and 100 soldiers which it carries on a more than 13 ft (4 m) tall air cushion, the total weight can reach 555 tons. Four engines supplying 55,000 hp allow the *Zubr* to reach a maximum speed of 62 mph (100 km/h). The *Zubr* is equipped with 6, 1.2 in. (30 mm) cannons, 10 rocket launchers, and 2 anti-aircraft missiles.

SAS-100

PROJECT HABAKKUK

During World War II, German submarines sunk many British civilian and military ships in the Atlantic Ocean. Lord Louis Mountbatten, admiral of the British fleet, suggested to English prime minister Winston Churchill that they construct unsinkable aircraft carriers. The idea was to make an impregnable, 1,968 ft (600 m) aircraft carrier out of 280,000 blocks of ice, or out of pykrete (a mixture of wood pulp and ice). Given that ice weighs less than water, despite the aircraft carrier's enormous potential weight (estimated at 2 million tons), it was assumed that it would be able to float on water like an iceberg.

The engineers planned to build a cooling system in the heart of the ship to protect it from melting in the sun. The intention was to equip the ship with 26 electric motors that would power it at a speed of 11 mph (18 km/h). The builders proposed to have it carry 150 twin-engine bombers or fighters.

A small, experimental model was built and successfully launched on Lake Louise in Alberta, Canada. The project, however, was scrapped due to its high cost. Construction of the real aircraft carrier would require 8,000 workers working for 8 months, at a cost of $70 million.

The project was named Project Habakkuk, based on the verse in the book of Habakkuk: "Be utterly amazed, for I am going to do something in your days that you would not believe, even if you were told" (*Habakkuk* 1:5).

FIRST MILITARY SUBMARINES

In 1775, an American student named David Bushnell invented the first military submarine. The submarine was shaped like a standing egg and was named the *Turtle*. A sailor would sit inside in very tight quarters and turn 2 hand-cranked propellers — a vertical one for rising and a horizontal one for moving forward.

The *Turtle* also had an oversized wooden screw coming out of its top, with the crank handle inside the vessel. Attached to it was a waterproof fuse that led to a floating mine which would be fastened to the wooden outer hull or keel of an enemy ship. Bushnell's plan of attack was for the operator to stealthily steer up under an enemy ship, drill the wood screw deep enough into the keel to anchor it, then detach both the screw and the mine from the *Turtle*, set the underwater fuse burning, and quickly move off undetected. The mine would then explode and sink the ship.

The *Turtle* entered its first mission during the American War of Independence with the intent of sinking the British flagship, HMS *Eagle*, which was blockading the New York Harbor. On the night of September 7, 1776, Sergeant Ezra Lee piloted the *Turtle*. However, he could not actually drill the wood screw through the copper-plated hull of the *Eagle*. The bomb floated away and blew up at a distance, where it did not cause any damage. The submarine had enough oxygen to remain underwater for only half an hour. Lee had no choice but to rise to the surface in order to replenish his air supply, and though he was discovered he managed to escape.

Over the years there were other attempts to sink British ships with the *Turtle*, but they all failed. The final attempt was 36 years after the first one, during the War of 1812.

FIRST SUBMARINE TO SINK A SHIP

H. L. Hunley was a submarine of the "Confederate States of America," which was the name of the American South during the American Civil War (1860–1865). On February 17, 1864, the *Hunley* attacked and sank the USS *Housatonic* of the Union States' (the North's) fleet in Charleston Harbor, SC, making it the first submarine to sink an enemy warship.

The *Hunley* was 39.5 ft (12 m) long with a crew of 7 squeezed into a cubicle only 3.9 ft (1.2 m) high and 3.3 ft (1 m) wide. The crew would turn a long pole, which would turn the hand-cranked propeller that powered the submarine. The "torpedo" which sunk the *Housatonic* was nothing more than a cask containing 90 lb (41 kg) of gunpowder attached to a 22 ft (6.7 m) long wooden spar mounted on the *Hunley's* bow. The spar torpedo had a barbed point, and would be rammed into the side of the enemy vessel. The submarine would then back away and one of the crew would pull a rope, which activated the explosive.

After it successfully sank the *Housatonic*, the *Hunley* itself sank deep into the sea along with all its crew. On August 8, 2000, the *Hunley* was discovered at the bottom of the sea at the point where it had sunk.

FIRST ISRAELI SUBMARINES

The first 2 submarines purchased by Israel were the INS *Tanin*, which arrived in Haifa Port on December 15, 1959, and her sister, INS *Rahav*, which arrived a few months later. Both ships were built in Britain during World War II and after they had been removed from active duty, were specially renovated for the Israeli Navy in the shipyard of the British naval fleet.

In 1965, the Israeli government purchased another 3 submarines which had served the British Navy in World War II. The 1st was the INS *Livyatan*, which arrived in Israel on the last day of the Six Day War (June 1967). The next to arrive was the INS *Dakar*, which began its journey on January 9, 1968. However, on January 15, contact was lost.

Thirteen months later, Dakar's emergenc buoy was discovered off the Gaza strip by a resident of the Arab town of Khan Yunis. Thus, the *Dakar* was at first assumed to hav been sunk by the Egyptians. However, not a single part was found in searches around Egypt. The Nauticos company was hired to renew the search along the submarine's route. On May 28, 1999 — 31 years after it disappeared — the *Dakar* was found sunk 1.9 mi (3 km) deep between the Mediterranean islands of Cyprus and Crete.

The 3rd submarine, the *Dolphin*, arrive in Israel a few days after the disappearanc of the *Dakar*.

The bridge of the INS *Dakar*

The *Dakar's* emergency buoy

FIRST NUCLEAR SUBMARINE

The first submarine powered by a nuclear reactor was the *Nautilus*, which was launched by the American military in 1955. In 1958, the *Nautilus* traveled 1,864 mi (3,000 km), and among other things it passed under the ice cap of the North Pole. Two years later, another American nuclear submarine, the *Triton*, circumnavigated the entire globe submerged in water, without rising to the surface even once. Nuclear submarines service only the American, Russian, British, and French military.

HOW DOES A SUBMARINE SUBMERGE AND FLOAT?

Submarines have an inner and an outer steel shell, called a hull. The area in between the two hulls is divided into sections called ballast tanks. They can b filled with either air or water. When the submarine is on the surface, the ballast tanks are filled with air and the submarine's overall density is less than that of the surrounding water. Thus, it floats.

Ballast tanks are open at the bottom. For the vessel to go down, the submarine operator opens up valves at the top and lets air out. Seawater rushes in to fill the space that was taken up by air. This changes the ship's density. When the density of the submarine is greater than the surrounding water, it begins to sink. This is called negative buoyancy. A movable set of wings, called hydroplane helps control the angle of the dive.

To keep the submarine at any specifi depth, the crew adjusts the mixture of air and water in the ballast tanks. The operator tries to keep the submarine's overall density about the same as the surrounding water. This is called neutra buoyancy. When the submarine reache its cruising depth, the hydroplanes are straightened so the craft can travel leve through the water. If something change the submarine's weight and density, such as firing torpedoes, the operator must make further adjustments of the water/air mixture in the ballast tanks.

Submarines

A nuclear submarine

The launching of a missile from an Ohio submarine

ORLD'S LARGEST SUBMARINE FLEET

he American Navy has 77 active submarines, 18 of the Ohio class which ach carry 24 Trident ballistic missiles ith 8 nuclear warheads apiece. Four dditional submarines are used for carying guided missiles, and another 55 ttack submarines attack boats and ather information. The Ohio class ubmarines can launch missiles while ubmerged 165 ft 0 m) under water.

ARGEST SUBMARINE FLEET EVER

uring World War II, the Germans onstructed 1,162 submarines. hese sank more than 2,800 ships. he Germans lost 821 submarines – 433 were hit by planes and 252 y ships. The rest were damaged y aerial bombing of the ports, it by mines, or sunk in accients. Approximately 30,000 out f the 40,000 sailors who served the German submarine fleet rowned at sea.

ARGEST SUBMARINES

he world's largest submanes are the nuclear submanes that are powered by a 0,000 hp nuclear reactor nd equipped with launch ads for nuclear missiles. he largest of these are the ussian nuclear submarine eet of the Typhoon class, ith a displacement of 5,000 tons. The submanes are 558 ft (170 m) long nd are equipped with 20 R-39 RIF missiles with warheads hat split into 7. Each sub has a range of 5,527 mi ,895 km).

The American Ohio class submarines are slightly longer, 561 ft (171 m), but their capacity is a third smaller, disacing 16,700 tons. The Ohio is able to coast at a speed of 9.2 mph (47 km/h) when submerged, and can go down to maximum depth of 984 ft (300 m). The crew of 140 and he 15 officers live comfortably aboard the sub: they enjoy ean air, water for showering, a laundromat, nice ood, snack bar, fitness room, and even a small wimming pool, as well as hothouses for rowing flowers.

ASTEST SUBMARINE

he Russian nuclear submarine *Alfa* can each a speed of 48 mph (78 km/h), making it he fastest submarine in the world.

The first tank

The Panzerkampfwagen VIII V2

FIRST TANK

At the beginning of World War I (1914), British lt. col. Ernest Swinton thought of the idea of inventing reinforced crawling vehicles that would be able to cross over trenches and break through barbed-wire fences in order to counteract and destroy enemy machine-gunners, who were killing literally thousands of foot soldiers advancing toward the enemy trenches.

Swinton's first proposal was rejected, but he tried again and this time Minister of the Navy Winston Churchill convinced the British Ministry of Defense to study the possibility of developing a new war machine.

The first tank prototype, nicknamed Little Willie, was demonstrated in September 1915. Little Willie became the foundation for the first war tank, named Mark I.

Mark I was 33 ft (10 m) long and 7.9 ft (2.4 m) high, and weighed 28 tons. It was shaped like a rhombus surrounded by two large caterpillar shapes. On the back were added a pair of huge and heavy wheels for stability. It traveled at a speed of only 3.4 mph (5.5 km/h). However, it could cross trenches 10.8 ft (3.3 m) wide and bypass obstacles 4.6 ft (1.4 m) tall.

Since the tank did not have a rotating turret, turrets were set on each of its two sides, each containing a 2.2 in. (57 mm) cannon and a .303 in. (7.7 mm) machine gun. The tank was .4 in. (10 mm) thick. Light ammunition could not pierce it, but it offered no protection against cannons.

The Mark I operated with 8 crewmen under very unpleasant and difficult conditions. Temperatures inside the tank were very high. Ventilation was inadequate, so the air was contaminated with poisonous carbon monoxide, fuel and oil vapors from the engine, and fumes from the weapons.

Three crewmen were in charge of the steering — 1 driver and 2 working the gears. The first time Mark I tanks were used was in World War I in the Battle of Somme (1916). They didn't help much in battle, as most of them broke down or became stuck. Their main success, however, was that they broke the enemy's morale: many of the German soldiers fled or surrendered upon seeing this frightening, monstrous-looking machine.

MOST POPULAR TANK

The Russian tank T-54 is the most used tank in the world. Altogether, between the years 1954 and 1981, more than 95,000 T-54 tanks have been in operation. In the Soviet Union alone, 50,000 tanks were built, and an additional 45,000 were constructed by fellow Warsaw Pact countries as well as by China. The T-54 has participated in dozens of wars throughout the world, at times being used by both sides. The tanks were also used in wars against Israel, and more than 1,000 were captured. The Israeli tank corps replaced the motors, upgraded the tanks, and gave them a new name — the Tiran.

A Russian T-54 tank belonging to the Iraqi army during the Gulf War (1991)

HEAVIEST TANK

The heaviest tank ever built was the German Panzerkampfwagen VIII V2, which weighed 192 tons. The tank was never used because by the time World War II ended in 1945, the tank was still in the experimental stage.

The heaviest tank that saw battle was the French Char 2C, which weighed 75.2 tons. It was powered by two engines of 250 hp each and could reach a maximum speed of 7.5 mph (12 km/h).

The Scorpion S-200

WORLD'S FASTEST TANK

The world's fastest tank is the British Scorpion S-200, which serves 23 armies in the world. The tank's maximum speed has been clocked at 51.3 mph (82.5 km/h).

WORLD'S BEST TANK

The Merkava Mark IV tank, whose production began in 2003, is considered the world's best. The tank, which was developed and assembled in Israel, weighs 70 tons, is 30 ft (9 m) long, 13 ft (4 m) wide, and 8.2 ft (2.5 m) high. The tank has a 1,500 hp engine, which gives it a maximum speed of 40 mph (64 km/h). The 1,400 liter diesel fuel capacity allows it to travel for a distance of 311 mi (500 km) in one go.

The Mark IV includes the larger 120 mm cannon which can fire both cannon shells and missiles. It is also equipped with 60 mm mortars, 2 MAG machine guns, and a 0.5 in. (12.7 mm) heavy machine gun.

By the year 2006, $10 billion had been invested in the development and production of the Merkava. If we were to divide the total cost by 1,730 — the number of tanks so far produced — we would arrive at an average cost of $5.8 million per tank — very inexpensive compared to modern-day tanks.

HIGHEST NUMBER OF TANKS

Russia owns the most tanks in the world, with 21,000. The United States has 16,000 and China has 11,000. Israel has 4,300 tanks — one tank for every 1,700 residents, which is more than 10 times the number of tanks per capita in the United States.

A Russian T-54 tank

LARGEST CANNON EVER USED IN BATTLE

The capture of Constantinople, the capital of the Byzantine Empire, in 1453 is called the Fall of Constantinople. It was carried out by the Ottoman Empire, under the command of Sultan Mehmed II. The Ottomans used huge cannons made from a special type of bronze in distant Hungary. These cannons looked like pipes. They were 17 ft (5.18 m) long and had a 2.5 ft (762 mm) diameter barrel. Each weighed 17.3 tons and each fired 1,500 lb (680 kg) of granite stones. It took 200 men to clear a path to transport the cannon, which was dragged by 60 oxen, and 200 additional men who held ropes and made sure that it would remain upright. After a week of preparations, the cannons began firing the granite 7 times a day over the walls of the city. After 90 days of firing, the Ottomans managed to break through the wall, and finally the city of Constantinople was captured.

In 1464, Mehmed II ordered 42 even larger cannons weighing 18.3 tons each in order to protect the Straits of Dardanelles. Some 350 years later, in 1807, when the British Royal Navy began the Dardanelles Operation during the Anglo-Turkish War, these large cannons worked as well as when first produced.

In 1867, Turkish sultan Abdulaziz presented Queen Victoria with a cannon, which today is on display at the Tower of London Museum.

LARGEST CANNON

In the siege of Sevastopol (Russia) in July 1942 (World War II), the Germans used two cannons named Dora and Gustav. Their diameter was 31.5 in. (800 mm), with a 95 ft (29 m) long barrel. The guns fired bullets weighing 8.1 tons each, for a distance of 13 mi (21 km), and shells of 4.1 tons for a distance of 30 mi (48 km). The entire cannon weighed 1,350 tons and was 141 ft (43 m) long. A crew of 2,000 soldiers (250 just for firing) was required to operate them. The cannons were transported to their destination on railroad tracks via 24-car trains.

HIGHEST-SHOOTING CANNON

In November 1966, the joint U.S.-Canadian High Altitude Research Program (HARP) cannon fired a 185-lb (85 kg) Martlet projectile to an altitude of 112 mi (180 km). The cannon's barrel was 118 ft (30 m) long and weighed 150 tons. The HARP was an experimental cannon used to research how quickly it is possible for a projectile to leave the earth's atmosphere. The experiment was performed in the Arizona desert as part of the United States' outer space research.

MACHINE GUN WITH THE FASTEST RATE OF FIRE

The American-made M-61 Vulcan machine gun has the highest rate of fire. It is 10 times faster than a conventional machine gun. The Vulcan has 6 rotating barrels which can fire 6,000 rounds per minute from a .787 in. (20 mm) diameter cartridge. It takes the Vulcan half a second to accelerate to a maximum speed in which 100 rounds per second are fired — therefore, in the 1st second, the gun can fire "only" 75 rounds. The Vulcan was first manufactured in 1946 and since then has been installed on battle planes such as the F-15 and F-16, tanks, armored vehicles, and battleships.

DID YOU KNOW?

The Kalashnikov gun is on Mozambique's national flag, symbolizing its fight for independence, and is the logo of the Islamic terror organization Hezbollah. Lieutenant General Mikhail Timofeyevich Kalashnikov, the inventor of the submachine gun, was a tank commander in the Russian army during World War II. During the course of the war, Kalashnikov took note of the deadly use the Germans were making of the Schmeisser MP-40 submachine gun, compared to the outdated guns used by the Red Army. While recuperating from battle wounds in an army hospital, he read a book about development of firearms and began designing the gun that bore his name. Kalashnikov claimed that the most important characteristic of a gun is its beauty.

MOST POPULAR GUN

The Kalashnikov AK-47 submachine gun is the most popular and most widely used assault weapon in the world. From the time it first came out in 1947, Russia has produced more than 70 million AK-47s, supplying left-wing, anti-Western groups throughout the world. The gun is 34.3 in. (87 cm) long with a barrel length of 16.3 in. (41.5 cm). The Kalashnikov comes with a 40-round box magazine or 75-round drum magazines. It is capable of firing 600 rounds per minute, for a maximum distance of 1,378 ft (420 m).

KING OF CANNONS

The widest barrel attached to a conventional cannon belonged to the Tsar Cannon, manufactured in Russia in 1586. The cannon weighed 38 tons, was 17.5 ft (5.34 m) long, and had a barrel of 35 in. (890 mm) in diameter — with an outer diameter of 47 in. (1,200 mm). The huge cannon was never fired and is now on display at the Kremlin. The largest diameter of any cannon today, in modern times, does not reach even half the diameter of the Tsar Cannon.

Cannons and Guns

LARGEST CANNONS IN MODERN HISTORY

The largest modern-day cannons used were installed on two Japanese battleships: the *Yamato* and the *Musashi* — the largest battleships ever built (see page 130). Each ship was equipped with 9 cannons, firing shells 18 in. (460 mm) in diameter which were installed in 3 turrets. Each cannon was 75.5 ft (23 m) long and weighed 162 tons, and each shell weighed 3,219 lb (1,460 kg).

The main weaponry used by the Iowa class of American navy battleships is 9 cannons able to fire shells 16 in. (406 mm) in diameter installed on 3 turrets containing 3 cannons each. Each cannon is 66 ft (20 m) long and weighs 238,000 lb (108,000 kg) — almost as much as a spaceship. The shells weigh between 1,918 lb (870 kg) and 2,778 lb (1,260 kg) and can fire at a distance of 25 mi (40 km). When the shell is fired its full distance, it remains in the air for a minute and a half until it reaches its target.

EXPERIMENTAL GUN WITH THE FASTEST RATE OF FIRE

. Michael O'Dwyer, CEO of Metal Storm Ltd., a weapons research and development company in Australia, invented the first electronic gun. The prototype was a 36-barreled, stacked projectile machine gun, boasting the highest rate of fire in the world — 1.62 million rounds per minute (27,000 per second), for a 180-round burst. The company developed the first electronic handgun which in theory can fire more than 1 million rounds per minute (17,000 per second).

O'Dwyer's gun does not have movable parts. There are no locking mechanisms, hammers, firing pins, or ammo clips. There is no chance of jamming, and safety features include a coded receiver that prevents unauthorized use by children or criminals. The gun can be set to kill (with bullets) or to stun (with bean bags), and features "rapid reload" capability. A recoil barrel allows several bullets to be discharged, one after another, so that you feel a kick only after the last shot is fired, thereby improving accuracy.

With 1 press of the trigger, an electric spark ignites the fire behind the first bullet, and before it even leaves the barrel, the second one is already on its way pushing the first one, giving it a higher speed, greater strength and a more effective range. With this speed there is no movement, and the gun remains steady in the firer's hand such that 3 bullets will hit precisely the same spot.

This gun is deadly. However, Metal Storm plans many civilian uses for their advanced electronic weaponry technology, such as firing projectiles containing fire-suppressant products to help firefighters target fires that are more difficult to access, and firing small sacks of sand or other non-lethal munitions for dispersing protests.

SMALLEST GUN

The smallest gun in the world is the Swiss Mini-Gun, manufactured in Switzerland. The gun is 2.16 in. (5.5 cm) long and its bullets have a diameter of .092 in. (2.34 mm).

MOTHER OF ALL BOMBS

The GBU-43/B Massive Ordnance Air Blast bomb (MOAB — colloquially said to stand for the Mother Of All Bombs) is a large-yield, satellite-guided, conventional bomb that was developed for the United States military by Albert L. Weimorts, Jr., to be used in the American invasion of Iraq in 2003. However, the bomb was never used in battle. It weighed 21,700 lb (9,840 kg).

Weimorts also developed the Guided Bomb Unit 28 (GBU-28) Bunker Buster. It was specifically developed for use in Operation Desert Storm (1991) to penetrate Iraqi command centers located deep underground, yet the Americans hoped it would help them in striking Osama bin Laden in his mountain hideout.

Weimorts was reported to have said that it took 1 month to design and build the MOAB, but an entire year to fill out the paperwork.

MOST POWERFUL NON-NUCLEAR BOMB

The Russian answer to the American MOAB is an air-delivered bomb 4 times more powerful than the American bomb, dubbed "the Father of all Bombs." The bomb's explosives were developed with the use of nanotechnology. Although they weigh only 7 tons, they yield the equivalent of 45 tons of regular explosives. The American bomb yields 11.5 tons of explosives.

The bomb releases a fog of explosives when it hits the earth. As a result, everything within a radius of a few hundred yards is burned. The cloud of the explosion can rise as high as 9,842 ft (3,000 m), and the shock waves produced can destroy an area the size of a small city.

LARGEST NON-NUCLEAR BOMB USED IN BATTLE

The largest and heaviest conventional bomb ever used was the British Air Force's Grand Slam, which weighed 10 tons. The bomb, which was dropped over railroad tracks in Germany in March 1945 (World War II), was 25 ft (7.5 m) long.

SUPER-SHELLS

Although the largest cannons today are found aboard the American Battleships of the Iowa class, new and larger shells have been developed with technological advances:

- APC (Armor Piercing, Capped) 8 — as its name suggests, is capable of piercing through armored vehicles. The shell weighs 2,700 lb (1,225 kg) and can pierce even when fired from a distance of 11 mi (18 km). It can pierce an armored vehicle 1.6 ft (.5 m) thick — the equivalent of 21 ft (6.4 m) of reinforced concrete.
- Naval HC-13 — diameter of 1.33 ft (406 mm), weighing 1,900 lb (860 kg). This shell was designed mainly for non-armored shore bombardment. When the shell strikes, it creates a crater 20 ft (6 m) deep, with a diameter of 49 ft (15 m).
- KT-23 — in 1953, the United States Navy began secret development of nuclear underwater shells with an estimated output of 20 kT. It appears that the shells were ready for use in 1956. However, the American military does not confirm or deny reports of nuclear weapons on the decks of its boats.

BULL'S EYE

The world's most accurate air bomb is the Dual Mode Guided Bomb, manufactured in the United States. After it is dropped, it is guided by laser beams sent from a satellite — allowing it to strike within 6.5 ft (2 m) of its target.

Bombs and Missiles

GRAPHITE BOMB

A graphite bomb (also known as the "Blackout Bomb" or the "Soft Bomb") is a non-lethal weapon used to disable electrical power systems. Graphite bombs work by spreading a cloud of extremely fine, chemically treated carbon filaments over electrical components, causing a short circuit and thus disruption of the electrical supply. The filaments are only a few hundredths of an inch thick and can float in the air like a dense cloud. The United States used this bomb for the first time in the Gulf War of 1991 in order to neutralize 85% of Iraq's electricity.

Graphite bombs

QASSAM

The Qassam rocket is a simple steel artillery rocket manufactured by terror organizations in the Gaza Strip. The Qassam is very primitive, very inaccurate, and has a very short range. The main damage it causes is interference with daily life and the fear and shock it has brought to residents.

Qassam rocket fragments

Scud missile

Scud ready for launching

SCUD

The SS-1 Scud is a short-range ballistic missile 36 ft (11 m) long, with a diameter of 2.9 ft (.88 m). It was developed during World War II by the Russians in their war against the Nazis. The more advanced models of Scuds can carry standard explosives, chemical warheads, or nuclear warheads with a power of between 5 and 8 kT.

KATYUSHA

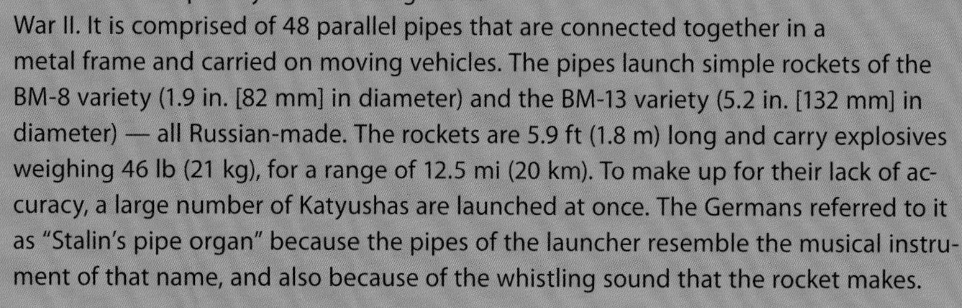

Katyusha is the name for an extremely simple and primitive moving rocket launcher that was developed by Russia during World War II. It is comprised of 48 parallel pipes that are connected together in a metal frame and carried on moving vehicles. The pipes launch simple rockets of the BM-8 variety (1.9 in. [82 mm] in diameter) and the BM-13 variety (5.2 in. [132 mm] in diameter) — all Russian-made. The rockets are 5.9 ft (1.8 m) long and carry explosives weighing 46 lb (21 kg), for a range of 12.5 mi (20 km). To make up for their lack of accuracy, a large number of Katyushas are launched at once. The Germans referred to it as "Stalin's pipe organ" because the pipes of the launcher resemble the musical instrument of that name, and also because of the whistling sound that the rocket makes.

A Katyusha rocket launcher

LARGEST HYDROGEN BOMB EVER DETONATED

Tsar Bomba is the nickname given by the Western nations for the AN-602 hydrogen bomb. It is the largest, most powerful nuclear weapon ever detonated. Project Tsar Bomba, referred to by the Russians as Big Ivan, began in July 1961 at the instruction of Soviet leader Nikita Khrushchev. The team of Soviet scientists who manufactured the bomb included Andrei Sakharov, the famous nuclear phycisist and peace activist. Shortly after the "successful" detonation of Tsar Bomba, Sakharov began speaking out against nuclear weapons, which led to his becoming a Russian dissident.

The experimental detonation took place in October 1961 over the Mityushikha Bay nuclear testing range, north of the Arctic Circle. Its yield was reduced to 50 mT of TNT instead of the planned 100 mT, in order to reduce the nuclear fallout.

The bomb weighed 27 tons. It was so large (26 ft/8 m long, 6.6 ft/2 m in diameter) that the plane that flew it to the test site had to have its bomb bay doors and fuselage fuel tanks removed. It was attached to a 1,764 lb (800 kg) fall-retardation parachute, which gave the release and observer planes time to fly about 28 mi (45 km) from ground zero.

The bomb was dropped from an altitude of 6.5 mi (10.5 km) and was designed to detonate at a height of 2.5 mi (4 km) over the land surface. Witnesses standing as far as 620 mi (1,000 km) away described it as a giant ball of fire in the sky. The heat from the explosion could have caused 3rd degree burns 62 mi (100 km) away from ground zero. The fireball reached nearly as high as the altitude of the release plane. The subsequent mushroom cloud was about 40 mi (60 km) high (nearly 7 times the height of Mt. Everest). The base of the cloud was 25 mi (40 km) wide.

Tsar Bomba is the single most physically powerful device ever utilized by humanity. The Soviet Union's goal was to compete with the West and prove its own nuclear capability. The experiment renewed the dormant nuclear weapons race among the superpowers.

LARGEST NUCLEAR TEST BOMB EVER DETONATED

The largest atomic bomb ever tested was dropped by the United States in March 1954 on Bikini Island in the South Pacific. The bomb, called Bravo, had a yield of approximately 20 mT of explosives. The blast eradicated the island completely, and left a half-mile (80 m) crater in the sea.

An SS-18 intercontinental missile

HEAVIEST INTERCONTINENTAL MISSILE

The Soviet Union's SS-18 intercontinental missiles are the heaviest intercontinental ballistic missiles in the world. Each one weighs 19,400 lb (8,800 kg) and can deploy 10 smaller missiles which are able to arrive at their destination on their own. The explosive yield of each of these smaller missiles can reach as high as 750 kT. Their flight range is 9,950 mi (16,000 km).

For comparison sake, the heaviest American ballistic missile weighs "only" 8,820 lb (4,000 kg) and carries 10 warheads with an explosive yield of 330 kT each.

HEAVIEST ATOMIC BOMBS

The heaviest atomic bombs weighed 4 tons and were 13 ft (4 m) long. They were carried by B-52 planes and had the explosive power of 9 million tons of dynamite. These bombs were taken out of service in 1984.

SMALLEST NUCLEAR BOMB

In the 1960s, the United States developed the smallest nuclear bomb. Called the W-54, it was 30 in. (76 cm) long, with a diameter of 10.75 in. (27 cm). It weighed only 51 lb (23.13 kg). Its explosive yield was 0.1 kT and it was slated to be used by commando units to destroy ports or bridges, and at times in the battlefield.

HIGHEST NUMBER OF ATOM AND HYDROGEN BOMBS

The Center for Strategic and International Studies in the United States estimates that approximately 22,000 nuclear warheads exist in the world today. The following is the breakdown by country:

United States	10,500
Russia	10,000
France	460
China	410
Israel	200-400
Britain	185
India	60
Pakistan	15-25

The United States and Russia signed a Nuclear Non-Proliferation Treaty in the 1990s to neutralize and destroy 2/3 of their nuclear weapons.

Many experts are of the opinion that Iran has nuclear warhead technology.

LARGEST NUCLEAR WARHEADS

The explosive power of the W-53 nuclear warhead of the American Titan II rocket had a yield of between 5 and 9 mT of TNT. However, these rockets were taken out of active service. The missile with the highest yield in the United States today is the W-56, which has a yield of "only" 2 mT.

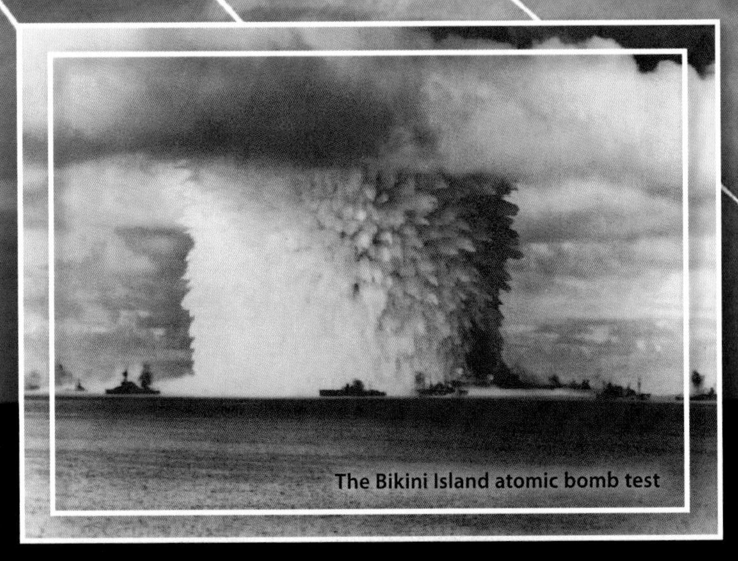

The Bikini Island atomic bomb test

Unconventional Weapons

Szilard and Einstein

EINSTEIN'S LETTER

The capability of splitting atoms and its possible use as a nuclear bomb of great strength was discovered in Berlin in the laboratory of Otto Hahn and Fritz Strassman. During the splitting process the atom's nucleus (center) splits when a neutron comes in contact with it, transforming the nucleus into massive energy.

Three Jewish physicists who had escaped from Nazi Germany to the United States — Leo Szilard, Edward Teller (known for having invented the first hydrogen bomb), and Eugene Wigner — concluded that the process would result in a chain reaction of splitting. The nucleus which splits releases 2 neutrons. One of them is intended to come in contact with the nucleus of another atom and split that one. The process continues and this chain reaction causes a massive amount of energy to be released. This is the gist of the production of this weapon of mass destruction.

These physicists were aware that nuclear research in Nazi Germany was very advanced and they asked Albert Einstein to warn the American president of this fact. Einsten responded by drafting a letter along with Leo Szilard and sending it to President Franklin Delano Roosevelt on August 2, 1939. As a result, Roosevelt ordered an acceleration of nuclear research.

A few days later, Einstein regretted having sent the letter. The Germans, despite their interest in the atomic project, were unable to actualize their efforts, and instead they concentrated on upgrading and increasing the number of weapons in their possession.

THE HUMAN FACTOR

Niels Bohr, one of the scientists developing the atom bomb, tried to convince American army officers not to drop the bomb in a populated area. He suggested dropping it from a height of 6 mi (10 km) in Japanese skies to produce an explosion that the Japanese could not ignore but that would result in little loss of life.

President Harry Truman made the critical decision to drop the bomb. He called it "the easiest decision I have ever made." Pilot Col. Paul Tibbets of the *Enola Gay* never expressed any regret or remorse, and on several occasions declared, "I would do it again." Although Tibbets might not have regretted his share in the attack, other crew members did.

THE MANHATTAN PROJECT

In 1942, soon after entering World War II, the United States began construction of the first nuclear bomb in Los Alamos, NM. The project was named The Manhattan Project. Top physicists were enlisted for this purpose. Research was directed by American Jewish physicist J. Robert Oppenheimer and among the other scientists were Enrico Fermi, Niels Bohr, and Werner Heisenberg.

The project had four main locations. Research in uranium enrichment took place at the University of California at Berkeley, Uranium 235 was produced in Oak Ridge, TN, plutonium was produced in Hanford, CA, and the first nuclear reactor was developed at the University of Chicago.

Many of the physicists who worked on this project were Europeans who had been exiled from occupied Europe. They were excited to join a group that was working on producing weapons aimed at rescuing their homeland from Nazi occupation — or to at least intimidate the enemy who was armed with nuclear weapons on a similar scale. Two bombs were developed: a uranium bomb known as Little Boy, and a plutonium bomb called Fat Man. Germany surrendered before construction of these bombs was completed.

Intercontinental ballistic missile deploying its smaller missiles

FIRST ATOMIC BOMB

The first atomic bomb was dropped during World War II, on the morning of August 6, 1945, by the American Air Force on the city of Hiroshima in Japan. It created a blast equivalent to about 12.5 kT of TNT. The bomb, known as Little Boy, was 10 ft (3 m) long and weighed 4 tons. It exploded 1,640 ft (500 m) above the city in order to achieve the most destruction possible. Col. Paul Tibbets took off in his B-29 plane called the *Enola Gay* with a crew of 10. None of the crew was aware of the true purpose of the mission they were on.

In 1945, Hiroshima (literally, "wide island") was the 6th largest city in Japan. It has an area of 350 mi^2 (905 km^2), and before the atomic bomb was dropped on it, it had a population of 250,000.

When the *Enola Gay* attacked, Hiroshima's air-raid alarm was not sounded, which raised the number of casualties by hundreds of percentages.

At 8:16 A.M., the atom bomb was dropped above the center of the city from a height of 5 mi (8 km). Tibbets immediately flew 180° upward to escape the massive shockwaves.

The bomb exploded 650 ft (200 m) above the local hospital. For a 1,000th of a second, the heat which had been generated by the bomb was equivalent to that of 1,000 suns, and for 1 second the temperature reached that of the sun. Most of the city simply disappeared. A massive ball of fire brightly lit up the sky and rose to an incredible height in the shape of a mushroom. Below was a massive shock wave that moved at the speed of sound for several miles, destroying everything in its path.

A few hours later black rain began falling. The drops which had passed through the mushroom turned black from the radioactive radiation. The survivors, most of whom suffered severe burns, ran for water and drank radioactive water. Thus, a large number of those who had survived the bomb were killed.

The explosion killed 70,000 people on the spot, and thousands more died the following day. An additional 100,000 died from injuries and radiation during the following years.

For the few moments after the explosion the Japanese radio stations and telegraph stations noticed that broadcast had ceased in the region. The Japanese army command tried to make contact with the army units stationed in Hiroshima, and was frightened by the total silence. They could find no plausible explanation for the massive explosion that had struck the city. Only 16 hours later did the United States inform the world about the new weapon of mass destruction in their hands.

Despite the large number of casualties, the Japanese army could not bring itself to surrender, and on August 9 a second atom bomb was dropped over Nagasaki. Only then did the Japanese emperor surrender.

Col. Paul Tibbets, *Enola Gay*'s pilot

A nuclear bomb

Nuclear Warfare

NUCLEAR TESTING

Since nuclear arms were invented, there have been more than 2,000 explosions for experiment and demonstration throughout the world. The countries which are known to have conducted these tests are the United States, the Soviet Union, the United Kingdom, France, the People's Republic of China, and North Korea. In 1963, most countries possessing nuclear weapons — and many others as well — signed the Limited Test Ban Treaty. As of today, 116 countries have signed and ratified it. The treaty obligates the signatories to refrain from testing nuclear weapons in the atmosphere, under water, or in outer space. The treaty permits underground nuclear testing.

INTERNATIONAL CITY OF PEACE

Although the buildings in Hiroshima had been constructed mainly from wood, there were some built of reinforced concrete that were particularly strong. Among them was the exhibition hall and conference center, which remained standing even though the atom bomb was dropped close to it. Since then it has never undergone repairs or renovations. In 1966, UNESCO (United Nations Educational, Scientific, and Cultural Organization) declared it a World Heritage Center.

After World War II the city was rehabilitated, and it declared itself the International City of Peace. Every year on August 6, Hiroshima marks the day with memorial services to teach the world about the horrors of war and the deadly results of the dropping of the atom bomb.

Hiroshima's exhibition hall and conference center, which survived the atomic bomb attack

THE PLUTONIUM BOMB

Fat Man was the code name given to the plutonium bomb that was dropped over the Japanese city of Nagasaki on August 9, 1945 — 3 days after the first atom bomb was dropped over Hiroshima. This was the 2nd and last time in which nuclear weapons were used in war. This bomb exploded with a destructive power equivalent to 21 kT of explosives.

The Nagasaki bombing

The "Fat Man" bomb

DID YOU KNOW?

Simply knowing that nuclear weapons exist has created a mutual intimidation between the two major blocs that have ruled the world since World War II: the Western bloc referring to the United States, and the Eastern bloc referring to the Soviet Union. This fear and intimidation have kept the peace. This "peace" is referred to as the Cold War.

After World War II, the United States invested great resources in the nuclear industry. At the beginning of 1946, the United States had only 6 bombs. However, 14 years later, it had more than 30,000 nuclear missiles of all classes and sizes.

The Russians managed to produce a nuclear bomb only in 1949 and immediately entered the nuclear arms race. England, France, and China joined the race only in 1960.

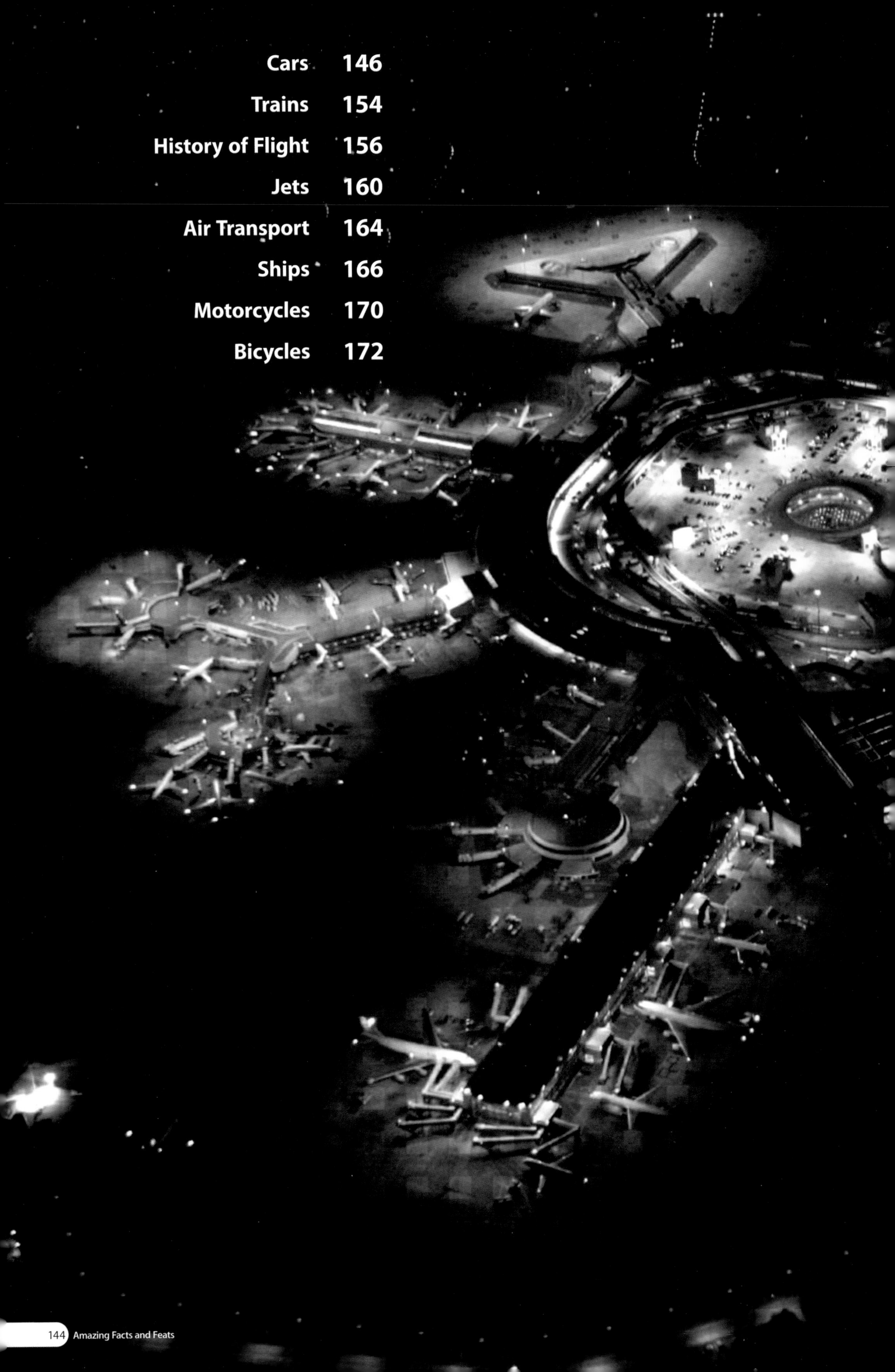

Cars 146

Trains 154

History of Flight 156

Jets 160

Air Transport 164

Ships 166

Motorcycles 170

Bicycles 172

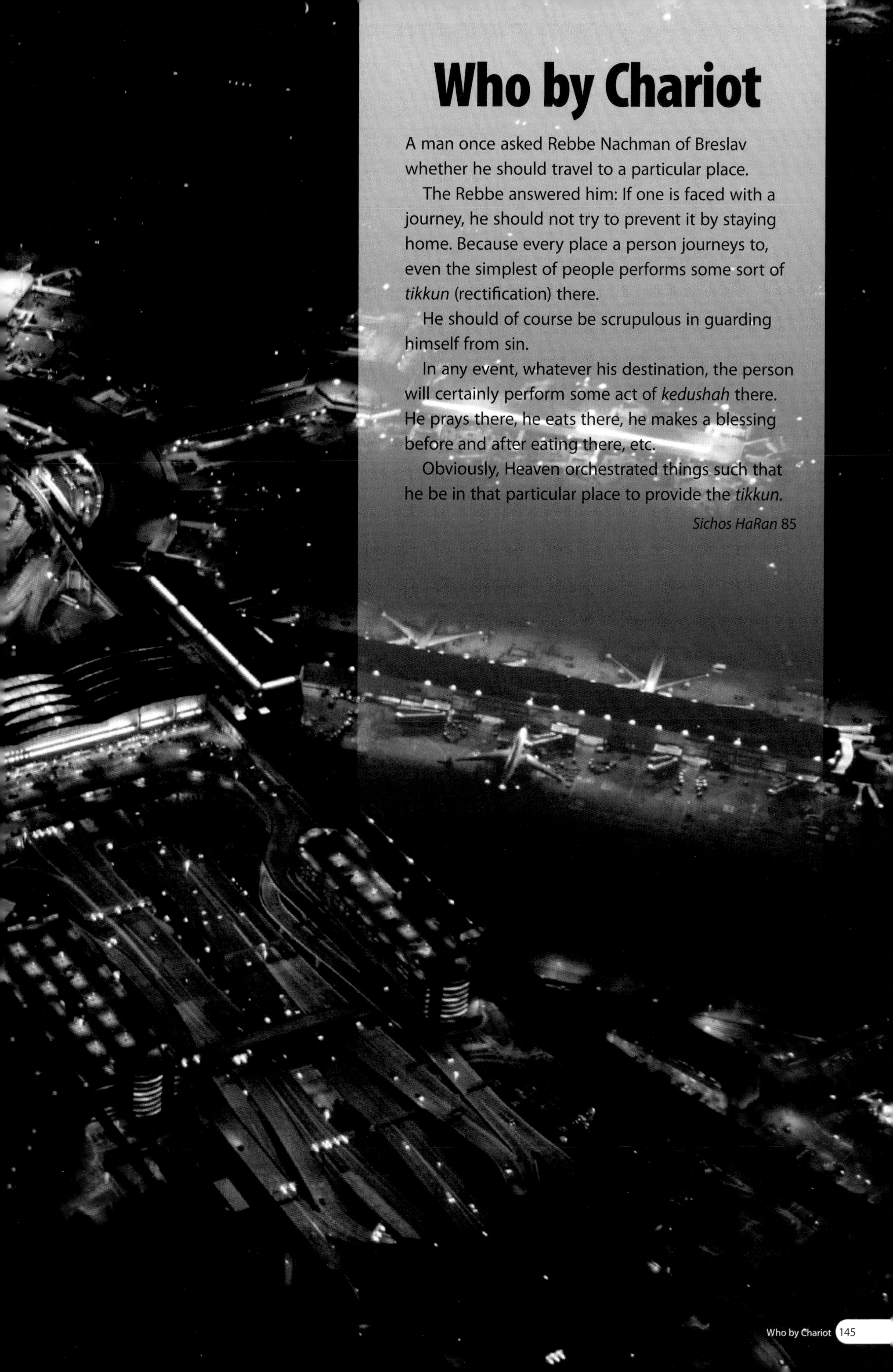

Who by Chariot

A man once asked Rebbe Nachman of Breslav whether he should travel to a particular place.

The Rebbe answered him: If one is faced with a journey, he should not try to prevent it by staying home. Because every place a person journeys to, even the simplest of people performs some sort of *tikkun* (rectification) there.

He should of course be scrupulous in guarding himself from sin.

In any event, whatever his destination, the person will certainly perform some act of *kedushah* there. He prays there, he eats there, he makes a blessing before and after eating there, etc.

Obviously, Heaven orchestrated things such that he be in that particular place to provide the *tikkun*.

Sichos HaRan 85

Siegfried Marcus

Siegfried Marcus's car

FIRST CAR

The world's first car was invented by a Jew named Siegfried Marcus. As early as 1875, he drove his gasoline-driven car through the streets of Vienna. Because of his Jewish origin, during the Nazi regime (1933–1945), book publishers were ordered to take his name out of all encyclopedias and replace it with the names of German car inventors Gottlieb Daimler and Karl Benz (photocopies of these instructions still exist). Another reason Marcus is not given credit as the inventor of the car is that he never registered a patent for his automobile inventions and he dismantled his original car.

History books therefore record Daimler and Benz as the inventors of the car.

A model of Marcus' second car from 1888 is displayed in Vienna's Technical Museum. A sculpture of Marcus stands by the entrance to a technical high school in the city.

Daimler worked for an engine-manufacturing company. After being fired in 1880, he began experimenting with improving the engine his former boss invented, and 4 years later he decided to incorporate it into the car which he was yet to name.

Two years later, Karl Benz — who had no idea that Daimler had already constructed something similar — registered the first true patent for an automobile that ran on gasoline. It was a tall wagon with three wheels and was named the Benz Patent Motorwagen. The car had a 1.7 liter engine with 1.5 hp and could travel at a speed of 12.5 mph (20 km/h). Benz' invention enjoyed immediate success, and he was able to sell one car every 2 months — 25 cars within 4 years.

Incidentally, Benz himself was afraid to drive and handed the wheel over to his wife.

FIRST PATENT FOR A CAR

In 1879, a sophisticated New York lawyer by the name of George Selden registered a patent for his abstract idea for an engine-powered vehicle. Selden himself could not even build a bicycle and had no intention of investing any money into actually building the vehicle. However, he refused to forego his rights, and using his legal skills he managed to delay paying the patent fees for 16 years. His patience and perseverance paid off, and he eventually managed to collect royalties for every car sold in the United States for 17 years, beginning in 1895. The end result was that Henry Ford took Selden to court and his victory resulted in a basic change in American patent laws.

FIRST AUTOMOBILE COMPANY

Frenchmen René Panhard and Emile Levassor were partners in a machinery business when they decided to become the first automobile manufacturers. This is why many words in the car industry are French in origin: garage, carburetor, chassis, limousine, and others.

The first car manufactured by the Panhard et Levassor factory in 1889 is considered the first modern car. The engine was a German Daimler mounted in front. The basic design of almost all future cars became known as Systeme Panhard: it consisted of 4 wheels with rear-wheel drive operated by a pedal, a clutch pedal to operate a chain-driven gearbox, a front-mounted radiator, the first modern transmission, and differential gearing. In 1900, French roads had some 1,200 cars — many with 20 hp motors.

Incidentally, in 1897, Levassor became the first casualty of motor sports when he was killed while driving a company car in the Paris-Marseilles race.

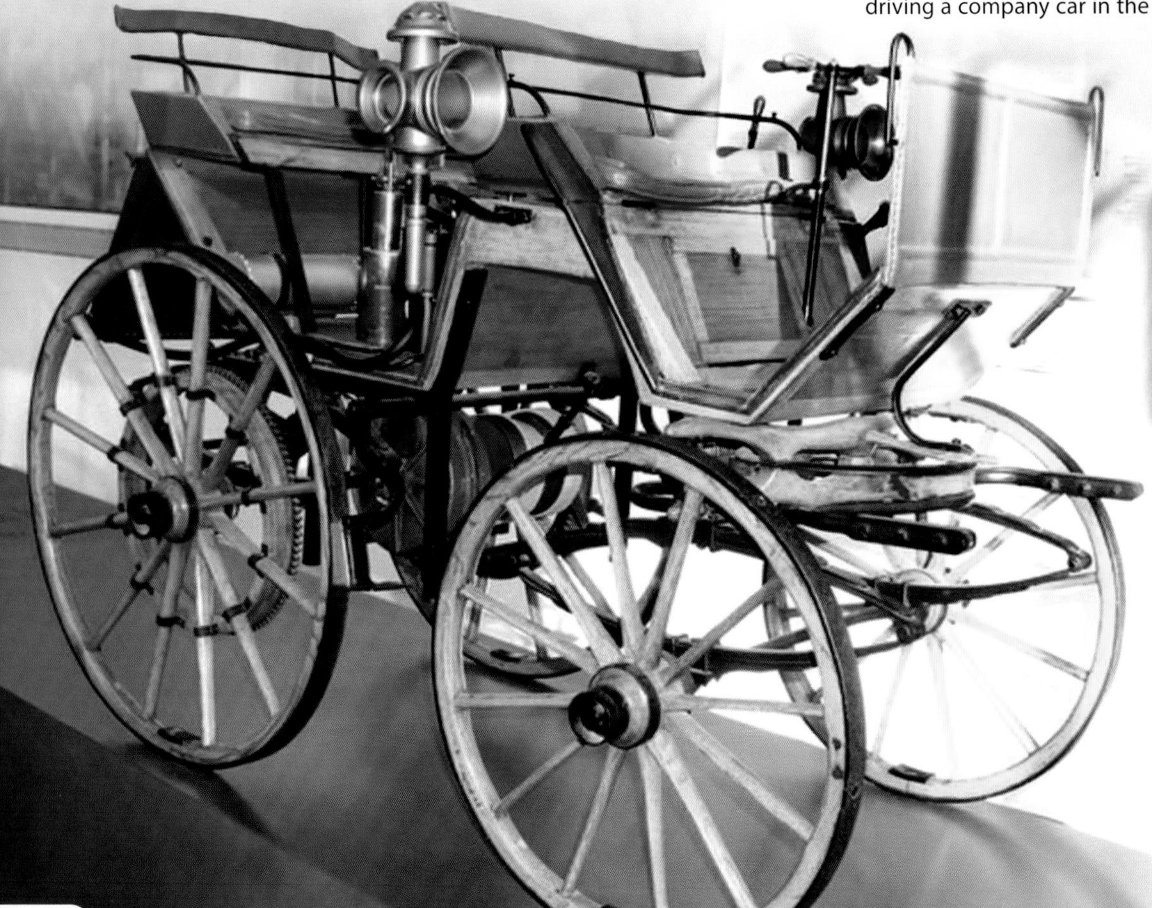

Gottlieb Daimler

Karl Benz

FIRST TRAFFIC ACCIDENT

In 1769, a French inventor by the name of Nicolas-Joseph Cugnot built a "Carriage Without Horses," which was like a 3-wheel tractor designed for towing artillery powered by a giant steam engine in the front. Cugnot called his machine a "fardier a vapeur." On an early test run in the streets of Paris, after a short ride at a speed of 1.9 mph (3 km/h), it failed to make a sharp turn and crashed into a stone wall. The project was scrapped, while Cugnot went down in history as the man involved in the first motor vehicle accident.

In the 2nd half of the 19th century, the English Parliament enacted a series of laws called "Red Flag Laws" (listed below). The Red Flag laws were designed to control the use of self-propelled vehicles such as trains and agricultural engines. British lawmakers were concerned that these newfangled vehicles would endanger pedestrians and horses, as well as damage carriages and public roads. The Red Flag laws were repealed in 1896, the same year that American Henry Ford opened his car manufacturing plant in Great Britain — which went on to become the largest car manufacturer in Britain.

ɪRST STEERING WHEEL

ɔr a 15-year period, all cars were ɫeered with the aid of a control ːick — even in races where cars ɏould drive as fast as 24 mph ʒ8 km/h). It was only in 1901 ɪat Peugeot revolutionized ɪe car industry with their ew model, Peugeot Type 36, ɪanufactured between 1901 ɲd 1902. This was the first car to ɐature a steering wheel rather than a control stick.

RED FLAG LAWS:

The Locomotive Act (Red Flag Laws) of 1865

- The speed limit was 4 mph (6 km/h) in the country and 2 mph (3 km/h) in the city.
- Self-propelled vehicles had to be accompanied by a crew of 3: the driver, a mechanic, and a man with a red flag (or lantern) walking 60 yards (55 m) in front of each vehicle. The man with the red flag or lantern made sure the vehicle would stay within the speed limit, and warned horse riders and horse-drawn traffic of the approach of a self-propelled machine.

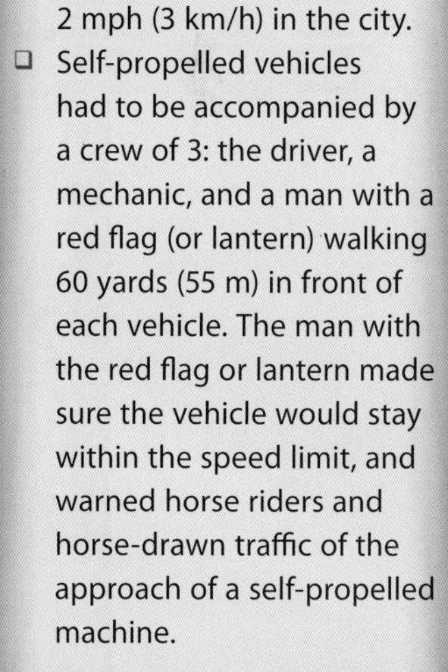

In 1878 the following changes were made to the Red Flag laws:

- The red flag was optional under local regulation.
- The distance between the vehicle and the man with the red flag was reduced to 20 yards (18 m).
- Vehicles were required to stop on the sight of a horse.
- Vehicles were forbidden to emit smoke or steam, in order to prevent horses from being alarmed.

The Benz Patent Motorwagen

FIRST RUBBER TIRES

Armand Peugeot started out manufacturing steel rods to shape dresses. This led to his manufacturing umbrella frames, saw blades, wire wheels, and ultimately bicycles. From there the move to cars was only natural. By 1892, he had already manufactured 20 different models of Peugeot cars to which he introduced one of the most important inventions to the world of cars — rubber tires. In 1894, Edward Michelin improved on this invention: instead of hard rubber tires, he introduced the air-filled tire.

Ransome Olds

FIRST PRODUCTION LINE

In order to make the car affordable to everyone, the price of production had to be drastically cut. The only way to do this was to transform it from an individual, made-to-order vehicle, to a mass-produced one.

The first assembly-line automobile to be mass produced was in Detroit, MI (USA), in 1901. The car, known as the Curved Dash Oldsmobile, was manufactured by American car manufacturer Ransome Eli Olds. Olds was able to sell 425 cars in 1901.

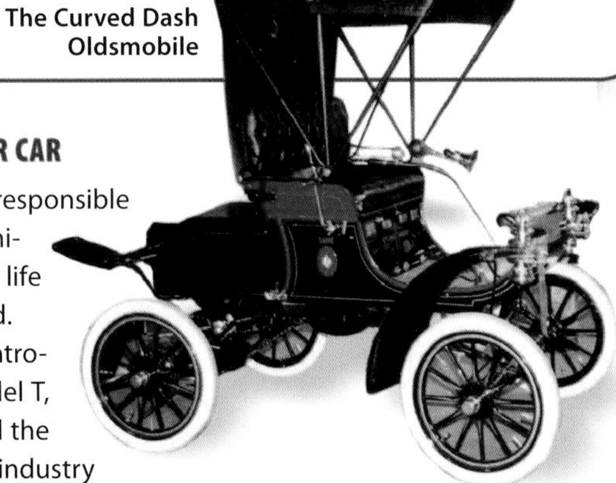

The Curved Dash Oldsmobile

FIRST POPULAR CAR

The man truly responsible for the car dominating modern life was Henry Ford. In 1908, Ford introduced the Model T, which changed the face of the car industry in the United States and throughout the world. The Model T weighed 1,323 lb (600 kg) and was powered by a 4 cylinder, 2.9 liter, 20 hp engine.

Ford was a brilliant manager. He insisted on uniformity in manufacturing and therefore was able to maintain a very low price of only $825 per car. The result was that in the year 1912, 75% of cars sold were Fords. By 1914, Ford had sold almost 310,000 cars. The explanation for their success is quite simple — by 1914, the assembly process for the Model T had been so streamlined that it took only 93 minutes to assemble a car! By 1916, the price had dropped to a mere $345.

Ford's uniformity and insistence on making his product affordable can be summed up in his motto: "You can order a Model T in any color, so long as it's black."

Incidentally, the first car imported to Israel was the Ford Model T, purchased by botanist Aharon Aharonson from Zichron Yaakov.

Reliant cars

SAVINGS ON WHEELS

In January 1935, the first Reliant car was manufactured by British engineer Tom Lawrence Williams. The Reliant had only 3 wheels - 2 in the back and 1 in the front. In 1953, the Reliant Regal model was able to reach a speed of 60 mph (96 km/h) and became the first car manufactured from fiberglass. The Regal continued to be manufactured until 1973, whereupon it was given a new body, an improved motor of 750 cc and a new name: Reliant Robin. But ... it still stuck to its 3 wheels.

In September 2000, to mark 65 years of 3-wheeler production, Reliant introduced a limited run of 3-wheelers called Robin 65.

Only 65 Robin 65s were made. Each came with a numbered plaque with the owner's name on the dashboard. All 65s were painted in a gold metallic paint and featured alloy wheels, a stainless steel exhaust pipe, and a host of internal additions such as leather trim, walnut dashboard, chrome door handles, and a high performance sound system.

In December 2000, the last Reliant rolled off the production line, and the company closed its doors. A company spokesman explained that although Reliant car owners were very loyal, with the passage of time many of them were simply no longer alive.

The Model T Ford

The Sussita

LONGEST ROAD IN ISRAEL

The longest road in Israel is Route 90. It is 297.4 mi (478.7 km) long and runs from Taba (next to Eilat) on the Israeli-Egyptian border in the south, to Metulla (near the Israeli-Lebanese border) in the north.

GREATEST CAR CONGESTION IN THE WORLD

Israel is the country with the greatest congestion of cars in the world. Since 1960, the population has increased 400% — from 1.3 million to 7.1 million. The total number of motor vehicles, however, has risen by 3,670% — from 70,000 to 2,573,000. The number of passenger cars alone has risen by 8,300% — from 24,000 to 1,995,000.

In 1960, the entire population of Israel drove 1.2 billion mi (1.94 billion km) per year — 575 million mi (925 million km) in passenger cars, 122 million mi (197 million km) in buses, and 508 million mi (818 million) in other forms of transportation. In 2008, this number had risen by 2,240%, to 27.7 billion mi (44.6 billion km) — 18.9 billion mi (30.4 billion km) in ordinary cars, 568 million mi (914 million km) on buses, 7.8 billion mi (12.5 billion km) on trucks, 516 million mi (830 million km) on motorcycles and other vehicles.

In the year 1960, Israel had 4,039 mi (6,500 km) of paved roads, which by 2009 had increased 275%, to 11,245 mi (18,096 km). In 1960, there were 12 cars per km of road in Israel, while in 2009 there were 142.9 cars per km of road.

Incidentally, there are 2,283 traffic lights in Israel.

THE ONLY ISRAELI-MANUFACTURED CAR

The only car which was designed and manufactured in Israel was the Sussita. At the beginning of 1955, the Autocars Company in Haifa was granted a license to manufacture the British Reliant. The Reliant did not enjoy much success in Israel, but 5 years later, in 1960, the first Sussita produced by Autocars (with help from Reliant) was introduced. Over the next few years, 70,000 Sussitas were manufactured, although only a few of them are still in existence. The last model was the Rom Carmel, which was manufactured from 1975 until 1981, at which point the Autocars factory closed down.

In the mid-1960s, the Autocars Company introduced a sporty 2-seater called Sabra in the United States. This model was sold with either a hard roof or an open roof. Today, the Sabra is considered one of the most valuable collectors' items.

"Bon Appetit"

What was unique about the Sussita was that its external body was made from fiberglass (a type of plastic) rather than from metal. The skeleton was very light and did not rust — very strong and very advanced for that time-period. The fiberglass also drastically reduced the price of the car in comparison to other cars. The only problem was that hungry camels in the Sinai Desert found the fiberglass very tasty and were caught chewing on cars. The Sussitas were also not very safe.

Incidentally, the name Sussita was chosen in a competition. The winner received a prize of 500 Israeli lira.

INVENTION THAT SAVED THE MOST LIVES

The seat belt, which was invented in 1959 by the Swedish Engineer Nils Bohlin and patented by Volvo, has saved the highest number of lives in the automobile industry. The original seat belt was anchored in 3 places, and in 1970 Volvo developed its roller-type storage system for the belt.

The United States National Highway Traffic Safety Administration estimates that in the past decade, seat belts prevented approximately 56,000 deaths and 1.5 million injuries in the United States. This is not to mention the monetary savings, which includes insurance and medical costs, estimated at $110 billion.

SEAT BELTS IN ISRAEL

It is estimated that 90% of Israeli drivers and 84% of front-seat passengers wear seat belts. Studies have shown that women take this more seriously than men (87% of female front-seat passengers wear seat belts, as opposed to only 76% of the men). The Afula/Jezre'el Valley area seems to have the least number of belted travelers — 71% of drivers and 64% of front-seat passengers.

According to a survey conducted by the National Road Safety Commission in Israel, among Jewish travelers, 92% of drivers, 81% of front-seat passengers, and 41% of back-seat passengers belted up. In the non-Jewish sector, however, only 61% of front-seat passengers use seat belts, while 31% of those seated in the back do so. In that same year, traffic fatalities were 16% higher among those not wearing seat belts.

THE WAY THEY USED TO DRIVE

Cars of the past were recipes for driving disasters. Three pedals stuck out of the floor: the right one was for braking, the middle one for driving backwards, and the left one would go into 1st gear when pressed and 2nd gear when released. This of course depended on whether the gear stick protruding from the floor pointed inwards. The gear stick served no function in the middle position, while anyone who needed to make an emergency stop would pull the stick backwards. There was another stick on the right of the steering wheel which served as a gas pedal, and a stick to the left that turned on the ignition.

MOST SOLD MODEL OF CAR

The Japanese Toyota Corolla, which was first introduced in 1966, is the best-selling car in the world, with over 35 million sold. Over the past 40 years, one Corolla has been sold on average every 40 seconds.

LEAST NUMBER OF CARS

The country of Somalia in Africa has the least number of cars per capita — 1 car per 10,000 residents.

MOST EXPENSIVE CAR

The most expensive car in the world is the Ferrari FXX, which sells for $2,078,000, not including taxes. The vehicle is equipped with a V12 6.3 liter engine which supplies 800 hp. The price of a Ferrari in Israel including taxes amounts to NIS 35 million. Only 20 such cars are manufactured per year, each of them ordered in advance.

A Ferrari race car

MOST EXPENSIVE VINTAGE CAR

In April 1990, Nicholas Harley from England sold a 1931 Bugatti Royale 41 to a Japanese company for $15 million. This is the highest recorded price ever paid for a car. In 1931, the Bugatti Royale sold for $30,000 — less than 1/500th of the price paid for it 60 years later. Nevertheless, it was still considered expensive at the time.

A 21st century Bugatti

Bugatti Royale

Italian car manufacturer Ettore Bugatti had planned to build 25 Royales and sell them to royalty. But because this was during the Great Depression (1929–1939), even the wealthy and noble weren't buying. Thus, he sold only 3 out of the 6 cars he built between 1927 and 1933. All 6 are still in existence.

LARGEST CAR MANUFACTURER

Toyota of Japan is the largest car manufacturing company in the world. In 2009, Toyota manufactured 7,051,000 cars — 1.5 million less than it did in 2008. Toyota manufactures Toyota, Lexus, and Scion, and controls the Japanese manufacturer Daihatsu. Toyota employs 320,808 people.

The company started in 1933 as a division of Toyoda (with a "d") Automatic Loom Works. Toyota Motor Co. was established as an independent company in 1937.

During World War II, Toyota was mainly involved in manufacturing trucks for the Japanese army. The company has established manufacturing and assembly plants in 15 countries besides Japan.

In April 2007, Toyota replaced General Motors as the car manufacturer with the highest number of sales in the world. However, by the end of that year, General Motors regained this distinction.

General Motors Corporation was founded in 1908, and from 1931 until April 2007 was the largest car manufacturer in the world. Despite regaining its position at the end of 2007, today General Motors remains in 2nd place.

In June 2009, General Motors filed for bankruptcy due to its $172 billion debt. The American government intervened and saved the company — 61% of its stock is now owned by the American government. General Motors employs 204,000 workers. The company also manufactures GMC, Buick, Cadillac, and Chevrolet cars.

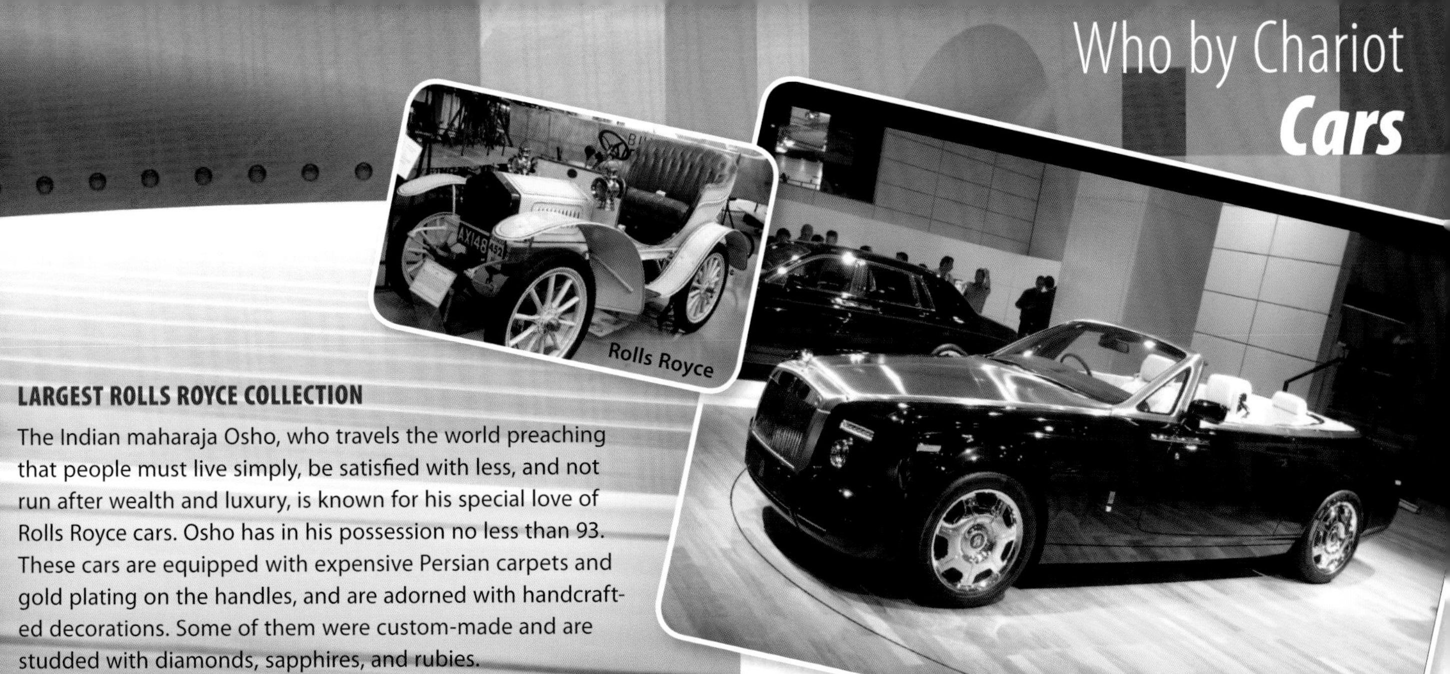

Rolls Royce

Rolls Royce

LARGEST ROLLS ROYCE COLLECTION

The Indian maharaja Osho, who travels the world preaching that people must live simply, be satisfied with less, and not run after wealth and luxury, is known for his special love of Rolls Royce cars. Osho has in his possession no less than 93. These cars are equipped with expensive Persian carpets and gold plating on the handles, and are adorned with handcraft-ed decorations. Some of them were custom-made and are studded with diamonds, sapphires, and rubies.

VOLKSWAGEN BEETLE

In the 67 years since Volkswagen introduced their first and classic Beetle model, 21,529,500 Beetles have been sold around the world. The first Beetle was designed at the behest of the evil archenemy of the Jewish people, Adolf Hitler, *yimach shemo*, when he first rose to power in Germany. He asked sports car manufacturer Ferdinand Porsche to design and manufacture a car that could transport 5 people and travel at a speed of 37 mph (60 km/h), whose cost would not exceed DM 1,000 (half a year's average salary), and which would travel at least 10.6 mi (17 km) per liter. Porsche got together with German industrialist Dr. Fritz Neumeyer and created the Volkswagen Company with the aim of meeting the Führer's demand.

In 1936, the V3 model, the first version of the mass-produced "Beetle," was introduced. During the next 44 years, the Beetle underwent only minor changes. In 1980, the 20 millionth Beetle was manufactured in Mexico. In 1994, Volkswagen came out with a new and more advanced model. It was stronger and safer, and aside from the familiar Beetle look had no connection to the original model. Even the price was far from the economical price of the original. In 2003 sales plummeted, and only 30,000 were sold, until finally at the end of July 2003, production was stopped entirely. However, there are still many of the old model Beetles on the road, mainly on the streets of Mexico and its neighboring countries in Central America.

Top 20 Motor Vehicle-Manufacturing Companies

Toyota
General Motors
Volkswagen
Ford
Honda
Nissan
PSA
Hyundai
Suzuki
Fiat
Renault
Daimler
Chrysler
BMW
Kia
Mazda
Mitsubishi
AvtoVAZ
Tata
FAW

Top 10 Motor Vehicle-Producing Countries

Japan
China
United States
Germany
South Korea
Brazil
France
Spain
India
Mexico

Total global production: approximately 70 million vehicles per year

LARGEST TRUCK

Although the length of the Liebherr T282, the world's largest truck, does not appear particularly impressive — only 47.5 ft (14.5 m) — its height (45.6 ft/13.9 m), width (28.5 ft/8.7 m) and net weight (201 tons, not including the weight of the driver), make it clear that this is no ordinary truck.

The Liebherr T282 is a mining truck. It has a 21.3 ft (6.5 m) dump bed which can carry slightly more than 528 tons of dirt and can operate with the aid of a 3,500 hp engine, traveling at a maximum speed of 37 mph (60 km/h). What about the price? Well, it can be yours for only $3 million.

Volvo's B12 bus

LONGEST BUS

The B12 bus manufactured by the Volvo Company of Sweden is 85.3 ft (26.8 m) long. The bus, which consists of 2 other buses attached to it from behind, has a total of 300 seats and is powered by a 12 liter, 340 hp engine. Among the fleet of 4,000 buses belonging to Brazilian company Viação Campo Belo, 30 of them are B12s.

A 10,000 MILE JOURNEY ON ONE GALLON OF GAS

The Japanese Fancy Carol-NOK team designed a super-economical car. In a test drive from the city of Hiroshima, it passed the 100 km (62 mi) mark using only .0244 liters of gasoline — in other words, slightly more than 10,240 mpg (4,100 km/liter). The flat car, which is slightly less than 27.6 in. (70 cm) high, is covered with special aerodynamic coating which lessens air resistance and prevents excess energy waste.

DRIVER'S LICENSES FOR CHILDREN

In the United States, there are 13 states that issue driver's licenses at the age of 14. In each of these cases, the licenses have special limits and conditions. In Hawaii, you can receive a driver's license for a private car from age 15. In the state of Mississippi, one can receive a license without taking a driving course.

The Radiance

HARNESSING THE POWER OF THE SUN

The Radiance car is powered by solar energy. In the year 2000, the Radiance completed a 4,377 mi (7,044 km) Canadian journey which began in Halifax, the capital of the province Nova Scotia, and ended in Vancouver, the capital of the province British Columbia. The car drove at an average speed of 50 mph (80 km/h).

The Radiance was staffed by members of Queen's University in Canada who built the car. Its flat, aerodynamic shape lessens air resistance and insures that the energy consumption does not exceed that of an electric kettle. In order to drive the low, flat car, the driver needs to lie down. The journey took 29 days at a total cost of $2,525 — $5 for the 1,000 watts of power consumed by the solar car, and an additional $2,520 of gasoline consumed by the accompanying staff who were driving conventional cars.

LONGEST CAR

Jay Ohrberg from Burbank, CA (USA), designed and built a 100 ft (30.5 m) limousine, making it the longest car in the world. Inside the car can be found a luxurious living room, swimming pool with a diving board, and a retractable roof. The roof can also be used as a helipad. (See inside cover for a picture of the limousine.)

DID YOU KNOW?

Air bags open at a speed of 199 mph (320 km/h).

* * *

Electric-powered cars were first manufactured in 1896, and until the end of that century almost half the cars on the road ran on electricity. However, in 1905, 80% of the cars were manufactured with gasoline motors, and by 1920 all electric cars were removed from use.

WORLD'S CHAMPION CAR-PARKER

What is the best method for parking in a narrow space? Russ Swift of England can park his Mini-Minor with "breathing room" of only 12.6 in. (32 cm). He drives at a high speed until he is parallel to the desired parking spot. He then slams on the brakes, "breaks the wheel" completely (spins the steering wheel all the way), and within 1 second spins the car 180° and slides it into the parking space.

DID YOU KNOW?

Trucks, buses, and taxicabs make up for 19% of cars on the road, yet are involved in 40% of fatal traffic accidents.

SUBMARINE CAR

The sQuba, manufactured by Swiss automobile manufacturer Rinspeed, is a 2-seater sports car which, when necessary, can submerge in water to a depth of 33 ft (10 m). Despite its light weight of only 2,028 lb (928 kg), the sQuba is not particularly fast, because it is powered with only a 50 hp engine. However, the pair of propellers in the front and the jet stream motor in the back are all electric, causing no pollution, and it is certainly more pleasant to dive into the water than to sit in traffic jams. A pair of oxygen tanks provides the driver and passenger with sufficient air to breathe.

FASTEST AMPHIBIAN CAR

The same Swiss automobile company Rinspeed manufactured a sophisticated car called Splash, which set the record for the fastest crossing of the English Channel in an amphibian (land and sea) vehicle. The car's driver, Frank M. Rinderknecht — coincidentally the CEO of Rinspeed — left Dover Beach in England and crossed the Channel in 193 minutes and 47 seconds. The Splash's maximum land speed is 124 mph (200 km/h), and it can float on the surface of the water with the aid of wing-fins at a maximum speed of 50 mph (80 km/h).

FASTEST TRAINS

The world's fastest train is the Harmony express train, which swept across 714.6 mi (1,100 km) in China at average speeds of 217.5 mph (350 km/h) on its 1st run. Its record-setting speed during pre-launch trials was 288.4 mph (394 km/h). The Chinese government spent $17 billion to develop the Harmony express line and $2.4 billion to create a French-designed train station, with 20 tracks and 11 platforms.

The German InterCity Express (ICE3) travels between the cities of Frankfurt and Cologne at a speed of 205 mph (330 km/h). More than €2 billion was invested in its development.

The Shinkansen, also known as the bullet train, is a network of high-speed railway lines in Japan. The 1,528 mi (2,459 km) long network links most major cities on the islands of Honshū and Kyūshū at speeds of up to 186 mph (300 km/h). Test runs achieved a speed of 275 mph (443 km/h) for conventional rail in 1996, but in 2003 a world record of 361 mph (581 km/h) was set with a Maglev rail system (see page 155).

The TGV (French: Train à Grande Vitesse, meaning high-speed train) is a long-distance train that travels its regular route at a speed of 186 mph (300 km/h). In a special test run, the TGV reached a speed of 357.2 mph (574.8 km/h) — half the speed of sound.

FASTEST UNMANNED TEST-TRAIN

The fastest speed attained by an unmanned rocket sled that rides on train tracks was 6,450 mph (10,380 km/h) — Mach 8.43. The test was carried out at the Holomon missile base in New Mexico (USA).

A high-speed train

FIRST STEAM LOCOMOTIVE

George Stephenson

In 1829, brothers George and Robert Stephenson developed the "Rocket," the first steam locomotive, which became the most important mode of transportation at that time.

The first steam locomotive

FIRST PASSENGER TRAIN

The first passenger train service began in Kent, England, in 1830. The train traveled at a speed of only 5 mph (8 km/h) and its entire route was only 1 mi (1.6 km) long.

LONGEST TRAIN IN REGULAR SERVICE

The longest train in regular service is 1.9 mi (3 km) long. The train's route, which travels the Nouadhibou-Choum route in Mauritania (on the northwest African coast), is 286 mi (460 km) long. The entire journey takes 12 hours at an average speed of 25 mph (40 km/h).

TOTAL LENGTH OF TRAIN TRACKS WORLDWIDE

The total length of all the train tracks in the world is 692,988 mi (1,115,205 km). Of these, 159,999 mi (257,481 km) are extra-wide tracks, 417,216 mi (671,413 km) are standard tracks, and 115,774 mi (186,311 km) are narrow tracks.

COUNTRY WITH THE MOST TRAIN TRACKS

The country with the longest ne work of train tracks is the Unite States, with a total track length 184,425 mi (296,500 km).

LONGEST RAILWAY LINE

The longest train route in the w is the Trans-Siberian Proper rout the Trans-Siberian Railway, whic 5,866 mi (9,440 km) long. It star Moscow, the capital of Russia, a travels east through Russia, end in the Russian city of Vladivosto on the Sea of Japan. The route 97 stations, and it takes 8 days t travel the entire way.

There are 2 other trans-Sibe routes on the Trans-Siberian Railway: the Trans-Mongolian r from Moscow to Beijing (China) Mongolia, and the Trans-Manchurian route from Moscov to Beijing through Siberia and Chinese Manchuria.

STRAIGHT-AS-A-RULER TRACK

The longest straight portion o track in the world is found on Australia's Trans-Australian line 298 mi (480 km) of completely straight track, though not alwa on the same level.

Who by Chariot
Trains

The Maglev train

LARGEST TRAIN STATION

The world's largest train station is New York's Grand Central Station. The station, built in 1903, covers 48 acres in area and has 2 levels of tracks: 41 tracks on the upper level and 26 tracks on the lower level. On an average day, 550 trains carrying 180,000 people pass through the station.

MOST CONGESTED TRAIN SYSTEM

The most congested train system in the world is found in Japan, where there are 16 million daily train travelers.

MOST CONGESTED SUBWAY SYSTEM

Moscow's subway system is considered the most congested in the world. Every day, 8.7 million people ride the trains, totaling 3.2 billion passengers per year — almost half the world's population. This amounts to more train travelers than the total number of subway riders in London, Paris, and New York combined. There are over 150 stations along Moscow's subway network, with more than 124 mi (200 km) of track.

THE MAGLEV TRAIN

Maglev, or magnetic levitation, is a transportation system that lifts up, guides, and moves vehicles — mainly trains — using a very large number of magnets to lift and move the vehicle. Maglev could potentially be faster, quieter, and smoother than wheeled mass transit systems.

Magnets hold the train afloat about .4 in. (1 cm) above the track. The train moves forward quietly and at incredible speed, without gasoline expenses and air pollution. The highest recorded speed of a Maglev train is 361 mph (581 km/h), clocked on an experimental run in Japan between 2 cities.

The main drawback of the magnetic levitation train is the cost of establishing a network of special tracks. Today, the only maglev line train in operation connects the city of Shanghai, China, with its airport.

ISRAEL'S ONLY UNDERGROUND TRAIN

In 1956, the municipality of Haifa began to build a subway known as the Carmelit, which even today is Israel's only underground train system. The Carmelit connects the 3 main sections of Haifa: the lower city, the Hadar level, and the Carmel. In 1986, after 30 years in operation, the Carmelit was closed down due to serious safety problems. It was reopened in September 1992 after extensive renovations.

FIRST TRAINS IN ISRAEL

In September 1892, the first train in Eretz Yisrael began to operate as the Jerusalem-Jaffa line. The route was 54 mi (87 km) long, and the trip took 3 hours and 50 minutes. It ran almost continuously until 1998.

The construction of train tracks in Egypt in 1852 gave Sir Moses Montefiore the idea of extending the Egyptian tracks. In 1857, he brought an English engineer who was an expert in train tracks to Eretz Yisrael, to conduct a feasibility study. The engineer suggested the route which still operates today.

By 1905, there was a Haifa-Damascus line, and in 1915 the ruling Turks opened a military line from Afula in the Jezre'el Valley to the Sinai Desert. After the British took over Palestine in 1917, they opened up an Egypt–Lod–Haifa line, a Cairo-Haifa line, and a Haifa–Beirut–Tripoli line.

There is a story that after Israeli independence was won in 1948, Israel Railways was going to operate on Shabbos. But one man traveled to the railway headquarters and convinced the chief executive to cancel the plan. Some people acquire for themselves the World to Come in just a few minutes — and for just one seemingly small act.

DID YOU KNOW?

In the Soviet Union, train tracks were intentionally built at first to a different standard than the European one in order to make it difficult for foreigners and residents to enter and leave the country. At the border, they would raise the locomotive and the cars and switch the axles so that the wheels would fit the Russian train tracks. Today, following the dismantling of the Soviet Union and the opening of the borders, there is a movement to convert the Russian tracks to conform to European standards.

THE TRANS-SIBERIAN RAILWAY AND YESHIVAS MIR

In 1938, right before the outbreak of World War II, ships stopped sailing from Europe to the Far East. Between 1938 and 1941, thousands of Lithuanian and Polish Jews fled from the Nazi occupiers, mainly to Shanghai (China) and to Japan by means of the Trans-Siberian Railway. Among those who were saved were all the rabbis and students of the Mir yeshiva. The Jews were aided by 2 righteous gentiles: the Japanese Consul in Kovno, Lithuania, Mr. Chiune Sempo Sugihara, who issued more than 2,150 visas (assisted by Mir student Yisrael Zupnick), and the Dutch consul in Kovno, Jan Zwartendijk, who also issued thousands of permits for Jews to travel — all against the official instructions of their governments.

The government of the Soviet Union classified these Jews as tourists and allowed them to travel on the Trans-Siberian Railway to the Far East in exchange for money that was transferred to them by the Jewish Joint Distribution Committee.

e Sempo Sugihara

THE BEGINNING OF FLIGHT

French brothers Joseph-Michel and Jacques-Étienne Montgolfier were the inventors of the hot-air balloon. They began their "airborne" career by investigating smoke, which they thought had "light" properties and could cause objects to rise.

The brothers constructed a globe-shaped balloon of sack-cloth with three thin layers of paper inside. They coated it with aluminum to prevent burning and connected the parts with more than 2,000 buttons. In their public demonstration in June 1783, the brothers made a fire from straw, cotton, and even old shoes. They filled the balloon with a volume of 31,780 ft^3 (900 m^3) of smoke. It flew for 10 minutes for a distance of 1.24 mi (2 km), and reached an estimated height of 3,280 ft (1,000 m).

In September 1783, the *Aerostat Réveillon* balloon was flown with the first living beings in a basket attached to it: a sheep called Montauciel (Climb-to-the-sky), a duck and a rooster. This demonstration was performed before a crowd at the royal palace in Versailles in front of King Louis XVI and Queen Marie Antoinette of France. The flight lasted approximately 8 minutes, covered 2 mi (3 km), and obtained an altitude of about 1,500 ft (460 m). The craft landed safely after flying.

In November of the same year, the first free flight by humans was made in a balloon by physicist Jean-François Pilâtre de Rozier along with the Marquis d'Arlandes. The flight began from the grounds of the Château de la Muette (close to the Bois de Boulogne park) in the western outskirts of Paris. They flew aloft about 3,000 ft (910 m) over Paris for a distance of 5.6 mi (9 km). After 25 minutes the machine landed safely between the windmills outside the city ramparts, on the Butte-aux-Cailles. This ushered in the era of hot-air balloon passenger flights.

David Schwarz' airship

David Schwarz

FIRST TRUE AIRSHIPS

David Schwarz was a Jewish wood merchant from Zagreb, then part of Austria-Hungary, now Croatia. He was hired by the German army to build the first true airship, and the ship successfully took off. In 1894, Carl Berg was hired to build an airship for Prussia, and he gave Schwarz credit as the idea-provider. Schwarz died of a heart attack a few years later.

In 1898, Schwarz' widow sold the plans for the ship to Count Ferdinand von Zeppelin on condition that it would be named the Schwarz. Zeppelin ignored the agreement and called the airships by his name. He also did not pay Schwarz' widow the entire sum for purchasing the plans.

Count Zeppelin founded Luftschiffbau Zeppelin GmbH (Airship Construction Zeppelin Ltd.) in southern Germany. There he developed the LZ-1. It was 420 ft (128 m) long and was equipped with 2 Daimler engines, 14.2 hp each.

The ship flew at a speed of 19.7 ft (6 m) per second and broke the speed record for airships. But Count Zeppelin ran out of money and had to take apart the LZ-1 and sell it for scrap, as well as to close the company.

The 2nd Zeppelin, LZ-2, was built 6 years later thanks to donations, a raffle, and the mortgaging of Countess Zeppelin's family estates. LZ-2 made its only flight in January 1906. It had 80 hp Daimler engines, which gave it more speed. However, engine failure forced an emergency landing during the ship's very 1st flight. The plane was completely destroyed on the ground by a storm that evening.

The LZ-3 was Zeppelin's 1st true success. The German military bought it and renamed it Z-1, and it served as a training ship until 1913. The army was also willing to buy LZ-4, but wanted to see it make a 24-hour trip. However, during a stop near Stuttgart, a storm tore away the airship from its anchorage. The LZ-4 crashed into a tree, caught fire, and quickly burned up. No one was seriously hurt, although there were close calls as 2 technicians trying to fix the engines managed to escape only by making a dangerous jump.

FIRST PARACHUTES

In 1495, the great Italian artist and inventor Leonardo da Vinci designed and sketched the first parachute. Like many of his inventions, the parachute never got off the ground. However, 100 years later, the Venetian inventor Fausto Veranzio took a look at da Vinci's parachute sketch and set out to implement a chute of his own. It had a square, lightweight wooden frame over which fabric was stretched. It was to be used to save people from burning buildings.

Louis-Sébastien Lenormand, a French physicist and inventor, further developed the parachute. (*Para* means "against" in Greek, and *chute* means "fall" in French.) After making a jump from a tree with the help of 2 modified umbrellas, Lenormand refined his contraption and in December 1783, jumped from the tower of the Montpellier observatory in southern France, 66 ft (20 m) above the ground, using a 14 ft (4.2 m) parachute with a rigid wooden frame.

FIRST TRUE PARACHUTIST

The first parachutist was Frenchman André-Jacques Garnerin, who in October 1797 jumped from a flying balloon which was floating 3,280 ft (1,000 m) above the skies of Paris. The parachute was made from 32 pieces of white canvas which were sewn together into one giant cloth with a diameter of 23 ft (7 m). A basket large enough to transport an adult was attached to it. Garnerin repeated this frightening demonstration more than 200 times in exchange for payment, throughout Europe. The strong current of air underneath made the ride bumpy. He eventually swapped the hard canvas cover for silk, which was soft and strong and softened the turbulence.

Louis-Sébastien Lenormand's parachute jump

André-Jacques Garnerin

The Zeppelin hangar

MOTORIZED FLYING BALLOONS

Early balloons could not be truly navigated; they depended on the grace of the wind. The first to invent what became known as a motorized airship was French engineer Henri Giffard. In 1852, Giffard attached a small, steam-powered engine weighing 353 lb (160 kg) to his airship, and took off from Paris. He chugged through the air for 17 mi (32 km) at a top speed of 5 mph (8 km/h).

Brazilian Alberto Santos-Dumon improved on the motorized airship by installing an internal-combustion motor in which the gasoline was burned inside and not outside. This made it possible to fly more safely and for greater distances.

WORLD'S FIRST AIRLINE COMPANY

DELAG, Deutsche Luftschiffahrts-Aktiengesellschaft (German Airship Travel Corporation), was founded in 1909 as the world's first airline company. The company purchased several Zeppelin airships for transporting passengers.

During the course of their service to DELAG, the Zeppelins flew a total of approximately 124,280 mi (200,000 km), transporting approximately 40,000 passengers.

Four of the ships were destroyed through accidents. There were no casualties because most of the accidents happened when the ships were brought into the hangar.

In 1914, new Zeppelin airships were manufactured. They were 525 ft (160 m) long and had a volume of 883,000 ft^3 (25,000 m^3). This allowed them to transport loads weighing as much as 9 tons. The ships were powered by 550 hp Maybach engines, which enabled them to fly at a speed of 50 mph (80 km/h).

The first Zeppelin flight around the world

The Zeppelin in the skies above Jerusalem

FIRST FLIGHT AROUND THE WORLD

In September 1928, the airship Graf Zeppelin (named for Count Ferdinand von Zeppelin — Graf is German for Count) was inaugurated. The Graf Zeppelin was 776 ft (236.53 m) long, with a volume of 3,700,000 ft^3 (105,000 m^3), the largest of airships until that point in time. The plan was for the Graf Zeppelin to be used for test flights and demonstrations, with the hope that one day passengers and mail could be transported on it.

On October 1928, the airship flew to Lakehurst, NJ (USA). Afterwards it flew to Europe, visiting Spain, Italy, Germany, and even Eretz Yisrael. In August 1929, the airship began its journey around the entire earth. The expedition began in Lakehurst, stopping first at its home terminal in Friedrichshafen, Germany. From there it continued to Tokyo, onward to Los Angeles, and back to Lakehurst. The airship completed its journey in 21 days, 5 hours, and 31 minutes. In May 1930 it was decided to open a regular transatlantic route, and in July 1931 the Graf Zeppelin flew over the North Pole.

END OF THE ZEPPELIN ERA

In 1935, the Nazi Hermann Göring, *yimach shemo*, commander of the Luftwaffe (German Air Force), created a new airline company which controlled the Zeppelin flights. The predominant feature on the outside of the airship was the Nazi swastika. The Zeppelins flew over Nazi party meetings throughout Germany, playing songs and broadcasting propaganda speeches from the air. On March 4, 1936, the LZ-129 ship took off on its first flight. The Zeppelin company's CEO, Dr. Hugo Eckener, refused to cooperate in any way with the Nazis. Thus, he named the airship the *Hindenburg*, after German president Paul von Hindenburg, in order to prevent the Nazi party from calling the ship the *Hitler*. Due to the military boycott against Germany, Eckener couldn't get the helium gas required to fill the ship. Instead, the *Hindenburg* was filled with hydrogen gas, and it began regular transatlantic flights along with the Graf Zeppelin.

On a journey in May 1937, while landing in Lakehurst in front of a crowd of thousands, the ship's tail caught fire and the *Hindenburg* was consumed by flames. The incident killed 35 people and injured 97 passengers as well as a spectator on the ground. Even replacing the flammable hydrogen gas with non-flammable helium did not erase the tragedy from people's memories, and the Zeppelin stopped transporting passengers.

Incidentally, following the tragedy there were still 400 people who had paid for a flight on the Zeppelin and who were left without transportation. Their money was finally refunded in 1940.

The Zeppelin going up in flames

LIFT FORCE

Weight is a force that is always directed toward the center of the earth. Given that an airplane is heavier than air, it requires an opposing force which will hold it in the air. To overcome the weight force, airplanes generate an opposing force called *lift* that is generated by the motions of the airplane through the air — mostly by the wings. The front portion of the wing is thicker than the back portion and it is curved downward. This special shape causes the air above the wing to flow at a faster speed than the air beneath it.

Air pressure of a fast-moving object is lower than that of a slow-moving object. Therefore the pressure on the upper part of the wing is lower than under the wing. This pressure "pushes" the plane upward almost as if the plane were "floating" in the air. The exact way this happens depends on the size of the wings and their shape.

The higher the plane rises, the thinner the air and the lower the air pressure, until the plane reaches its maximum altitude and cannot climb higher.

When it comes to a helicopter, the lift force is produced by the fast rotation of the blades, which causes differences in pressure between the air above the wings and the air below. In a helicopter, rather than the entire plane moving at a high speed against the wind, only the rotor blades installed above move at a fast pace and serve as wings, which produce the lift force.

The main rotor creates a bending force which tries to move the helicopter in the opposite direction from which it is moving. To combat this, a small vertical rotor is placed at the tail of the helicopter, which prevents it from spinning. Raising and lowering the speed of the tail rotor turns the helicopter in the desired direction. Another solution is to make use of two upper rotors spinning in opposite directions, where each one negates the influence of the other.

FIRST HELICOPTERS

Sikorsky's 1st helicopter, the VS-300

Though the first actual helicopter wasn't built until the 1940s, it is believed that Leonardo da Vinci's sketches from 1640 were the predecessor to this modern-day flying machine. As with many of da Vinci's ideas, he never actually built and tested it — but his notes and drawings mapped out exactly how the device would work.

Da Vinci scrawled next to his sketches of the "aerial screw" the words, "If this instrument made with a screw be well made — that is to say, made of linen of which the pores are stopped up with starch and be turned swiftly — the said screw will make its spiral in the air and it will rise high." Without the benefit of a motor, however, da Vinci was unable to realize his dream.

One of the earliest breakthroughs in helicopter advancement was made by George Cayley, who produced a converti-plane in 1843 with 2 rotors turning in opposite directions. However, the 2 steam motors which powered them were so heavy that there was no chance of the craft taking off.

In 1907, French brothers Louis and Jacques Breget rose some 2 in. (5 cm) off the ground in their helicopter model, Sadler 2. Paul Cornu of France also achieved free flight in his model in 1907. His flight lasted only 20 seconds and the helicopter rose only 12 in. (30 cm), but it was still a landmark development.

The first real helicopter was developed by an American engineer originally from Russia named Igor Sikorsky. After working several years on his own to develop aircraft, he convinced the government of the United States to allocate $2 million (an astronomical amount at that time) for research and development of "flying machines." This led to the construction of the first helicopter in 1939 — the VS-300. Sikorsky also developed the first commercial helicopter, the S-55.

The Sikorsky S-55, the 1st commercial helicopter

FIRST PILOTS — ORVILLE AND WILBUR WRIGHT

The Wright brothers were bicycle manufacturers by profession. They began their path to the world of flying by constructing gliders. They read all that was written at that time about gliders and flight. They learned from the mistakes of inventors who had preceded them — mostly from the detailed research of German inventor Otto Lilienthal. Lilienthal flew more than 2,000 times in gliders which he built.

In 1899, the Wright brothers built the first 2 winged "kite." Because they were afraid to fly in it, they connected ropes to the wings and to the back, and managed to control it with the ropes from the ground. They discovered that the craft did not have enough lift force, and that the calculations of their predecessors regarding lift force were wrong. In order to figure out the correct data, they constructed a wind tunnel and blew air into it at 37 mph (60 km/h) with a large fan.

Inside the wind tunnel they placed different models of wings to find out which one had the greatest lift force. They finally chose the model they wanted and built a new plane. They named their plane *Flyer I*. Its wingspan was 43 ft (13 m) and it weighed 750 lb (340 kg) and was powered with a 12 hp engine. A sprocket chain drive, borrowed from bicycle technology, powered the twin propellers, which moved in opposite directions. Steering was accomplished by a complex system of cradles and ropes.

When the plane was ready to fly, the brothers drew straws to see who would have the honor of operating the 1st airplane. Orville, the younger brother, won the draw, and on December 17, 1903, he took off from Kitty Hawk, NC (USA). The plane remained in the air for 12 seconds, reaching a height of 9.8 ft (3 m), and flying for a distance of 128 ft (39m) — less than the wingspan of a jumbo plane. Taking turns, in their 4th and last attempt of the day, Wilbur managed to remain in the air for 59 seconds, flying a distance of 915 ft (279 m) and reaching an altitude of 9.8 ft (3 m). This flight was longer than the other 3, and it marked the 1st flight in which the pilot was able to control a plane and gear heavier than the air.

Slowly but surely, the brothers' planes developed further and further. In 1908, Wilbur managed to attain a height of 361 ft (110 m) and remain in the air for 2 hours and 20 minutes.

Incidentally, the Wright brothers never married, claiming that they did not have enough time to care for both a wife and an airplane.

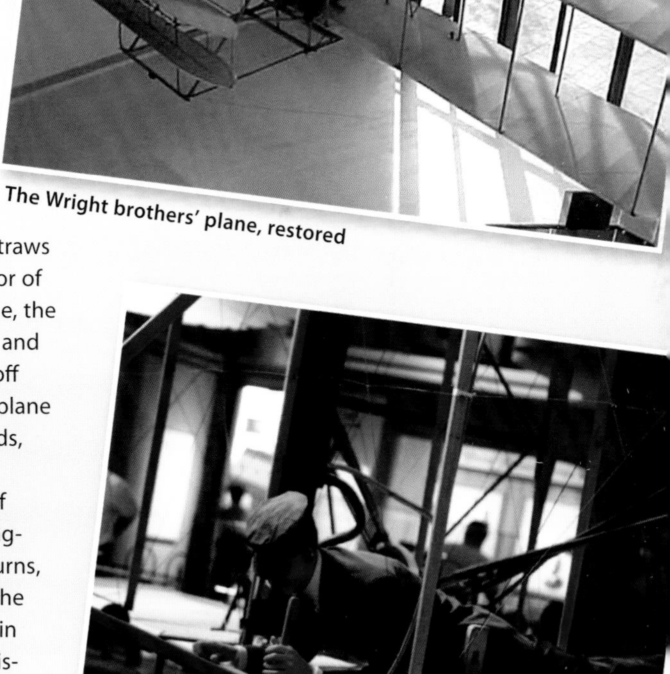

The Wright brothers' plane, restored

Reconstructing the Wright brothers' flying method

Orville Wright

Wilbur Wright

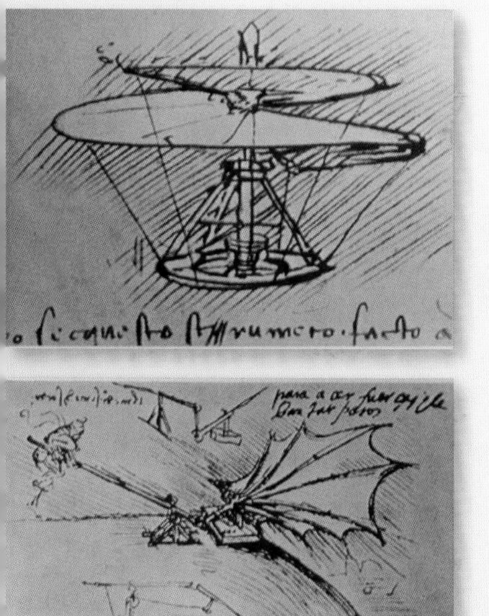

Da Vinci's sketches of the "aerial screw"

A Blackbird landing

The scramjet engine begins operation only at a speed of Mach 6. There are no movable parts, and the oxygen which is compressed into it gets mixed with hydrogen in a special container. The mixture of hydrogen and oxygen produces a thrust which brings the plane to very high speeds.

FASTEST UNMANNED EXPERIMENTAL AIRCRAFT

The fastest unmanned aircraft in the world is the X-43A. A winged booster rocket with the X-43 at the tip, called a "stack," is launched from a carrier plane. After the booster rocket brings the stack to the target speed and altitude, it is discarded, and the X-43 flies free using its own state-of-the-art engine, which is called a scramjet.

One of NASA's B-52 planes was the carrier plane which released the X-43A. This unmanned aircraft is 13 ft (4 m) long and weighs 3,087 lb (1,400 kg). The winged booster rocket accelerated the X-43A and brought it to an altitude of 112,000 ft/ 21.2 mi (34,000 m) before releasing it.

After being released, the scramjet engine accelerated the X-43A for 10 seconds to its record-breaking speed of 7,369 mph (11,858 km/h, Mach 9.68), and after a series of short maneuvers it exploded into the Pacific Ocean.

A conventional rocket engine absorbs air which is mixed with fuel and powers a turbine, which in turn rotates the blades.

FASTEST MANNED EXPERIMENTAL AIRCRAFT

The American Air Force's experimental X-15A-2 rocket is the fastest manned plane in the world — twice as fast as its nearest competitor. In a test run in 1967, the X-15A-2 was carried under the belly of a plane which propelled it into the air at a very high altitude. The pilot of the rocket then descended to an altitude of 62 mi (100 km) where the air resistance is lowest, and attained the highest speed ever reached by a manned plane — 4,474 mph (7,200 km/h, Mach 5.8). The X-15A-2 is unable to take off on its own power and resembles a missile more than a jet.

HIGHEST ALTITUDE

The highest altitude ever reached by a non-spaceship aircraft was achieved by a gas-filled air balloon. Two pilots from the United States Navy flew this balloon to a height of 113,780 ft (34,680 m), 3 times the height of a regular passenger flight. In an air balloon filled only with hot air it is possible to reach a maximum altitude of 65,616 ft (20,000 m).

FASTEST PASSENGER PLANE

The British-French Concorde, developed in 1962, was 1 of only 2 supersonic passenger planes in the world. It flew at an altitude of almost double that of ordinary planes — 59,710 ft (18,200 m), at double the speed of sound, thus reducing the journey by half.

The Concorde, however, was a dismal commercial failure. The plane generally had 100 seats — 4 in a row, with an aisle in the middle. Although it was considered a luxury plane, it was not long before passengers realized just how uncomfortable it was. The height of the ceiling in the middle aisle was barely 6 ft (1.8 m) high, leaving no room for hand luggage or any sort of entertainment. These deficiencies would at times overshadow the main benefit — the extremely short flying time of only 3.5 hours from New York to London. The price of a ticket on the Concord was $10,000 and even so, the venture did not make a profit.

On July 25, 2000, Air France Concorde flight 4590 crashed in Gonesse, France, shortly after takeoff from Charles de Gaulle airport. All of the passengers plus 4 people on the ground were killed.

The crash happened because a Continental Airlines passenger DC-10 airplane had lost a metal piece about 1.2 in. (3 cm) wide and 17 in. (43 cm) long during takeoff from Charles de Gaulle. During the Concorde's subsequent take-off, this piece of debris, still lying on the runway, ruptured a tire which then burst. A large chunk of tire struck the underside of the aircraft's wing structure and ruptured one of the fuel tanks.

Altogether only 20 Concorde planes were manufactured. Its "retirement flight" took off on November 26, 2003.

The Concorde

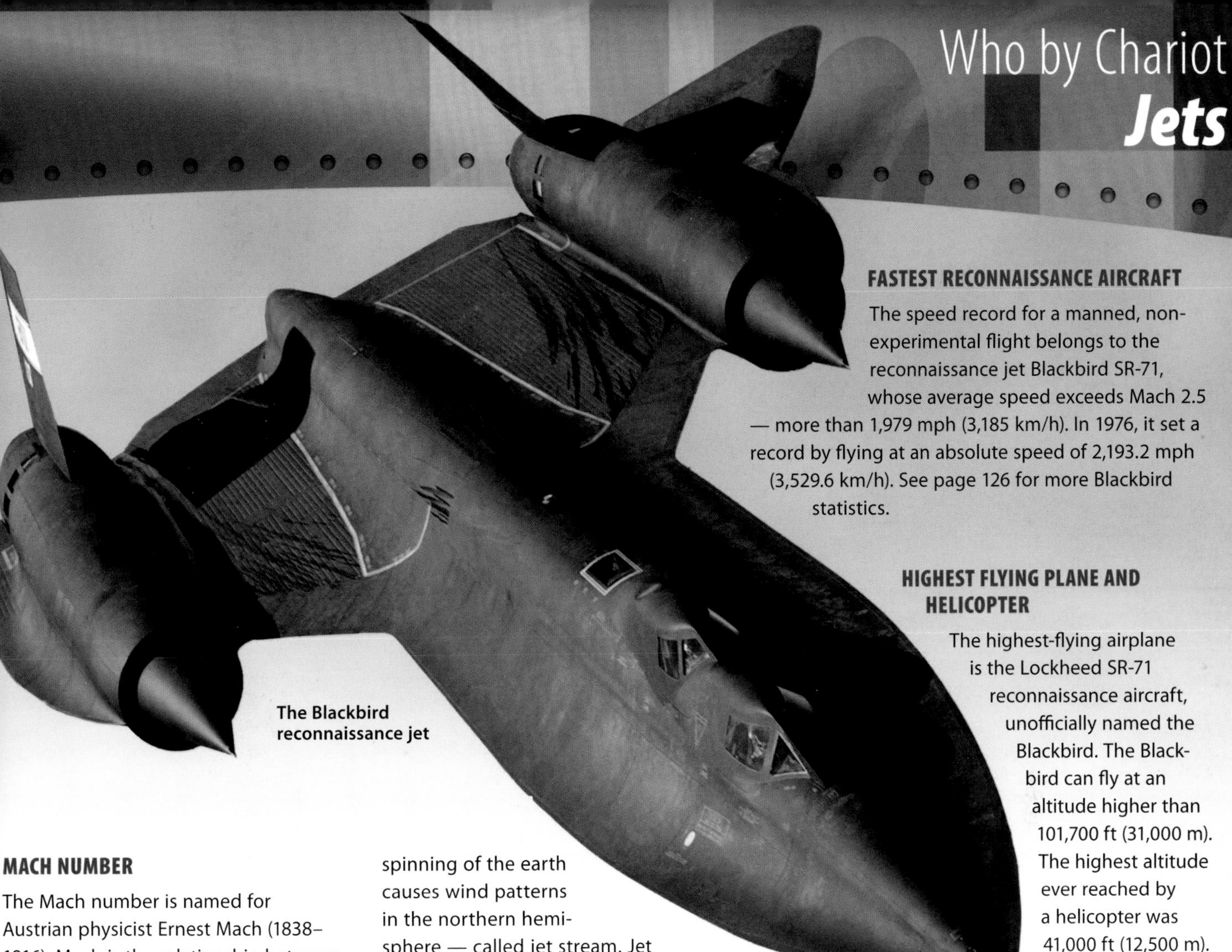

The Blackbird reconnaissance jet

FASTEST RECONNAISSANCE AIRCRAFT

The speed record for a manned, non-experimental flight belongs to the reconnaissance jet Blackbird SR-71, whose average speed exceeds Mach 2.5 — more than 1,979 mph (3,185 km/h). In 1976, it set a record by flying at an absolute speed of 2,193.2 mph (3,529.6 km/h). See page 126 for more Blackbird statistics.

HIGHEST FLYING PLANE AND HELICOPTER

The highest-flying airplane is the Lockheed SR-71 reconnaissance aircraft, unofficially named the Blackbird. The Black-bird can fly at an altitude higher than 101,700 ft (31,000 m). The highest altitude ever reached by a helicopter was 41,000 ft (12,500 m).

MACH NUMBER

The Mach number is named for Austrian physicist Ernest Mach (1838–1916). Mach is the relationship between any speed and the speed of sound — Mach 1 being the equivalent of the speed of sound. Mach 2 is double the speed of sound, and so forth. Speed in which the Mach number is greater than 5 is called hypersonic speed.

Mach 1 is equal to 738 mph (1,188 km/h) at sea level, or 1,082 ft/sec (330 m/sec). Given that the speed of sound varies with temperature and pressure, a speed of Mach 1 can vary depending on the surroundings. In water, for example, the speed of sound is 4 times greater than in the air, while in a complete vacuum, sound cannot travel at all. Therefore, to make things more convenient, Mach 1 was standardized to 660 mph (1,061 km/h) in the stratosphere — a height of 36,089 ft (11,000 m). The main use of the Mach number is to measure the speed of planes in the air. However, it also describes the speed of liquids through canals and various pipes such as wind tunnels.

ONE WAY IS LONGER THAN THE OTHER

A flight from New York to Tel Aviv is an hour shorter than a flight in the opposite direction. This is because the spinning of the earth causes wind patterns in the northern hemisphere — called jet stream. Jet stream winds consistently blow from west to east at a speed of between 31 and 62 mph (50 and 100 km/h). Thus, if an airplane is flying west, its engine has to work harder and it consumes more gasoline. A plane's flying route is determined not only by which route is shorter but by the path in which the wind patterns at that particular time are weaker.

The spinning of the earth does not effect the flight time because the plane, the atmosphere, and the earth are within one system, just as a bee flying inside a moving car is not affected by the speed at which the car is traveling.

FUEL USED FROM TEL AVIV TO NEW YORK

The 3 fuel tanks in a Boeing 747 (2 in the 2 wings and the large one in the center of the plane) are filled with 160 tons of jet fuel. Every hour of flight, the 4 engines consume 11 tons, totaling 130 tons of fuel burned on a flight from Tel Aviv to New York. A ton of jet fuel costs approximately $500. Thus, on this flight, the Boeing 747 uses $65,000 worth of fuel.

THE "BLACK BOX" IS REALLY ORANGE

The purpose of the Black Box is to track and record various data during a flight or other journey: speed, conversations, computer activity, etc. This is done via analog and digital means. It helps in investigating accidents and even allows investigators to hear conversations that took place in the pilot's cabin during the half hour before an accident.

The box is commonly found in planes, helicopters, spaceships, trucks, and even some cars. The unique shape and color of the box make it easy to locate after accidents and at times even after explosions. Contrary to its name, the box is generally painted orange.

The Antonov An-225 cargo plane

LARGEST CARGO PLANE

The world's largest cargo plane and the heaviest fixed-wing aircraft is the Antonov An-225, made in Russia. It has a wingspan of 290 ft, 2 in. (88.5 m), and it is 60.6 ft (18.5 m) high and 279 ft (85 m) long. It can transport a cargo of 270 tons, with a maximum takeoff weight of 660 tons — requiring 32 wheels for support.

What is quite impressive about the Antonov An-225 is its flight range. It is capable of flying 9,570 mi (15,400 km) empty, and 2,500 mi (4,000 km) with a maximum payload.

SMALLEST PLANE

The Bumble Bee II has the distinction of being the smallest plane in the world. It was designed and manufactured in 1988 by Robert H. Starr in Arizona (USA). It was 8.9 ft (2.7 m) long, with a wingspan of 5.6 ft (1.7 m), and weighed only 397 lb (180 kg) when empty. Its fuel tank held only 3.2 gal (12 liters) of fuel.

Unfortunately, on its 1st flight, after making several circuits around Starr's neighborhood at a height of 400 ft (120 m), the aircraft's engine quit and the plane crashed and was totally destroyed. Starr, the pilot, was seriously injured but eventually recovered from his injuries. There has not yet been a successor to Bumble Bee II.

SMALLEST JET

The smallest jet in the world is the Bede Microjet BD-5J, which belongs to Juan Jimenez of Puerto Rico. The Bede Microjet BD-5J weighs only 357 lb (162 kg), is 12.1 ft (3.7 m) long, and has a wingspan of 18.7 ft (5.7 m). The jet can attain a maximum speed of 298 mph (480 km/h).

Bede Microjet BD-5J

MOST SOLD PASSENGER PLANE

In 2005, 38 years after the first Boeing 737 rolled off the production line, the 5,000th plane of this model was manufactured. Boeing's order book contains 1,100 orders for the plane, which is known as "the most successful passenger plane of all times." The first model, the Boeing 737-100, which flew in 1967, carried 100 passengers and weighed in at 50 tons. The latest model in development — the Boeing 737-900ER — can carry 215 passengers and weighs 85 tons.

MOST SOLD CARGO PLANE

The DC-3 Dakota jet is a twin-engine cargo plane manufactured by Douglas. It was first flown in 1935 and is considered one of the most successful cargo planes in aviation history. The Dakota is so reliable that it has been said, "The only replacement for a Dakota is another Dakota."

The DC-3 is also the most sold cargo plane in history, with more than 10,000 having been manufactured. The Dakota flew the first quick American coast-to-coast flight with only 1 stop for refueling. This brought about a revolution in the commercial flight industry — airline ticket prices dropped and many airline companies purchased Dakota planes.

The DC-3 Dakota

LARGEST AIRPLANE IN THE WORLD

The A-380 airbus is a double-decker plane which earned the name "flying city." It is so gigantic that it cannot fit into most departure and boarding areas, and its massive weight cannot be supported by most landing paths.

The plane is 246 ft (75 m) long and has a wingspan of 262.5 ft (80 m). The height of its two decks is 78.7 ft (24 m), and its takeoff weight is 550 tons. The large space underneath the floor of the main deck includes a café, a workout room, and duty-free stores. Airports wishing to provide landing for airbuses will have to invest huge sums in infrastructure, runways, landing paths, and new arrival and departure areas.

GREATEST NUMBER OF PEOPLE ON A FLIGHT

El Al Airlines holds the world's record for the most passengers on a single flight. In November 1991, the Israeli government planned and carried out Operation Solomon, airlifting 14,400 Ethiopian Jews safely to Israel on 30 planes. The operation lasted 3 days and during one of the flights 1,087 passengers jammed into a Boeing 747 — the seats were removed and the passengers all sat on the floor.

Japanese 747 planes typically have 500 seats, while El Al generally operates with approximately 430.

Cockpit of a Boeing 737

The A-380 Airbus

ɪOST AIR ACCIDENTS

ʜe Airbus Company holds a ɛcord it is definitely not proud f — the highest number of air ccidents. The primary cause f air accidents is the "human ɑctor" (59%). Many of these ccidents could have been revented. The high reliability f advanced planes and the ase in which they are flown reates an atmosphere of omplacence, causing the pilot ɔ rely more heavily than he hould on autopilot and other utomatic systems.

The other main cause of air ccidents (22%) is mechanical r maintenance problems.

Statistics have shown that ɪost fatal air accidents have ccurred over Eastern Asia.

PATHWAYS IN THE SKIES

Passenger planes fly at an altitude of between 6.8 and 8.1 mi (11 and 13 km). The lower air pressure at this altitude causes much lower air resistance. The plane is therefore able to fly at a much higher speed with very low fuel consumption.

At an even higher altitude, the air is much thinner and the jet fuel does not receive the amount of air it needs in order to create a thrust pushing the plane forward. The supersonic Concorde would fly at a height of 12.4 mi (20 km) at double the speed of sound. Despite the relatively low air pressure at that height, its very high speed insured that enough air needed to power the motors was able to enter.

TRAFFIC CONGESTION IN THE AIR

According to data compiled by the United States Federal Aviation Authority, at any given moment there are 4,800 planes flying over American airspace, and 14,400 flying throughout the world. There are set air traffic lanes, just as there are lanes for cars driving in the street. These air lanes are monitored by hundreds of control centers as planes fly and pass from one supervised area to another. A radar screen helps insure that the plane stays in the lane it was assigned. When flying above the oceans, where there is no supervision center, the automatic pilot makes sure that the plane stays strictly within the confines of its assigned lane.

When 2 passenger planes are assigned the same lane, they generally keep a distance of 3 flying minutes from each other and a vertical separation of approximately 1,970 ft (600 m). Incidentally, the more precise the plane's navigation instruments and the more refined the monitoring systems on the ground, the less space between planes is needed. This allows for more planes to fly in the same lanes, thereby easing congestion at the major airports.

A TRULY HUGE HELICOPTER

The Russian helicopter MIL MI-26 is the largest helicopter in the world. It weighs 28 tons, is 131 ft (40 m) long, and its main rotor of 8 blades has a diameter of 105 ft (32 m). The helicopter is powered by 2 engines which produce 11,000 hp, and it can transport 30 tons of cargo.

SMALLEST HELICOPTER

The tiny, 1-seater MiniCopter developed by Aerospace General, is the world's smallest helicopter. The MiniCopter weighs 161 lb (73 kg) and can fly a distance of 249 mi (400 km) at a speed of 85 mph (137 km/h).

FASTEST HELICOPTER

The British Air Force's Westland Lynx is the fastest helicopter in the world. In 1986, pilot John Egginton broke the world record for helicopters when he reached a speed of 249.1 mph (400.87 km/h). For the sake of comparison, the maximum attainable speed for battle helicopters is only 168 mph (270 km/h).

The Westland Lynx

HIGHEST HELICOPTER TAKEOFF AND LANDING

In 2005, the Eurocopter AS350B3 helicopter set the world's record for highest-ever helicopter takeoff and landing. The helicopter landed on the top of Mt. Everest — 29,134 ft (8,880 m) high. The helicopter remained on top of Mt. Everest, which is the highest mountain in the world, for 120 seconds before taking off on its return journey.

FIRST SOLAR PLANE

Helios is a light, unmanned plane powered by solar energy, weighing only 1,300 lb (590 kg). It has a wing span of 246 ft (75 m) — 49 ft (15m) longer than a Boeing 747. The 6,000 solar cells above its wings provide energy for 14 propellers installed on the plane's wings. These cells enable the plane to fly at approximately the speed of a bicycle and remain in the air for 6 months without having to refuel.

The Helios holds the altitude record for an unmanned propeller plane — 96,784 ft (29,500 m). The AeroVironment Company, manufacturer of the Helios, also manufactures small planes equipped with video spy cameras that weigh less than a coin.

HOW A PLANE TURNS AND DESCENDS

There are 3 surfaces on an airplane that control its movement: the ailerons on the wings, the rudder on the tail, and the elevators on the tail. All of these control surfaces are like flaps. When they move, they change the way the air flows around the airplane. Airplanes make use of a control stick rather than a steering wheel.

When the pilot moves the control stick to the right, the aileron on the right wing tilts up and the aileron on the left wing tilts down. The right aileron then makes less lift when it tilts up and the left aileron makes more lift when it tilts down. The airplane then rolls to the side with less lift — in this case, to the right. When the pilot moves the control stick to the left, the aileron on the left wing tilts up and the aileron on the right wing tilts down. The airplane rolls to the side with less lift, which is the left side this time.

The elevators at the back of the airplane control whether the nose at the front of the airplane points up or down. When the pilot pulls the control stick back, the elevators tilt up. This causes less lift, so the tail goes down. When the tail goes down, the nose goes up. This is called pitching up.

When the pilot pushes the control stick forward, the elevators tilt down. When the elevators tilt down, they create more lift in the same way that the ailerons do. This causes the tail to rise and the nose to point down.

The rudder is a vertical flap on the tail. It controls the sideways movement of the airplane's nose to the left or to the right. This sideways motion is called yaw.

Two pedals at the pilot's feet control the rudder. When the pilot pushes on the right pedal, the rudder tilts to the right. This makes the airplane's nose yaw to the right because more lift is created on the right side. This extra lift pushes the tail to the left, which makes the nose yaw to the right. When the pilot pushes on the left pedal, the rudder tilts to the left. This makes the airplane's nose yaw to the left.

Air Transport

The Michelob Light Eagle pedal plane

Pilots have to use the ailerons and the rudder controls to turn the airplane. The whole flight path needs to curve, so the airplane must roll to the left or right while the rudder helps keep it pointed in the proper direction. Otherwise, the force of air pushing against the control surfaces would make the airplane go off course.

When an airplane is flying in thin air, it takes longer to change direction when moving the control surfaces.

The Ekranoplan

JUST LIKE A HUGE PLANE

The Ekranoplan, known as the Caspian Sea Monster, looks like a huge plane without wings. It is 328 ft (100 m) long and weighs 540 tons. It can hover a few meters above the sea and travel at 249 mph (400 km/h). It can "fly" over ice, snow, and level ground. It can also take off, fly, and safely "land" in waves of up to 16 ft (5m) high. Another name for the Ekranoplan is "ground-effect vehicle."

Ekranoplans were originally developed by the Soviet Union as high-speed military transports able to transport up to 100 tons of cargo,

and were based mostly on the shores of the Caspian and Black Seas.

In 1987, a model was developed to transport anti-ship missiles, and today a number of small advanced models have been manufactured for the purpose of civilian transportation.

BICYCLES IN THE SKY

In 1987, a world record was set for flying a plane with human-operated pedals. The Michelob Light Eagle, weighing only 90 lb (41 kg) and with a wingspan of 115 ft (35 m), flew 37 mi (60 km) at an average speed of 16.8 mph (27 km/h). The record was set at Edwards Air Force base in California (USA).

FIRST AUTOMATIC PILOT

The DC-4 Skymaster was the first plane to have automatic pilot installed. The system, which has since been installed in every commercial plane and most newer-model private planes, helps the pilot establish and stay in his flying lane. The system is so advanced that it can even control takeoff, the entire flight, and landing, without any pilot intervention. Most pilots, however, are not willing to let the automatic pilot control takeoff and landing, as well as flying during severe weather conditions. For the automatic pilot, there is no distinction between day and night flights.

PRESSURE IN THE EARS

At very high altitudes, the air column is higher and therefore the air pressure is lower. When one is going up or down in a fast elevator or during plane takeoff and landing, the change in air pressure is manifest by pressure or pain in the ears. This is caused by differences in pressure between the middle ear and the outer air.

For the passengers' comfort and protection, all planes flying at an altitude of over 1.9 mi (3 km) have an air compression system installed in the passenger compartment which converts the passenger compartment into a type of compressed air balloon. As the plane rises, the compression maintains inner cabin air pressure slightly higher than the pressure outside. As the plane passes the 1.9 mi (3 km) altitude, the same atmospheric pressure inside is retained regardless of the outside air pressure. The opposite effect takes place as the plane descends for landing.

Most of us believe that should one of the plane's windows break, the inner pressure would go out through the window and suck out all the passengers and anything else in the plane. We always thought this was the reason for the double glass in which we rarely ever see even the thinnest of cracks.

You need not worry, because the difference between the inner cabin pressure and the pressure outside is not significant enough, so that even should one of the windows crack the pilot would have sufficient time to descend to a level where there is almost no difference in pressure between the inside and outside of the plane and would then be able to make an emergency landing.

Incidentally, at a height of 6.8 mi (11 km) above the ground, the temperature outside the plane can reach -68.8° F (-56° C).

DID YOU KNOW? AIR POCKETS

When the plane passes through rising warm air currents, they push the plane upward, and when the currents stop, the plane falls back to its original height. At times this can create whirlwinds with a sort of vacuum at its center, with the strong air movement in the downward direction. As the plane enters the whirlwind, it is tossed around very strongly and as it reaches the center it suddenly drops a few hundred meters. This phenomenon is referred to as an air pocket. At times the plane may pass through a strong wind blowing at the howling speed of 124 mph (200 km/h).

As the plane passes through the wind current, it gets thrown strongly from side to side. This can prove very time-saving and economical at times, because the plane is pushed in the direction of its flight, thereby saving on fuel consumption. This turbulence, however, is not a problem for the plane or the pilot.

Automatic pilot insures that the plane remains within its flying lane and at the right altitude at all times. The body of the plane is built to withstand much harder knocks and has no problem flying in severe, even hurricane conditions, while maintaining the flight path and protecting the well-being of the airplane.

Oasis of the Seas

"Central Park," Oasis of the Seas

LARGEST PASSENGER SHIP

Oasis of the Seas is the world's largest passenger ship, surpassing both *Freedom of the Seas* and the *Queen Mary II*. It is owned and operated by Royal Caribbean International, and made its 1st voyage in December 2009. It can carry 6,296 passengers and 2,165 crew. It services the Caribbean route.

The *Oasis* weighs 225,282 tons, and its displacement weight is almost the same as a Nimitz class aircraft carrier. It is 1,181 ft (360 m) long and 198 ft (60.5 m) wide, and rises 236 ft (72 m) above the water line. About 30 ft (9 m) sits under the water.

There are 16 passenger decks on the *Oasis*. It is driven by 3 diesel engines of 18,590 hp each and 3 diesel engines of 24,780 hp each. It can go up to 26 mph (41.9 km/h). It cost $1.4 billion to build.

Besides its regular rooms, the *Oasis* has 2-story suites as well as gigantic luxury suites with balconies. Among other features, it has a park with more than 12,000 plants and 56 trees, a mini-golf course, restaurants, shops, 5 swimming pools, volleyball and basketball courts, special areas for children and teenagers, entertainment areas, and a carousel.

FASTEST SPEEDBOAT

On October 8, 1978, Australian Ken Warby, navigating his *Spirit of Australia* on Blowering Dam near Tumut, New South Wales, Australia, set a speedboat record of 317.6 mph (511 km/h). Warby designed and built the boat out of balsa wood and fiberglass in his own backyard. He installed a jet-stream engine which he purchased at an army surplus auction for only $69.

There have been many attempts over the years to break Warby's record, including by large conglomerates who have invested millions of dollars building sophisticated speedboats. However, none of these boats have even matched the record.

FLOATING CITY

In 1996, American Engineer Norman Nixon presented his plan for the building of *Freedom Ship* — 5,315 ft (1,620 m) long, 755 ft (239 m) wide, 344 ft (105 m) tall, and weighing 3 million tons. The *Titanic*, the *Queen Mary*, the Nimitz class aircraft carriers, and the largest tanker in the world — the *Jahre Viking* — would all be able to fit on this ship with room to spare.

The *Freedom Ship* can be referred to as The City at Sea. It has 18,000 housing units for 40,000 permanent residents and 15,000 workers, and 10,000 hotel rooms with the possibility of lodging for 20,000 visitors daily. Its 100 engines would produce 350,000 hp and move the *Freedom Ship* around the world at an average speed of 11 mph (18 km/h). Due to its enormous size, however, the *Freedom Ship* would not be able to anchor at any port, and guests would have to be transported to and from the ship either via boats or by making use of the airport on its upper deck.

There are 100 engineers working for free until the $11 billion needed to build the ship is raised. These engineers claim that the *Freedom Ship* would be so big that it would not be affected by any strong gales or winds — kind of reminds us of what they said about the *Titanic*.

MOST EXPENSIVE SHIPS

Very few countries in the world are able to support the manufacturing and maintenance of an aircraft carrier. Approximately half of the world's 40 aircraft carriers are operated by the United States Navy. Their 9 Nimitz class aircraft carriers are the most expensive ships in the world. In fact, they are the most expensive structures in the world.

The manufacturing cost of an aircraft carrier can reach $4.5 billion and it can take up to 5 years to construct one. The annual operating costs are estimated at approximately $160 million. In addition, there are 90 airplanes aboard the ship worth $1.2 billion, not to mention the 6 accompanying battleships designed to protect it from enemy ships, submarines, and planes. Nimitz class aircraft carriers are designed to last at least 50 years in active service. For comparison's sake, the cost of building an American spaceship is "only" $2.2 billion.

LARGEST SHIP EVER DESTROYED

The 312,180 ton *Energy Determination* was the largest ship every destroyed at sea. In December 1979 it smashed into rocks in the Straits of Hormuz and broke in half. The value of the ship was estimated at $60 million.

LARGEST SAILBOAT

The largest sailboat ever built was *France II*. The 417 ft (127 m) long sailboat with a capacity of 5,800 tons was launched from Bordeaux, France, in 1911. The ship's body was made of steel and it had 5 masts. Despite its being planned as a sail ship, 2 steam motors were installed in addition to the sails. On July 13, 1922, it sank at sea opposite the shores of New Caledonia, an island in the South Pacific.

FASTEST TRAVELING SAILBOAT

On February 28, 2004, Steven Fosset and his crew sailed his boat, the *Cheyenne*, for 573 mi (922 km) in a period of 24 hours. The *Cheyenne* is 125 ft (38 m) long, and the height of its sail is 148 ft (45 m).

Fosset broke a 150-year record, which had been held since December 1854 by the *Champion of the Seas*. This sailboat traveled 535 mi (861 km) in 24 hours during a storm in the South Pacific.

LARGEST MAN-MADE MOVING OBJECT

The recently retired Norwegian oil tanker *Jahre Viking* is the largest man-made moving object in the world.

Weighing 575,000 tons, 1,504 ft (458.4 m) long, and 226.4 ft (69 m) wide, it covers an area of 7.7 acres. When at full cargo capacity of 564,763 tons of oil (4,240,865 barrels), the bottom 80.7 ft (24.6 m) of the ship becomes submerged under water. The *Jahre Viking* requires an area of 2 mi (3.2 km) in order to turn around and 5 mi (8 km) in order to come to a complete stop. It is incapable of entering most ports around the world. We do not even want to think what would happen to the ocean, if …

LARGEST SHIP PROPELLER

The world's largest ship's screw propeller was manufactured by Hyundai Heavy Industries for a 7,200 ton container vessel owned by Hapag-Lloyd. The diameter of the giant, 5-blade propeller is 30 ft (9.1 m), and it weighs 101.5 tons. The screw propeller is powered by the world's largest diesel engine, which weighs 2,157 tons and provides 93,360 hp.

The propeller was invented in 1836 by a British farmer from Kent named Francis Smith.

Planes landing and taking off on an aircraft carrier

An icebreaker

Above and below: hovercraft

LARGEST ICEBREAKER

The largest icebreaker in the world belongs to the Canadian Coast Guard's Polar Class 8, which cost $732 million to build. It is 636 ft (194 m) long and has a diesel-powered, 100,000 hp motor.

LARGEST DREDGER IN THE WORLD

The largest dredger in the world is the *Pearl River*. In less than an hour, it can suck up 20,000 tons of sand from 115 ft (35 m) deep via 2 suction pipes that are 3.9 ft (1.2 m) in diameter each. The dredger is 472 ft (144 m) long and is specifically designed to float and dig in shallow areas. Despite its vast size, the *Pearl River*, even at full capacity, submerges only 23 ft (7 m) below the surface of the sea.

FIRST HOVERCRAFT

A hovercraft, also known as an ACV (air-cushion vehicle), is a craft that travels over surfaces while supported by a cushion of slow-moving, high-pressure air which is ejected against the surface below and contained within a "skirt."

The inventor of the hovercraft was Sir Christopher Sidney Cockerell, a British engineer who formulated the idea in 1954. The 1st hovercraft was the English SR.N1. It came out in 1959. It weighed 4 tons, was powered by a propeller jet stream motor of 680 hp, and was able to reach a speed of 78 mph (126 kg/h).

LARGEST COMMERCIAL HOVERCRAFT

The largest civilian hovercraft in the world is the BHC SR.N4, which sails between England and France. It weighs 305 tons. The hovercraft, built in Britain, is 184 ft (56 m) long and powered by 4 Rolls-Royce Proteus gas turbine engines. It can transport 418 passengers and 60 cars. It can cross the English Channel at a speed faster than 73 mph (65 knots, 117 km/h) — the maximum speed allowed.

LARGEST CRANE VESSEL

The largest crane vessel is the *Thialf*. The 2 cranes provide for long lowering capacity as well as heavy lift capacity. The vessel is 661.4 ft (201.6 m) long and 290 ft (88.4 m) wide. When at full load, 141 ft (43 m) of the vessel is submerged underwater. The cranes can lift 312 ft (95 m) above the work deck, and can lower between 1,007 ft (307 m) and 1,500 ft (460 m) above the work deck. Each crane can lift a maximum of 7,100 tons.

The *Thialf* has 12 anchors, each weighing 49.6 lb (22.5 kg), which make sure it remains in exactly the right place. A computerized system uses propellers to correct any slight change caused by current or waves. When at full load, the *Thialf* can travel at a speed of 6.9 mph (11.1 km/h). The deck has a landing for a Boeing 234 helicopter and rooms for lodging its 736 workers.

LARGEST HOSPITAL SHIP

The largest hospital ship in the world is the American Navy's *Mercy*. The ship was built in 1976 as the SS *Worth* oil tanker by the National Steel and Shipbuilding Company in San Diego, CA. In July 1984 the ship was renamed the *Mercy* and converted into a hospital ship. It is sent to areas struck by natural disasters.

On September 15, 1990, the *Mercy* arrived in the Persian Gulf to support the allied forces in Operation Desert Shield. For the next 6 months, the *Mercy* admitted 690 patients and performed 300 surgeries in its operating rooms. The ship is 892 ft (272 m) long, 105 ft (32 m) wide, and has 12 operating rooms as well as 1,000 beds for patients — of which 80 are the Intensive Care Unit. In 2004, the *Mercy* aided victims of the tsunami in Southeast Asia.

DEEPEST SUBMARINE DIVE

On January 23, 1960, the research submarine *Trieste II* of the American Navy achieved the deepest submarine dive on record, when it submerged to the deepest point in the entire world — the Challenger Deep in the Pacific Ocean's Mariana Trench near the island of Guam. The depth of the Challenger Deep is 35,797 ft (10,911 m).

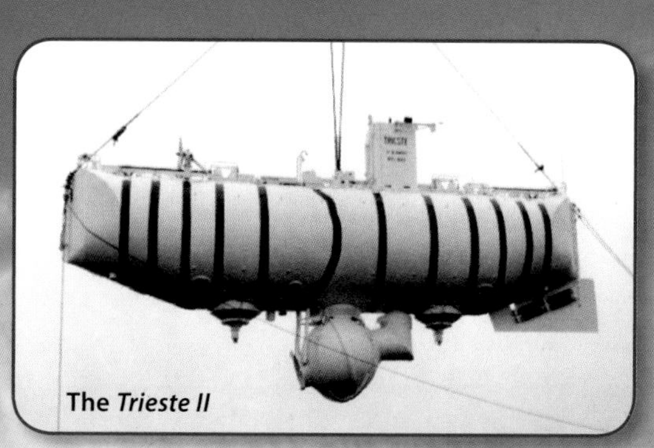
The *Trieste II*

THE MOST SOPHISTICATED FLOATING LABORATORY: LARGEST DEEP-SEA DRILLING TOWER

The deep sea drilling vessel *Chikyu* (Japanese for "Earth") is the most sophisticated floating laboratory in the world and carries on its deck the largest drilling tower in the world. The ship weighs 57,500 tons, is 689 ft (210 m) long, and cost $540 million to build. This ship carries out its exploration operations as part of the Integrated Ocean Drilling Program. The main participants of this program are Japan, the United States, and the European Union.

The drilling tower rises 367 ft (112 m) above the waterline and has a 5.9 mi (9.5 km) drilling pipe — 22 times the height of the Empire State Building. The ship carries out drilling experiments 22,966 ft/4.3 mi (7,000 m) deep into the crust of the earth while sailing in water 8,202 ft (2,500 m) deep.

A slight deviation of just a few yards from the point of drilling can easily break a pipe. The *Chikyu* is therefore equipped with an automatic satellite system which takes waves and water currents into consideration in order to make sure the vessel stays precisely above the drilling pit. Six propellers underneath the ship can turn 360° and help establish the precise location of the drilling. Drilling locations are in areas in which the earth's cover is relatively thin, such as the Nankai Trough on the floor of the Pacific Ocean opposite the shores of Japan.

FIRST MOTORCYCLE

German Gottlieb Daimler, known for having founded the Mercedes Company in conjunction with his assistant William Maybach, invented the first gas engine motorcycle in 1884. This motorcycle was basically an internal-combustion, 1-cylinder engine attached to a wooden bicycle. Daimler's motorcycle had 2 stabilizing wheels similar to a child's training wheels to prevent it from toppling. Daimler and Maybach named their motorcycle *Reitwagen*, which is German for "riding car."

FASTEST COMMERCIALLY SOLD MOTORCYCLE

The Kawasaki Company of Japan manufactures the ZX-12R motorcycle, known commercially as Ninja 12. The motorcycle runs on a 1,352 cc engine which produces 182 hp (1.5 times that of a family car). At 4,000 rpm, the motorcycle can go only 19 mph (30 km/h), although at 10,500 rpm it can attain a speed of 194 mph (312 km/h). The motorcycle sells for $30,000.

MOST RIDERS ON A MOTORCYCLE

The record for most riders on a motorcycle was set when 41 Brazilian military police stood one on top of the other in pyramid style while riding a Harley-Davidson. They journeyed in this manner for 0.9 mi (1.5 km).

In 2001, the Dare Devils Team of the Indian Army Signal Corps made a motorcycle pyramid consisting of 201 men balanced on 10 motorcycles. The pyramid traveled a distance of 424 ft (129 m).

LARGEST AND TALLEST MOTORCYCLES

American Gregory Dunham spent 3 years building the largest and tallest motorcycle. It is 16.4 ft (5 m) tall and 27.2 ft (8.3 m) long. Its handlebars are 20 ft (6.1 m) high. The motorcycle weighs 6,500 lb (2,948 kg) — the weight of 2 passenger cars.

LONGEST MOTORCYCLE

Rick Dozier, Bill Decker, Rob Moore, and William Longest (certainly an appropriate name), built a 29 ft, 3 in. (9.53 m) motorcycle which William Longest rode on June 15, 2003.

SMALLEST MOTORCYCLE

It is hard to believe how he managed it, but Tom Wilberg from Sweden built the world's smallest motorcycle, whose front wheel diameter is 0.63 in. (16 mm) and whose back wheel diameter is 0.87 in. (22 mm). The motorcycle is 3.1 in. (80 mm) long, with a 2.6 in. (65 mm) high seat. The motorcycle is powered by a 0.3 hp engine, and Tom manages to ride a distance of 33 ft (10 m) at a speed of 1.24 mph (2 km/h) — after much rigorous training in balancing.

MOTORCYCLE "SKIING"

In the middle of riding his motorcycle at a speed of 93 mph (150 km/h), Gary Rothwell gets off his motorcycle, places his feet on the ground, and continues holding on to the handle. He wears special titanium boots while the motorcycle drags him along with it. The motorcycle's speed increases to 156 mph (251 km/h). Gary is also known for riding his motorcycle at a speed of 133 mph (214 km/h) while seated facing the opposite direction.

FASTEST MOTORCYCLE

Since 2006, Chris Carr has held the world record for the fastest motorcycle. He rode at 352.8 mph (567.8 km/h).

Motorcycles

MOTORCYCLE JUMP RECORD

In 2005, while riding his Yamaha motorcycle, Jamie Barkla of Australia jumped into the air a distance of 148 ft (45 m).

FASTEST WHEELIE

In 2006, Terry Calcott of England set a world record for a motorcycle "wheelie" (riding on only the back wheel) as he rode his Suzuki GSX-R1000, with the front tire in the air, at a speed of 172.9 mph (278.2 km/h). Shortly thereafter, in May 2007, Calcott was killed in a motorcycle accident.

LONGEST WHEELIE

The record for the longest motorcycle wheelie ride was set by Kurt Osburn of Fullerton, CA (USA), as he rode on his rear wheel a distance of 2,840 mi (5,470 km). He began his journey in April 1999 from Hollywood, CA, and rode across the entire United States — coast to coast — until he arrived in Orlando, FL, in June.

LONGEST RIDE ON FRONT WHEEL

Englishman Craig Jones set the record for riding on the front wheel of a motorcycle (known as a "stoppie") in 2003, as he rode the front wheel of his Buell Firebolt XB12R for a distance of 873 ft (266 m).

DID YOU KNOW?

The noise emanating from a Harley-Davidson motorcycle has been registered as a patent by the company.

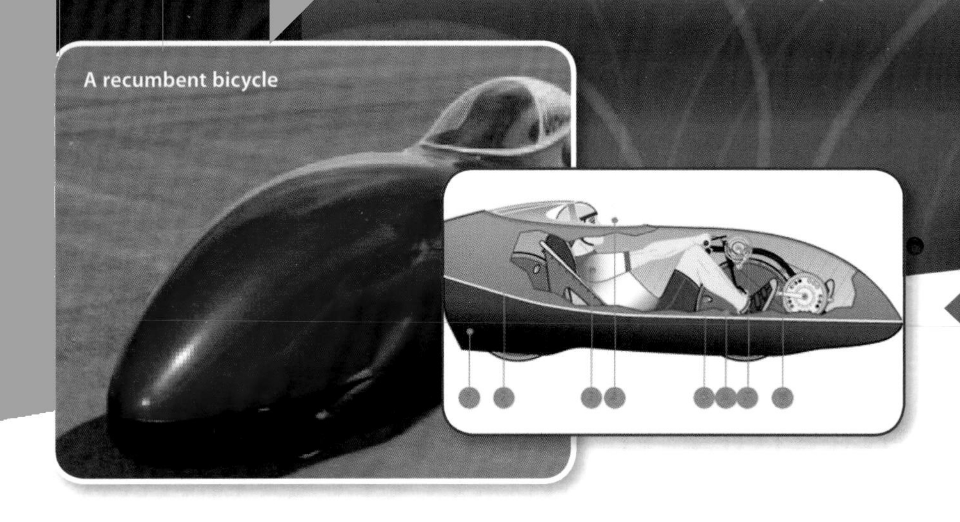
A recumbent bicycle

COUNTRY WITH THE MOST BICYCLES

Out of the approximately 1 billion bicycles in the world, 550 million of them can be found in China (1 bicycle for every 2 Chinese citizens). Ninety percent of these bicycles are simple bikes without any gears.

BICYCLE MANUFACTURERS

The largest bicycle manufacturer in the world is Hero Cycles located in Punjab, India, which was established in 1956 by the Munjal Brothers. The company manufactures 2.22 million bicycles per year.

LONGEST BICYCLE

The longest bicycle in the world was built by members of the mechanical engineering students association at Delft University of Technology in the Netherlands. The bicycle is 92.2 ft (28.1 m) long and is not supported by any "training wheels." In 2002, members of the group rode the bicycle for a distance of 328 ft (100 m).

SMALLEST BICYCLE EVER RIDDEN

The smallest bicycle ever ridden by a person had a front wheel that was 0.43 in. (1.09 cm) in diameter and a back wheel just over .5 in. (1.27 cm) in diameter. This absurdly small bicycle was built and successfully ridden a little over 16 ft (4.88 m) by a Polish man named Zbigniew Rozanek in 1998.

LARGEST BICYCLE

The world's largest bicycle is the Frankencycle built by Dave Moore of Rosemead, CA (USA). It is 11.5 ft (3.5 m) high and its wheels' diameter is 9.84 ft (3 m).

FARTHEST 24-HOUR BICYCLE RIDE

Greg Kolodziejzyk rode on a bicycle path a distance of 650 mi (1046 km) in 24 hours.

BICYCLE WITH THE MOST GEARS

In 1998, Leon Chassman of Michigan (USA) built a 1,500-speed bicycle.

LARGEST 3-WHEEL BICYCLE

K. Sukhakar of India holds the world record for the largest 3-wheel bicycle in the world. This tricycle is 37 ft, 4 in. (11.3 m) long, 47 ft, 7 in. (12.6 m) tall, and weighs 3 tons. The diameter of its front wheel is 17 ft (5.1 m).

FASTEST BICYCLE RIDER

The maximum riding speed of a racing bicycle on flat land is 48.5 mph (78 km/h). A recumbent bicycle is a bicycle that places the rider in a lying-down position. Because of the lower air resistance and more efficient push by the feet when the back is leaning, recumbent bicycles can reach a higher speed. Bike rider Sam Whittingham from Canada set the speed record for recumbent bicycles in 2002 at 81 mph (130.3 km/h) by riding on a recumbent bicycle wrapped in an aerodynamic covering.

Another method for avoiding air resistance is to ride on a bicycle behind a car which has a wind shield in back of it. The wind shield produces a vacuum and even a suction effect for the rider behind it. With the help of such a wind shield, Fred Rompelberg of Holland reached a speed of 166.7 mph (268 km/h) on a conventional bicycle.

LONGEST BICYCLE MOUNTAIN-JUMP

In 2006, Jason Rennie, riding on a Kona Stab downhill mountain bicycle, jumped a distance of 136.2 ft (41.5 m) in northern Wales. The bicycle was tied to a motorcycle which dragged him to a speed of 83 mph (133.5 km/h). The bicycle was then released from the motorcycle and Jason rode up a sloped ramp 13.1 ft (4 m) tall, and flew the record-breaking distance through the air, at which point he landed on a downward-sloped ramp which returned him to the street.

LIGHTEST RACING BICYCLE

In 2001, Dionisio Coronado of Spain built a racing bicycle that weighed only 9.9 lb (4.5 kg). The bicycle's chassis was built from beryllium, which is a very light metal used as a hardening agent in alloys. According to the rules of the International Cycling Union (UCI), the minimum permissible weight in bicycle races is 15 lb (6.8 kg). Incidentally, the cost of these professional racing bikes, which are built from lightweight titanium, can be several thousand dollars.

FIRST BICYCLES

In 1870, the first giant metal bicycles were introduced. The pedals were connected to the front wheel. What made them unique for their time was that the wheels were covered with hard rubber. This greatly reduced the bumpiness of the rides, which otherwise would have been extremely uncomfortable.

The front tire was of huge dimensions. The larger the front tire, the faster the bicycle could travel. The cost at the time for such a bicycle was the equivalent of half a year's average salary.

Early bicycle models

6–7	Shutterstock
8–9	Shuki, ויקיפדיה עברית — גל אמיר, Library of Congress
10–11	Shutterstock
12–13	Wikipedia — Keith Pomakis / David Dannenberg / הרב הלל בריסק שליט"א
14–15	Wikipedia — Henri Nissen, Almog
16–17	Wikipedia — Ramessos / ויקיפדיה עברית — דוד שי / שוקי פריימן יודאיקה
18–19	Wikipedia — Vissarion, Luc Viator / Shutterstock / Flickr — Hans Splinter / ויקיפדיה עברית — דוד שי
20–21	Shutterstock
22–23	PikiWiki_Israel — Ronia Harari / Shutterstock / Wikipedia — NehemiaG
24–25	Wikipedia — Ted Rufus Ross
26–27	Shutterstock / Wikipedia — Hans Hillewaert (Lycaon)
28–29	Wikipedia — Georges Jansoone, Gunkarta Gunawan Kartapranata, Deepak Gupta Flickr — eutrophication&hypoxia
30–31	Shutterstock / אלי אריאלי
32–33	Flickr — Rainer Ebert's photos, Bruno Deshayes-Mayer / Wikipedia — matthew / David Dannenberg
34–35	Wikipedia — Nomadtales / Shutterstock
36–37	Shutterstock / Wikipedia — ynhockey
38–39	Wikipedia — Musée des Arts et Métiers, Tomasz Sienicki, JoeTourist / Shutterstock
40–41	NASA / Shutterstock / Wikipedia — KennethHan
42–43	ויקיפדיה עברית — איתמר עצמון / Wikipedia — Douglas J. McLaughlin, Project Gutenberg
44–45	Shutterstock / Wikipedia — Timo Halén, Med, Sebastian Ritter, Hdekroon
46–47	Wikipedia — David Lliff
48–49	NASA / Shutterstock / Wikipedia — Richard Lazenby, Norwood, J. Patrick Fischer
50–51	Shutterstock / Wikipedia — Redcoat, koldo hormaza / U.S. Army
52–53	Shutterstock / Wikipedia — John O'Neil, Robert Isaac Nudel, Justin Paul Barras / ארכיון עיריית ירושלים
54–55	Shutterstock / Wikipedia — William Cho
56–57	Shutterstock / Wikipedia — Marcelo Montecino, Rifleman, U.S. Department of Defense / U.S. Federal Government / photobucket.com — Dolphin3254
58–59	Wikipedia — Lavaschlote, Rhaessner, Curtis Edward / Shutterstock
60–61	Wikipedia — Christophe Moustier, Padraic Ryan de Benutzer Eborutta / UN_General_Assembly
62–63	Wikipedia — MandyM, blueangel
64–65	Wikipedia — D ruchoy, Rüdiger Wölk, Edward Z. Yang, IdiotSavant
66–67	behn lieusong
68–69	Shutterstock / Wikipedia — Wieliczka, Erik Christensen, Hervé Cozanet, Lewis Wickes Hine, Grafikę Stworzy, Rj1979
70–71	Shutterstock / Wikipedia — Giovanni Lapolli's, Kwerdenker, Jfz, Dani 7C3, Macaddct 1984 Alex, BSMPS / Sandia National Laboratory
72–73	NASA / pingnews.com's photos / Wikipedia — Runningonbrains, U.S. Coast Guard / National Oceanic and Atmospheric Administration / Flickr — Isgcp's photos
74–75	Shutterstock / Flickr — Gwire's photos, Electrostatico's photos / Wikipedia — Jialiang Gao, David Rydevik
76–77	U.S. Air Force — Denise Gould / pingnews.com's photos, Wikipedia — Ali Imran, Federal Emergency Management Agency
78–79	NASA / Shutterstock
80–81	Shutterstock / U. S. Geological Survey — J.D. Griggs, McGimsey, Game / Wikipedia — Boaworm Henrik Thorburn / Shutterstock
82–83	Shutterstock
84–85	Shutterstock
86–87	Shutterstock / U.S. Federal Government — Cpl. Benjamin Cossel / U.S. Air Force — photo by Senior Airman Julianne Showalter / NASA / Wikipedia — John Atkins / Flickr — Shyam's photos

Credits

88–89 Wikipedia — IFCAR, muntuwandi, David Wilmot's / U.S. Federal Government

90–91 Shutterstock / Fan Yang / Cyberjunkie / Ashrita Furman / David Dannenberg

92–93 Flickr — Dean.Franklin's photos, Testimonials 125's photos / Wikipedia — Buphoff, kakuichi kai fabiano, Derek Cashman / U.S. National Park Service / San Alfonso del Mar / www.pbase.com/adnan_masood

94–95 Shutterstock / Flickr — GeoJono's photos, Nouveau's photos, Sling / Andrius Vanagas / Sidney Mobell

96–97 Sidney Mobell / Flickr — Ilkka Laukkanen, David Dannenberg, Eric Chan/ Shutterstock

98–99 Shutterstock

100–101 Shutterstock

102–103 F. Duerr and Sons / Caviar House and Prunier, London / Shutterstock

104–105 Shutterstock / U.S. Agricultural Research Service

106–107 Shutterstock / Wikipedia — Benjamin Zingg, Switzerland / Achichi / ויקיפדיה עברית — אחי רז

108–109 Wikipedia — Joy Schoenberger, Kowloonese, Claus Bunk / Shutterstock / U.S. Agricultural Research Service

110–111 Shutterstock / Flickr — hellochris, robstephaustralia / משתלת וולך

112–113 Shutterstock / petitchef.com / גלידות פלדמן / Wikipedia — Nsaum75

114–115 Shutterstock / petitchef.com / Wikipedia — Roland Zumbühl, fir0002 / Flickr — Jenni Jones-Kebler

116–117 National Institutes of Health / Flickr — Mr328K, Jordan Sim, Doc Searls / Shutterstock / Wikipedia — PhreddieH3

118–119 U.S. Air Force

120–121 Shutterstock / Wikipedia — pd

122–123 Wikipedia — Kevin Quinn, Ohio; pd

124–125 U.S. Air Force — photo by Staff Sgt. Derrick C. Goode / U.S. Navy — Ensign John Gay / Wikipedia — PH3 Colkitt

126–127 U.S. Navy / Wikipedia — MICROB1 / Israel Aerospace Industries / U.S. Air Force — Kenneth G. Takada

128–129 U.S. Air Force / U.S. Navy

130–131 U.S. Navy / U.S. Air Force — Scott Allen

132–133 Wikipedia — Ido 403, Bukvoed / U.S. Navy

134–135 Yad LaShiryon — Michael Mass, Wikipedia — PHC HOLMES, Superewer, Soviet Government Agencies / Imperial War Museum Collection / U. S. Federal Government

136–137 Wikipedia — GrahamColm, pd / David Dannenberg

138–139 Wikipedia — Fl295, Radomił Binek, ChrisO, Marko Milosavljevic / מרב מרודי

140–141 NASA / Wikipedia — pd / U.S. Army

142–143 U.S. Army / Flickr — Pierre J. / U.S. Federal Government / U.S. Air Force

144–145 Wikipedia — Andrew Choy

146–147 Wikipedia — Enslin, selbst fotografiert, Marcin Cieślak, Arnaud 25 / Photo et photographisme Roby avec l'aimable permission du Musée des Arts et Métiers, Paris

148–149 Wikipedia — Charles01, Chris McKenna / Lars-Göran Lindgren, Sweden / Jon Sullivan Petersen Automotive Museum, Los Angeles, CA / Shutterstock

150–151 Shutterstock / Wikipedia — Gérard Delafond, Stahlkocher, Zölle / Museum of Science and Industry, Manchester / Flickr — Steve Cadman

152–153 Rinspeed / Wikipedia — Rene Engle, Nuon Hans-Peter van Velthoven / Volvo

154–155 Wikipedia — Floflo, pd / Chris Howells / Alex Needham

156–157 U.S. Navy / Wikipedia — Murray Becker, pd

158–159 Flickr — dbking's photos, sujohndas' photos / U.S. Army / U.S. Federal Government

160–161 NASA / Wikipedia — Dotonegroup, Curtis L. Olson-Michael Lucan

162–163 Wikipedia — Bzuk, Chris Olsen, Alan Radecki Akradecki, Xeper / Flickr — billypalooza's photos

164–165 Wikipedia — Badseed / NASA / U.S. Navy

166–167 Wikipedia — Conollyb / U.S. Navy / Oasis.com

168–169 Wikipedia — BoH, Gleam, Jim Bedient, Jcmurphy, Andrew Berridge / U.S. Navy

170–171 Shutterstock / Flickr — cole24 / Wikipedia — Denkfabrikant, Softeis

172–173 Shutterstock

Inside covers: Shutterstock / University of California at Berkeley / Airunp / NASA / Flickr — Tlindenbaum's photos / Hyundai Motors / Wikipedia — Robin Chen, David Lliff, Scotto Bear, Tomasz Sienicki, Böhringer Friedrich, Suniltg

Coming Soon!
Volume 3

מה רבו מעשיך ה'

The Book of Amazing Facts and Feats 3

The Creator's World and All That Fills It

Volume 3 features…

The countries whose citizens have the highest average IQ in the world, the scariest (fake) radio broadcast in history, the origin of the phrase "Ponzi Scheme," a model of the *Beis HaMikdash* that took 33,000 hours to build, the man who went around the world in a motorcycle, the world's largest ferris wheel, and a ski resort in the middle of the desert.

Discover a host of strange and interesting bridges around the world: a "rolling bridge," a bridge made of water, the first suspension drawbridge, the highest bridge anchored by cables, the only suspension bridge connecting two continents, and more…

Learn about an astronaut's life in space, and about Jews in space. Gaze at the gorgeous blue-tongued skink, white tiger, and bird of paradise. And speaking of birds, read about carrier pigeons, warrior pigeons, the angriest bird, the most expensive bird, the most merciful bird, and other feathered facts.

And of course, collect more amazing facts about the world of Judaism and the Torah. You will be sure to appreciate even more The Creator's World and All That Fills It.

Have you seen or heard of a world record or amazing fact? You're invited to contact us at:

"The Book of Amazing Facts and Feats"
Email: seeim10@gmail.com

Your name will be publicized in the acknowledgments (if you wish) in the next volume.

EMPERORS HAVE NO REST

In March 1974, a Chinese farmer was digging a wel in his yard when he discovered ancient pottery shards. These turned out to be the 2,200-year-old remains of a life-sized, terracotta army consisting of more than 7,000 soldiers, 130 chariots with 520 horses, 150 cavalry horses, and weapons. The army had been buried with Qin Shi Huang, the first emperor of Qin (Shi Huang means "the first emperor").

Each soldier was molded with distinguishing differ- ences in the details of the faces and hairstyles as w as the clothing and arm positions, insuring that no two terracotta soldiers are alike – they vary in height, uniform and hairstyle in accordance with their rank, and many carried real weapons.

Many of the weapons were covered with a layer of poison, which resulted in the deaths of farmers anc the first curious people who touched the blades. The bows were in special casings and thus were pr served for thousands of years. They were designed to automatically fire arrows at anyone who disturb the soldier's "rest."

METAL SKELETON

Dozens of companies around the world are trying to develop an artificial metal skeleton consisting of small electric motors which have more than a hundred times the strength of ordinary motors. Th skeleton allows its wearer to lift hundreds of pounc and to run with them a great distance without effo He can climb high, steep mountains, and jump superhuman distances and heights. The artificial skel eton can greatly assist in the battlefield, and indust workers will be able to load and unload heavy equi ment without the aid of cranes and without hurtin themselves or becoming tired. In addition, rescue workers would be able to quickly remove rubble from disaster zones, and the handicapped would also benefit from its use.

However, like anything in life, it has its drawbacks. The skeleton contains electric motors and a computer, and even the slightest short circuit or any malfunction can cause the wearer to make unnatu movements and to place himself in life-threatenin danger.